Child Care: Kith, Kin, and Hired Hands

Child Care: Kith, Kin, and Hired Hands

Emmy E. Werner, Ph.D.
University of California at Davis

University Park Press
Baltimore

UNIVERSITY PARK PRESS
International Publishers in Medicine and Human Services
300 North Charles Street
Baltimore, Maryland 21201

Designed by S. Stoneham, Studio 1812, Baltimore
Typeset by The TypeWorks
Manufactured in the United States of America by The Maple Press Company

Photo Credits: Front and back covers and Chapters 1 and 10, respectively, "Grandmother story teller" (Taos), artist–Alma L. Concha, photographer–Eugene R. Prince, Lowie Museum of Anthropology, University of California, Berkeley, "Grandfather story teller" (Taos), artist and photographer as named above; Chapter 2, "Japanese snow monkey and infant" (Minneapolis Zoo), photographer–Annie Griffiths; Chapter 3, "An extended family" (Paraguay), photographer–David Mangurian, UNICEF; Chapter 4, "Two brothers on a sidewalk" (Monrovia, Liberia), photographer–Bernard Wolff, UNICEF; Chapter 5, photographer–Dick Swartz, U.S. Department of Health and Human Services; Chapter 6, photography–John Black and Associates, Davis, CA.; Chapter 7, "Alexander Spotswood Payne and his brother, John Robert Dandridge Payne, with their nurse," by the Paynelimner, c. 1790, oil on canvas, reproduced by permission of Virginia Museum of Fine Arts, Richmond, VA; Chapter 8, "Foster grandmother with child of single teenage mother in center for court-referred child abuse families" (Marshall, MO), ACTION photo; and Chapter 9, "The cast of *Sesame Street*, the popular television series for preschoolers produced by Children's Television Workshop," ©CTW, 1978.

Library of Congress Cataloging in Publication Data
Werner, Emmy E., 1929–
Child care.

Includes index.
1. Child rearing. I. Title.
HQ769.W444   1983   649'.1   83-14658
ISBN 0-8391-1805-8

Contents

Preface

This book presents a comparative view of alternate caregivers for the young. Worldwide, and especially in the contemporary United States, kith, kin and "hired hands" are the most common substitute parents in a domestic unit.

They provide physical care for young children, feed and protect them from harm, care for them when they are ill, play with them, and provide educational stimulation when parents, especially the mother, are not available or occupied with work. Their impact on America's families will increase with the dramatic rise in the number of women with young children who have joined the paid labor force and work full-time on a year-round basis outside of the household. Alternate caregivers also provide care for the growing number of children of unmarried teenage mothers, children with special needs, and families who suffer a prolonged and traumatic disruption of the household because of divorce, parental illness, or child abuse. In the closing decades of this century, they will affect about one out of every three Americans and about every other American child.

The book addresses a number of issues that are of importance for parents; students of family, child, and human development; the child care and child welfare professions; and social policy makers:

1. It examines, in a comparative fashion, the role of alternate caregivers in our evolutionary past, in history, and on the contemporary scene, in the industrialized as well as the developing world.

2. It focuses on economic and demographic factors that put constraints on the availability of alternate caregivers, and on differences in the choice of child care arrangements between parents who live in relative affluence and parents who live in relative poverty.

3. It evaluates the impact of alternate caregivers, such as siblings, grandparents, relatives, neighbors, family day care providers, nannies, and foster parents, on children within a variety of family life-styles that include extended, nuclear, and single-parent households.

4. It illustrates options as well as problems in shared child care that arise when families are confronted with rapid social change, and examines the role of educational programs, including television, that provide training and support for parent substitutes.

5. It concludes with a discussion of the implications of what we presently know about alternate caregivers for parents, child care professionals, and social policy makers, and points to priorities in social action programs and research that need to be addressed, so that we can better understand and support the contributions of such caregivers in the lives of children and families.

My special thanks go to my colleagues in Human Development at the University of California at Davis, who encouraged me in this venture, to Janis Castile, who typed the manuscript, and to Susan Oliver and the editorial staff of University Park Press, who transformed it into a book.

E. E. W.

To my kith and kin

CHAPTER *1*

Introduction

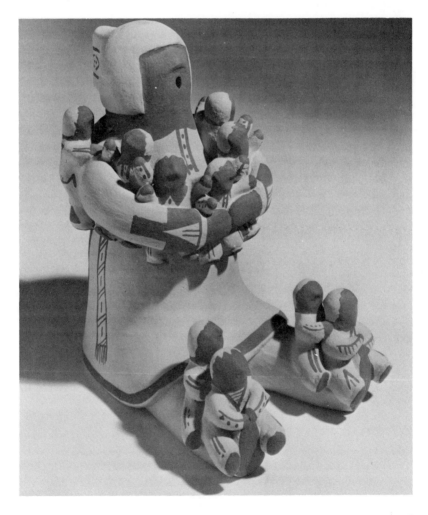

In the sense in which a man can ever be said to be at home in the world, he is at home not through dominating, or explaining, or appreciating, but through caring and being cared for . . .

Milton Mayeroff, *On Caring*

A quiet revolution has taken place in American families and around the world during the past decade: Fertility rates have declined; married women with children are entering the paid labor force in higher numbers and at younger ages; and divorce rates have risen, and so has the number of single-parent families, especially those with a female head of household.

In the 1980s about half of all American children will spend at least 2 years of their childhood in a "non-traditional" family, either in a family in which both parents are wage earners, or in a family that has gone through a divorce. About one-quarter of the total U.S. population must cope with the special problems that face families when both parents or the sole head of the family have work responsibilities outside the home and there are young children in need of care and supervision (Giraldo, 1980). By 1990, these concerns will directly affect one out of every three Americans.

The most dramatic increase is in the number of women with children under the age of 6 seeking paid employment outside of the home. According to the U.S. Bureau of the Census, some 51% of all married women in the U.S. were in the labor force in 1980, compared with 41% in 1970 and 24% in 1950. A large share of that growth was contributed by married women with children under 6 years of age: 45% of these women worked in the labor market in 1980, up from 30% in 1970 and 12% in 1950. Among women maintaining families on their own, the majority with children under 6 were employed in 1980. Not only are there more women with young children in the labor force, but the proportions engaged in full-time work year-round has increased more sharply than those who work part-time (see Figure 1).

It is estimated that by 1990 in the U.S. half of all preschool-age children—about 11.5 million—and close to 60% of school-age children—or 17.2 million—will have mothers in the labor force. At least 60% will have mothers who work full-time (Children's Defense Fund, 1982).

Masnick and Bane (1980), in their outlook report *The Nation's Families: 1960–1990*, predict that the revolution yet to come is in women's attachment to their work outside the home. Trends toward year-round, full-time, and contin-

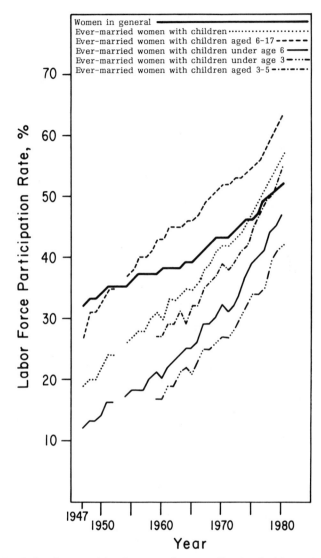

Figure 1. Labor force participation rates of women. (Reprinted with permission from Children's Defense Fund, 1982, The Child Care Handbook, p. 6.)

uous work, especially among younger women who are in their childbearing years, makes this revolution quite likely. If women in the U.S. develop more substantial and permanent attachment to work outside of the household, they will join, by necessity or choice, the majority of other women in the world. Throughout history, women have always been engaged in productive labor along with childbearing and child-rearing (Fisher, 1979; Rossi, 1977).

WOMEN'S TWO ROLES: WORK AND FAMILY

All cultures tend to have some division of labor by sex, in both the society at large and its family units. The specific tasks done by men and women vary from society to society, depending on ecological conditions, mode of production and technology, but some general trends can be found worldwide.

To date, one of the most comprehensive reviews of cross-cultural data on male-female division of labor is that done by D'Andrade (1966), who analyzed ethnographic material on over 600 of the world's societies: Women nearly always play an important role as producers of goods and services, just as in nearly all cultures of the world men make some contributions to the upkeep of their mates and offspring; but women almost universally are given child-rearing roles and perform the bulk of child-rearing in early childhood, at least until children reach age 6. This still holds today, even in societies that espouse complete economic, political, and social equality between the sexes, that is, in Cuba, The People's Republic of China, the Soviet Union, and the Israeli kibbutzim.

If women have outside employment and young children, they generally spend more time in fulfilling both their work and their family obligations than do men. This seems to be as true for capitalist societies as for socialist and Marxist countries (Roby, 1975).

Some detailed time-budget studies have been conducted in a number of industrial nations, including the U.S. (Bane, 1976; Szalai, 1973; Masnick and Bane, 1980). Summing time spent on child care, on the job, and on housework and other household obligations, these studies report that employed women everywhere work a very long workday and that they work longer hours than do employed men and housewives. In all 12 nations surveyed, employed mothers also spend more time with their children (both on workdays and days off) than employed fathers.

Recent research on time use and task allocation within households in the U.S. shows that working wives continue to do most of the cooking, housework, and child care[1] for their families, while husbands of working wives do not spend significantly more time on child care and housework than husbands of non-working wives (Masnick and Bane, 1980). Working mothers spend less time on child care than do non-working mothers, but the differences in the amount of time mothers spend exclusively with their children are surprisingly small, once family size and the children's ages are taken into account. Even the "average" non-working mother in the U.S. spends only 1.4 hours per day on child care (Bane, 1976).

---

[1] *Child care* refers to all activities performed by caregivers: physical care, feeding, protecting from harm, caring for illnesses, and educational stimulation and play.

CHILD CARE ARRANGEMENTS

Of particular concern today and in the closing decades of this century is the variety and quality of alternate child care arrangements available to parents. This issue has generated a great deal of public debate, for example in the White House Conference on Families (1980) and among child advocate groups. It is therefore worthwhile to examine some available data that show the options chosen by working mothers in the U.S. (see Table 1).

The Census Bureau of the U.S. Department of Commerce has published a nationwide survey of child care arrangements of employed mothers (1982). In

Table 1. Percent distribution of children under 6 years old of ever-married working women by type of child care arrangements and employment status of mother: 1958–1977

Type of child care arrangement and employment status of mother	1977[a]	1965	1958
Employed full-time			
Care in child's home	28.6	47.2	56.6
by father	10.6	10.3	14.7
by other relative	11.4	18.4	27.7
by nonrelative	6.6	18.5	14.2
Care in another home	47.4	37.3	27.1
by relative	20.8	17.6	14.5
by nonrelative	26.6	19.6	12.7
Group care center	14.6	8.2	4.5
Child cares for self	0.3	0.3	0.6
Mother cares for child while working	8.2	6.7	} 11.2
All other arrangements	0.8	0.4	
Employed part-time			
Care in child's home	42.7	47.0	NA[b]
by father	23.1	22.9	NA
by other relative	11.2	15.6	NA
by nonrelative	8.4	8.6	NA
Care in another home	28.8	17.0	NA
by relative	13.2	9.1	NA
by nonrelative	15.6	7.9	NA
Group care center	9.1	2.7	NA
Child cares for self	0.5	0.9	NA
Mother cares for child while working	18.5	32.3	NA
All other arrangements	0.4		NA

Source: U.S. Bureau of Census, 1982.
[a] Data are only for the two youngest children under 5 years old.
[b] NA, not available.

the late 1970s as in the two preceding decades the overwhelming majority of the children were taken care of in their own or someone's else's home, by members of their immediate family, or by family day care providers, many of whom were relatives or neighbors.

The future will undoubtedly see an increase in shared child care because it is essential for low-income and working parents, as well as for teenage mothers, parents of children with special needs, and families who experience a prolonged and traumatic disruption of their unit, as a result of death, desertion, divorce, parental illness, or child abuse. There will be demands for more child care, for better care, and for different options, but the overwhelming majority of American families, and families everywhere in the world, will still turn to "kith or kin" or to a "hired hand" to provide such care within the home.

This book takes a look at such alternate caregivers and their impact on the children, the parents, and the family system. Although they provide the lion's share of substitute parenting in this country and abroad, they have remained nearly invisible in the child development literature and in the child care debate (Woolsey, 1977).

ALTERNATE CAREGIVERS: A CROSS-CULTURAL PERSPECTIVE

From the 1950s to the 1970s, child development research in the U.S. and in the Western world has focused almost exclusively on only *one* group of caregivers—mothers in small, intact, nuclear, middle-class families (Clarke-Stewart, 1977). In the 1970s increasing attention was being paid to the role of fathers in child development (Lamb, 1981; Lynn, 1974) and to the impact of professional caregivers in early childhood intervention programs, day care centers, and residential institutions (Belsky and Steinberg, 1978; Brown, 1978; Rutter, 1981). But contemporary changes in work and family life-styles (whose impact on the children will extend into the next millenium) call for a consideration and evaluation of the role of other caregivers as well, be they siblings, grandparents, or family day care providers, and for a look at shared child care in a greater variety of family contexts in different socioeconomic strata and in different cultures as well.

The role of such alternate caregivers is especially important in the developing countries, where four out of five children on this planet live (Werner, 1979). Traditionally, extended families in the non-Western world have shared the care of young children, with the mothers assisted by siblings, grandparents, cousins, and other relatives. Beatrice Whiting (1972) has taken a look at women's contributions to the workload of work and family from a cross-cultural perspective and concluded that most women in non-industrial societies strike a better balance between drudgery and boredom than the alternatives of being employed outside the home or being housebound in U.S. society.

However, rapid social changes in the modernizing societies of Africa, Asia, Latin America, and Oceania have led to changes in women's roles (Tinker and Bromsen, 1976). There is a worldwide increase in single-parent families headed by women, the breakup of traditional marriages, and the contribution of women to paid labor (Newland, 1979). The International Year of the Child and the International Women's Year have focused the attention of international agencies, such as the United Nations Children's Fund (UNICEF), the United Nations Educational and Scientific Organization (UNESCO), the International Labor Organization (ILO), and the Ford Foundation on the intersecting needs of working mothers and their children (Engle, 1980). Often they find overburdened mothers, working the double shift of motherhood and low-paid employment (Fagley, 1976).

In both rural and urban areas of the Third World, older siblings, grandparents, and relatives continue to be major contributors to shared child care, but the introduction of formal elementary education may have some unintended consequences in the developing countries by depriving the family of a requisite child caregiver (Leiderman and Leiderman, 1977). In urban areas in which such education is now common around the world, child care services are often "purchased" from relatives. Other strategies reported are hiring the services of a neighbor or a domestic, boarding children out to a foster family, or leaving the children alone—a fate that some 1.8 million "latchkey" children in the U.S. share (Children's Defense Fund, 1982).

In many situations women use two or three different systems of alternate child care and different systems for different children (Engle, 1980); but there is one generalization that we can make with some confidence: worldwide the exclusive care of children by their mothers is an exception rather than the rule. Shared child care is here to stay.

A CROSS-CULTURAL PERSPECTIVE ON PARENTAL GOALS

What parents value in persons who share with them in the care of their children depends on what they want for and from their sons and daughters (Engle, 1980). LeVine (1980) has outlined a common set of goals that are shared by parents everywhere. He also notes some differences in parental strategies in child care that vary among cultures and families that live in relative poverty or affluence. LeVine proposes that all parents share three *universal* goals for their children: 1) physical health and survival until the child reaches the reproductive age; 2) the development of the child's ability for economic self-maintenance; and 3) the capacity to maximize other cultural values, for example morality, prestige, and intellectual achievement.

These goals are hierarchical. Under conditions of poverty prevalent in developing countries, the parental investment and allocation of time and resources will be designed to ensure the child's survival and his or her ability to offer long-term support to his or her parents. To accomplish this, the mother provides a nurturing environment for the infant, but delegates the actual child care to other family members, especially older children. *Obedience* and *compliance* are highly valued in the offspring.

LeVine (1980) notes a different investment strategy among the more affluent in the world, for example, middle-class Americans. Here survival is no longer a pressing issue, and children are not expected to contribute significantly to the economic welfare of the family. Parents value *independence* and *self-sufficiency* in their children instead. Parental investment strategies consist of a larger allocation of material and human resources (including personal attention) to a small number of children, with the goals of producing a self-reliant person who is able to cope with a changing environment and is achievement oriented.

It remains to be seen how much agreement there is in such goals and strategies between parents and other caregivers for their children. This agreement is probably greater in traditional, more homogenous societies and in modern nations that are "collectivist" in their political outlook (such as the People's Republic of China or the Soviet Union) than in a pluralistic society such as the U.S.

SOME CONCEPTUAL MODELS

Within the last decades, cross-cultural studies of child-rearing and child care have been successively influenced by the perspectives of social learning theory and cultural anthropology and, more recently, by attachment theory and sociobiology. Each of these theories offer some hypotheses about the role and impact of caregivers in children's lives. Relatively few of these hypotheses have been systematically tested, but they can provide some directions for future research, and some tentative order among the array of available data.

Whiting's (1977) model for psychocultural research divides the environmental determinants of personality into two parts: 1) the *maintenance system*, which is the institutionalized economic, sociopolitical, family, and household structure that assures survival of a group, in a particular ecological niche, at a particular point in human history; and 2) the child's *learning environment*, which shapes children's dispositions in accordance with the adaptive needs of the group and within the constraints set by the maintenance system.

Among the key variables in the child's learning environment on which Whiting (1977) has focused his attention are the relative salience of the mother and father as socializing agents, the number of caregivers, the mother's workload, the tasks assigned to older children, disciplinary techniques, and the frequency and strength of punishment and reward during the socialization process.

Whiting and Whiting (1975), in their research on *Children of Six Cultures*, borrow two assumptions from social learning theory: 1) reinforcement may be either *extrinsic*—such as rewards, non-rewards, or punishments administered by socializing agents—or *intrinsic*—that is, inherent in the nature of the act performed; and 2) the degree to which children will imitate the behavior of the socializing agent (caregiver) will vary with that person's salience and power, that is, control over services, goods, resources, and privileges desired by the child.

Another theory that has influenced cross-cultural research on child care is *attachment* theory (Ainsworth, 1967; Bowlby, 1969). Bowlby was the first to draw attention to the relevance of the concepts and methods of ethologists for the study of child development. Ethologists study animal behavior, emphasizing those patterns which are just as specific to a species as bodily structure. The biological determinants of social behavior, both infantile and parental, that favor the maintenance of physical proximity, protection, and nurturance are of particular interest to them.

The concept of attachment may be equated to what ethologists have called bonding (Ainsworth, 1977). It defines a relationship between two individuals that endures over a relatively long period of their life-span. The potential for attachmemt is part of the species-specific equipment of human newborns, as of many mammalian and avian species. Attachment itself is only gradually acquired in the course of interaction with caregivers in the environment and the feedback the young child acquires as a consequence of his or her actions. Ainsworth suggests two important ways in which the concept of attachment can make a special contribution to our understanding of human development:

> 1) It suggests that there are processes implicit in *social* development that cannot be inferred from a general knowledge of the process of *learning* and *cognitive* development; and 2) It implies that early social behavior has *genetic* determinants which set certain limits for all *cultures* beyond which a society cannot push its efforts to mold a child to conform to social demands without risking maladaptive anomalies (1977, pp. 64–65).

A number of biological and behavioral scientists, foremost Wilson (1975, 1978), and also Barash (1977), Dawkins (1976), and Freedman (1979), have combined the perspectives of ethology and population biology in their discussion of general laws of the evolution and biology of social behavior. Their books contain provocative extrapolations from comparative studies of animal behavior about parenting strategies, the asymmetrical investment of the sexes in child care, the relationship between generations and among siblings and kin, and the development of altruism.

The ethical and scientific issues surrounding the assumptions of the sociobiologists have generated a great deal of controversy (Caplan, 1978; Washburn, 1978), but also a series of testable hypotheses that can be confirmed or refuted.

Among the key concepts of sociobiology that are relevant to our discussion of the role of alternate caregivers in child development are the terms *inclusive fitness, kin selection*, and *reciprocal altruism*. The concept of inclusive fitness predicts that altruistic behavior is a function of two factors: the degree of relatedness between altruist and beneficiary, and the benefit-to-cost ratio of the altruistic act to recipient and altruist (Van den Berghe and Barash, 1977). Altruistic acts (for example, nurturant, protective behavior) that ensure the survival of the young of close kin (kin selection) will also ensure the preservation of the genes that the altruist shares with the beneficiaries (inclusive fitness). If individuals are only slightly related, however, or totally unrelated, altruism will more likely occur when the individual can expect at some time in the future an altruistic act in return (reciprocal altruism). If the cost to the altruist is relatively low, if the individual in need is well-known, if interactions are frequent, and if the population at large is exposed to a common risk, the probability of an altruistic act is increased (Trivers, 1971).

It should be emphasized that kin selection theory does not necessarily preclude conscious motivation and cognition. Thus altruistic, caring, nurturant behavior can be due to a combination of social learning and direct, genetically mediated predispositions. Sociobiologists do not deny the importance of culture in humans, but put it in the broader context and constraints of biological evolution (Konner, 1981; Van den Berghe and Barash, 1977).

There are differences in emphasis between Bowlby's theory of attachment and the sociobiological theories of kin selection and inclusive fitness (Porter and Laney, 1980). According to Bowlby, the infant is predisposed to become strongly attached to *one* person only (a concept that has been labeled *monotropy*), and this person is the primary caregiver, in most instances the natural mother. Inclusive fitness/kin selection theories focus instead on the selective advantages that accrue if reciprocal bonds of attachment develop between the infant and a wider range of caregivers, for example, relatives such as siblings, aunts, and grandparents.

A variety of empirical data on shared care support the contention that infants and young children can form a moderate number of secure affective bonds, but not a very large number. Smith (1980) suggests two constraints that set limits: the main constraint for the *child* seems to be the time required to learn and remember the interactional characteristics of the caregiver; the main constraint on the caregiver(s) may be the degree of control he or she can exert on the context of the relationship. These variables are examined in subsequent chapters.

AN OVERVIEW OF THIS BOOK

The role of alternate caregivers from an evolutionary perspective is examined in Chapter 2. "Aunting" behavior and babysitting has been observed in most group-living primates, among lemurs, Old and New World monkeys, and great apes, for example, chimpanzees. Field studies of such primate groups have shown that both siblings and grandmothers are involved in the care of the young, and there have been instances of fostering by older siblings after the mother's death. "Alloparental" care is also practiced by inexperienced females in primate groups who are not related and seems to be a training ground for acquiring mothering skills.

Chapter 3 provides a perspective on shared child care in human domestic groups and examines the changes in the role of alternate caregivers from the hunter-gatherer stage of subsistence economy to modern industrialized societies which are stratified by social class. It discusses the constraints of *economic* factors (for example, labor requirements and level of technology) and *biologic* factors (for example, levels of fertility and mortality) that define the context in which child care takes place.

Chapter 4 examines the roles of siblings and child nurses in the care of younger children. It deals with the prevalence, antecedents, and consequences of sibling caregiving among large, extended as well as small, nuclear families. It discusses the role of child caregivers as behavior modifiers, therapists, and tutors, and as links between the parents and a rapidly changing social world.

Chapter 5 focuses on the role of grandparents as alternate caregivers. It examines changing grandparent roles in traditional versus modern societies, and the difference in the centrality of such roles among the poor and the affluent. It discusses the consequences of supplemental and surrogate parenting by grandmothers and its effects on the children and on the parent and grandparent generation.

Chapter 6 deals with family day care, the largest natural system of alternative child care in the U.S., which serves predominantly poor and working-class parents. It examines the roles of the family day care providers (who are mostly relatives or neighbors), the characteristics and behavior of the children in family day care, and issues in parent-caregiver relationships. It contrasts available evidence on the effects of family day care on children's cognitive, affective, and social development with data on children raised at home or in center care. It also provides examples of community-based support and training programs that seem to enhance the quality of family day care.

Chapter 7 examines the roles of governesses, nannies, and their kindred who provide alternate child care for the affluent. It traces their transatlantic journey from the households of privileged families in Europe to the U.S. It also examines other contemporary contractual arrangements for child care within the home, such as the role of babysitters and "au pair girls."

Chapter 8 focuses on the changing role of foster parents from close kin (usually an aunt or uncle) in traditional societies to paid strangers in modern bureaucracies. It evaluates the few available longitudinal data on the development of children who are placed in foster care and examines recent efforts to provide community support and training programs for foster parents.

Chapter 9 takes a look at television, the newest child care arrangement on our planet. Watching television constitutes the most important activity of most contemporary children in the U.S. It occupies about one-third of the waking hours of the average preschooler and more time than school attendance and homework for the average sixth grader. Television's impact is rapidly spreading throughout the globe. Some of the effects of television on the social behavior of children, here and abroad, will be discussed, and the role of educational television programs as "trainer" of other caregivers will be examined.

The final chapter discusses the implications of what we have learned about alternate caregivers for parents and for social policy and social action on behalf of children and their families. It suggests some research priorities that need to be addressed if we want to have a more solid base of knowledge about the effects of shared child care on boys and girls, their parents, and the larger social system in which they live. It also ventures some predictions about the future that may stimulate the ongoing child care debate.

REFERENCES

Ainsworth, M.D.S. 1967. Infancy in Uganda: Infant Care and the Growth of Love. Johns Hopkins Press, Baltimore.

Ainsworth, M.D.S. 1977. Attachment theory and its utility in cross-cultural research. In: P.H. Leiderman, S.R. Tulkin, and A. Rosenfield (eds.), Culture and Infancy: Variations in the Human Experience, pp. 49–68. Academic Press, New York.

Bane, M.J. 1976. Here to Stay: American Families in the Twentieth Century. Basic Books, New York.

Barash, D.P. 1977. Sociobiology and Behavior. Elsevier, New York.

Belsky, J., and Steinberg, L. 1978. The effects of day care: A critical review. Child Dev. 49:929–949.

Bowlby, J. 1969. Attachment and Loss. Vol. 1: Attachment. Basic Books, New York.

Brown, B. (ed.). 1978. Found: Long-Term Gains from Early Interventions. Westview Press, Boulder, CO.

Calhoun, J.A., Grotberg, E.H., and Rackley, W.R. 1980. The status of children, youth and families. U.S. Department of Health and Human Services, DHHS Publication #(OHDS) 80-30274, Washington, D.C.

Caplan, A. (ed.). 1978. The Sociobiology Debate: Readings on the Ethical and Scientific Issues Concerning Sociobiology. Harper & Row, New York.

Children's Defense Fund. 1982. The Child Care Handbook: Needs, Programs and Possibilities. Washington, D.C.

Clarke-Stewart, A. 1977. Child Care in the Family: A Review of Research and Some Propositions for Policy. Academic Press, New York.

D'Andrade, R.G. 1966. In: E. Maccoby (ed.), The Development of Sex Differences. Stanford University Press, Stanford, CA.

Dawkins, R. 1976. The Selfish Gene. Oxford University Press, New York.

Engle, P. 1980. The intersecting needs of working women and their young children. A report to the Ford Foundation. Unpublished manuscript.

Fagley, R.M. 1976. Easing the burden of women: The 16-hour workday. Assign. Child. 36:October-December.

Fisher, E. 1979. Woman's Creation: Sexual Evolution and the Shaping of Society. Anchor Press/Doubleday, Garden City, NY.

Freedman, D.G. 1979. Human Sociobiology: A Holistic Approach. The Free Press, New York.

Giraldo, Z.I. 1980. Public Policy and the Family: Wives and Mothers in the Labor Force. Heath, Lexington, MA.

Konner, M.J. 1981. Evolution of human behavior development. In: R.H. Munroe, R.L. Munroe, and B.B. Whiting (eds.), Handbook of Cross-Cultural Human Development, pp. 3–52. Garland Press, NY.

Lamb, M.E. (ed.). 1981. The Role of the Father in Child Development. 2nd Edition. Wiley, New York.

Leiderman, P.H., and Leiderman, G.F. 1977. Economic change and infant care in an East African agricultural community. In: P.H. Leiderman, S.R. Tulkin, and A. Rosenfeld (eds.), Culture and Infancy: Variations in the Human Experience, pp. 405–438. Academic Press, New York.

LeVine, R.A. 1980. A cross-cultural perspective on parenting. In: M.D. Fantini and R. Cardenas (eds.), Parenting in a Multi-Cultural Society. Longman, New York.

Lynn, D.B. 1974. The Father: His Role in Child Development. Brooks/Cole, Monterey, CA.

Masnick, G., and Bane, M.J. 1980. The Nation's Families: 1960–1990. Auburn House, Boston.

Mayeroff, M. 1971. On Caring. Harper & Row, New York.

Newland, K. 1979. The Sisterhood of Man. W.W. Norton, New York.

Porter, R.H., and Laney, M.D. 1980. Attachment theory and the concept of inclusive fitness. Merrill-Palmer Q. 26(1):35–51.

Roby, P.A. 1975. Shared parenting: Perspectives from other nations. School Rev. 83(3):415–431.

Rossi, A.S. 1977. A biosocial perspective on parenting. Daedelus 106:1–31.

Rutter, M. 1981. Social-emotional consequences of day care for preschool children. Am. J. Orthopsychiatry 51:4–28.

Smith, P.K. 1980. Shared care of young children: Alternative models to monotropism. Merrill-Palmer Q. 26:371–389.

Szalai, A., et al. (eds.). 1973. The Use of Time: Daily Activities of Urban and Suburban Populations in Twelve Countries. Mouton, The Hague.

Tinker, I., and Bromsen, M.B. (eds.). 1976. Women and World Development. Overseas Development Council, Washington, DC.

Trivers, R.L. 1971. The evolution of reciprocal altruism. Q. Rev. Biol. 46:33–57.

United States Department of Commerce, Bureau of the Census. 1982. Trends in Child Care Arrangements of Working Mothers. U.S. Government Printing Office, Washington, DC.

Van den Berghe, P.L., and Barash, D.P. 1977. Inclusive fitness and human family structure. Am. Anthropol. 79:809–823.

Washburn, S.L. 1978. Human behavior and the behavior of other animals. Am. Psychol. May:405–418.

Werner, E.E. 1979. Cross-Cultural Child Development: A View from the Planet Earth. Brooks/Cole, Monterey, CA.

White House Conference on Families. 1980. Listening to America's Families; Action for the 80's. Washington, DC.

Whiting, B.B. 1972. Work and the family: Cross-cultural perspectives. A paper prepared for "Women: Resource for a Changing World," International Conference, Radcliffe College.

Whiting, B.B., and Whiting, J.W.M. 1975. Children of Six Cultures: A Psycho-Cultural Analysis. Harvard University Press, Cambridge, MA.

Whiting, J.W.M. 1977. A model for psycho-cultural research. In: P. Leiderman, R.S. Tulkin and A. Rosenfeld (eds.), Culture and Infancy: Variations in the Human Experience, 29–48. Academic Press, New York.

Wilson, E.O. 1975. Sociobiology: The New Synthesis. Harvard University Press, Cambridge, MA.

Wilson, E.O. 1978. On Human Nature. Harvard University Press, Cambridge, MA.

Woolsey, S.H. 1977. Pied piper politics and the child-care debate. Daedelus 106:127–146.

CHAPTER 2

Alloparental Care among Primates

"Men have forgotten this truth," said the fox. "But you must never forget it. You become responsible, forever, for what you have tamed . . ."

Antoine de Saint-Exupéry, *The Little Prince*

Individuals other than the mother provide care for the young in one or more representatives of seven orders of mammals (Spencer-Booth 1970) and among birds. Wilson (1975) has introduced the term *alloparental* care to denote these interactions with infants by individuals other than their genetic parents. Male and female alloparents are referred to as *allofathers* and *allomothers*, respectively. Others have called this behavior "aunting" (Rowell et al, 1964).

Alloparental behavior is especially characteristic of primates, both in captivity and in the wild, but it is also well developed in other social mammals, such as whales, dolphins, and porpoises (Caldwell and Caldwell, 1969; Essapian, 1963); elephants (Douglas-Hamilton and Douglas-Hamilton, 1975); lions (Bertram, 1975; Schaller, 1972); and wolves (Hall and Sharp, 1978; Mech, 1970), jackals (Moehlman, 1978; van Lawick and van Lawick- Goodall, 1971), and foxes (Kleiman, 1968; MacDonald, 1979).

The interested reader is referred to a number of recent reviews that deal with parental care in mammals (Gubernik and Klopfer, 1981) and in primates (Blaffer-Hrdy, 1976; Chevalier-Skolnikoff and Poirier, 1977). Harper (1981) has written an excellent review of the offspring's effect on such parenting.

This chapter presents a selective overview of some patterns of alloparental care among the primates, the order of mammals to which the genus *Homo* belongs. The primate order has two major divisions or suborders: the *prosimians* ("before apes") and the *anthropoids* ("like human beings"). Prosimians are small, nocturnal, and predominantly arboreal animals, found in Asia and Africa. They are only distantly related to *Homo sapiens*, and information on their caregiving behavior is still fragmentary (Redican and Taub, 1981); but we do know from some studies (Jolly, 1966; Klopfer and Dugard, 1976; Richard, 1976) that lemurs, which belong to the prosimian suborder, practice sibcare and "babysitting."

More data on alloparental care are available on the suborder of anthropoids which consists of three superfamilies: 1) New World monkeys; 2) Old World monkeys; and 3) great apes and humans. New World monkeys, such as the marmosets and tamarins, are found only in Central and South America, where they have evolved from New World prosimians independently of other monkeys—they are *not* ancestral to Old World monkeys and are all arboreal (Redican and Taub, 1981). Old World monkeys, such as langurs and macaques, are found predominantly in Asia and Africa (and in captive colonies in Europe and the U.S.A.) Most are semiterrestrial. Among the *apes* that are found in Asia and Africa, there are four principal groups: chimpanzees, gorillas, orangutans, gibbons, and related siamangs. All are tailless animals, and most are semiterrestrial. Recent progress in the study of biochemical evolution (the structure of DNA and the immunologic system) shows that humans, chimpanzees, and gorillas form a very closely related group (Goodman and Tashian, 1976).

Among specific groups of monkeys and apes, there are differences in social organization: Some live in monogamous groups, others in one-male/multi-female groups, and still others in multi-male/multi-female groups (Clutton-Brock and Harvey, 1978; Redican and Taub, 1981).

Multi-male/multi-female systems have evolved in habitats in which food is difficult to obtain and/or is relatively low in nutrients, and predation pressure is great. Most monkeys are organized in such social systems, for example, the Japanese and rhesus monkeys. Among the great apes, chimpanzees live in such a system as well. Most alloparenting is done by nulliparous females in these groups, and male care is relatively attentuated (Redican and Taub, 1981).

One-male/multi-female systems, such as the ones found among gorillas and Indian langurs, have evolved in habitats in which food resources are seasonally in short supply, so it is advantageous for the ratio of females to reproductive males to be at a maximum. Here alloparents are usually allomothers, and male caregiving is generally limited to the male's own offspring or relatives (Redican and Taub, 1981).

Monogamous systems consist of one adult male and one adult female mated for life, and their offspring. A relatively small number of non-human primates live in monogamous groups. They have evolved in habitats in which there is a relatively stable supply of food and predation pressure is not great. In such social units, for example, among the marmosets and tamarins, males as well as females act as alloparents (Redican and Taub, 1981).

Blaffer-Hrdy (1976) reminds us that in most primate studies firm data on kinship are still lacking. There are also relatively few longitudinal studies of monkeys and apes that trace the development of their offspring and the functions of alloparental care in the wild.

Long-term (5 years or more) genealogical information gathered under relatively natural conditions and used in behavioral analyses is available for the wild chimpanzees in the work of van Lawick-Goodall and her associates; for the Japanese monkeys in the work of Itani, Kawai, Kawamura, Koyama, Yamada, and others; and for the rhesus monkeys in the work of Breuggeman, Koford, Sade, and others.

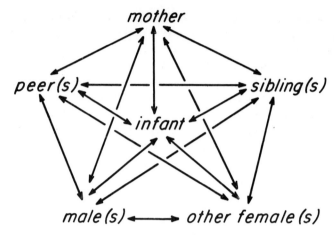

Figure 2. A general schema of the possible social interactions in a primate group in which there is an infant. (Adapted from Hinde, 1974. Reprinted with permission from McGraw-Hill Book Co., New York.)

In these species, which all live in multi-male/multi-female social systems, *matrilineal kinship* has emerged as a crucial determinant of both social status of the infant and the frequency of his association with other animals in "shared childcare." (Matrilineages in these social units are easier to ascertain than patrilineages.) Whether the importance of maternal kin holds for other species among primates remains to be demonstrated (see Figure 2).

GREAT APES

Chimpanzees

Of all the creatures in the animal kingdom, none so closely resembles humans as the chimpanzee. David Hamburg (1971) notes that in the nature of immune responses, the structure of blood proteins, and even in the structure of DNA, the hereditary material itself, the chimp is closer to man than any other primate. King and Wilson (1975) estimate that man and chimpanzee share some 99% of their genetic material. Recent research in biochemistry has shown that in some ways the chimpanzee is as close to man as he is to the gorilla, and neuroanatomists have pointed out that the circuitry of the chimpanzee brain resembles the circuitry of the human brain more closely than does that of any other species (van Lawick-Goodall, 1971; van Lawick-Goodall and Hamburg, 1975).

Thanks to the courageous and sustained effort of Jane van Lawick-Goodall and her co-workers at the Gombe Stream Research Center in Tanzania, East Africa, we now have genealogical information and long-term observations of the behavior of wild chimpanzees that document the social life of these animals, which are capable of close and enduring attachments and of care for offspring other than their own.

Among non-human primates, the period of infancy is longest for the chimpanzee, and, as among other *matrifocal* species in the primate order, the strongest and most persistent bond during that period is between mother and infant. Maternal contact remains important and preeminent for the young chimpanzee, even though peer contacts increase in the first 3 to 4 years. The young chimpanzee remains with the mother for 9 to 12 years, often with her and a sibling as its only companions (Clark, 1977).

Early on in her field studies, van Lawick-Goodall (1965, 1967) noted that adults and juveniles other than the mother would touch young babies, that older females showed interest in babies and might carry them, and that they displayed "maternal" protective behavior. Reynolds (1968) also observed that wild chimpanzee juveniles were sometimes carried by females other than their own mother.

Prolonged observations of chimpanzees in the wild as well as in captivity have made us aware that the mother closely controls the access of others to her infant, even if she has a relatively low rank in the social hierarchy of the group. Infants and juveniles maintain close contact with their mothers after weaning. After the birth of a new offspring, these siblings may have preferential access to the infant. In the wild, chimpanzee babies less than 5 months old are usually protected from contact with other animals in their social group, except their own siblings, which may "kidnap" their younger brother or sister as early as 4 months. From 5 months on, weanlings occasionally benefit from foster care by older siblings (van Lawick-Goodall, 1967, 1968). The most important relations a young chimp develops are likely to be with its siblings and other relatives within the maternal lineage.

Blaffer-Hrdy (1976) suggested that the preferential access of siblings to infants serves a number of purposes: It affiliates older siblings into the new mother-infant bond and may be extended to include more distant matrilineal relatives, for example, maternal grandmothers. Through early sibling-infant association, the foundation for care and potential adoption by older siblings is laid from birth. At the same time, the mother's female offspring have priority in learning to mother with her new infant.

Instances of *adoption* of orphaned babies by older siblings have been reported by van Lawick-Goodall (1971) among wild chimpanzees—two by older female siblings and one by a juvenile male who was an older brother. In another case, a 2-year-old male orphan was adopted by an older sister, and the adolescent brother of the pair "moved around with him and protected him on occasion" (report by Edna Konig in van Lawick-Goodall, 1967).

The eagerness of other females besides older sisters to assume "aunthood" may occasionally lead to subterfuge: Instances of a prospective aunt grooming the mother in order to gain access to the infant have been reported (van Lawick-Goodall, 1971).

In captivity, interactions between chimpanzee infants and individuals other than the mother tend to be similar in form and frequency to the high sibling contact observed in the wild in the Gombe Stream population. Nicolson (1977) suggests that the constant proximity of individuals in captive environments creates a situation analogous to the association of related individuals in a natural habitat. But here, too, the nature of each aunt's social relationship with the mother influences the interactions with her infant. Females generally spend more time in the "social grooming" of the chimpanzee infants than the males.

Gorillas

Although more than one sexually mature male is typically present in a multi-female group among wild gorillas, only the highest ranking silverback male in each group is reproductively active. Thus the mating system of the gorillas is functionally similar to that of the one-male/multi-female groups typical of other primates, and is different from that of the multi-male/multi-female social unit of the chimpanzees.

There have only been a few studies of free-ranging mountain gorillas and the development of their infants (Fossey, 1979; Schaller, 1963). Curiosity tends to be the most common response of other group members to the newly born infant, usually manifested by staring because of the protectiveness of the mother and her avoidance of proximity with other group members. Only siblings are allowed nearby for 1 to 2 weeks, and the last to be allowed in proximity are the adult silverback males (Redican and Taub, 1981).

During the course of infant maturation, that proceeds at a rate twice as fast as that of humans, the most important influence on degree and duration of mother-infant proximity appears to be the presence or absence of siblings. When an older sibling is present and acts as a mother substitute, the mother appears to be more permissive, and tolerates the infant's interactions with other peers.

On the few occasions when behavior akin to aunting was observed by unrelated adult females among gorillas in the wild, that female was always subordinate to the infant's mother (Fossey, 1979). Schaller (1963) observed gorilla infants who made contact with and were accepted by other females with infants of their own, and with pregnant females without infants. Younger females were more attracted to gorilla infants than adult females.

Two- to 3-year-old gorillas begin to approach silverbacks, and the males appear tolerant of them. Older males were observed grooming and cuddling 3 to 4 year olds with newborn siblings, and one silverback male was observed adopting an orphaned infant (Fossey, 1979).

OLD WORLD MONKEYS

Japanese Macaques

Care by conspecifics other than parents has been observed over prolonged periods of time among the free-ranging macaques in Japan, in a troop of Japanese monkeys on a ranch near Laredo, Texas, and in the enclosed troop at the Oregon Regional Primate Center (Alexander, 1970; Fedigan and Fedigan, 1977; Hasegawa and Hiraiwa, 1980; Itani, 1959; Kawai, 1965; Kawamura, 1965; Koyoma, 1967; Kurland, 1977; Yamada, 1963).

By a wide margin juvenile and subadult females play the most prominent role in aunting. Itani (1959) reports that nulliparous females are strongly interested in infants and make them their "playthings," but under the maternal supervision of the aunt. Some of the data on allomothering collected by Kurland (1977) support a "learning to mother" hypothesis: Older allomothers handle infants less awkwardly than younger ones.

The bulk of alloparenting that the Japanese macaque infant receives comes from non-kin (nulliparous females outside of the matrilineal line), but awkward handling of the infant decreases and more sustained contacts with the infant increase with increasing relatedness between allomothers. In turn, Japanese macaque mothers, similar to chimpanzee mothers, tend to be more tolerant of care extended by older siblings than by more distantly related or non-related alloparents (Kurland, 1977).

Yamada (1963) reports that the frequency of Japanese macaque infants feeding with their brothers and sisters is second only to the frequency of doing so with their mothers. By the time the infant is a juvenile, however, it may feed more often with siblings than with the mother. Thus, the basis for familiarity that could influence the choice of infants to care for or to foster or adopt is clearly established. Occasionally, the allomother can also be a grandmother. Itani (1959) reported that when a Japanese macaque gave birth to a pair of twins, one of these was cared for by the mother's presumed mother.

Alloparental care is also sometimes extended by males. For example, male rescue of an externally threatened infant has been reported by Itani (1959); and during the birth season, in some troops, males care for yearlings in the temporary absence of the mother (Alexander, 1970; Itani, 1959). This "baby-sitting" involves grooming, reassuring contact, or removal of the baby from harm's way.

Some instances of male "fostering" have been reported as well. Itani (1959) observed that a male of subleader status acted as the foster parent of a 6-month-old Japanese macaque infant who was separated from his mother. Although he never hugged or carried the infant, he groomed it and stayed with it for a period of 6 months. For those cases of allopaternal care in which information on relationship was available, foster parents were either the probable father or an older brother of the infant. Brothers are also reported to groom and protect younger siblings.

Orphans are uncommon in free-ranging monkey troops, but when a mother dies, her infant is invariably adopted, usually by someone who has formerly displayed some protective behavior toward them. Hasegawa and Hiraiwa (1980) found that adult males were the primary caregivers of orphaned infants, surpassing siblings, other relatives, non-kin peers, and other non-kin adult females. Adult males carried, groomed, and defended the orphan.

Kidnapping may occur when the mother has lost her own infant, and she attempts to steal another, often from a female of lower rank (Itani, 1959). If the foster mother ranks higher than the real mother, the infant stands to gain in fitness to the extent that the foster mother's rank entitles it to differential access to food and protection, and to higher status in dealing with other group members (Itani, 1959). Kurland (1977) also reports that Japanese monkeys "parked" their infants with new mothers while they foraged for provisions. The new mother "babysat" for groups of infants (average 2.8) with her own infant present.

Rhesus Monkeys

Long-term studies of free-ranging rhesus monkeys at the Caribbean Primate Research Institute at Cayo Santiago (Breuggeman, 1973; Loy and Loy, 1974; Sade, 1972) have shown the importance of caregivers with whom the rhesus monkey has a consanguineal relationship, especially among members of the matriline. Related animals were involved in grooming over five times more frequently than expected from random selection of grooming partners.

Kaufman (1966) found that in free-ranging rhesus monkeys, immature females as well as adult females without babies of their own, especially the newly mature females, were interested in infants. They watched and touched the babies, but would also cuddle and carry them, if permitted to do so by the mother. Rowell et al. (1964) and Spencer-Booth (1968), working with captive animals, have also described the intense interest by females in babies born into their group. However, siblings showed more attention toward an infant than did less closely related animals of the same age and sex in the group.

Aunt-infant relationships were first observed in a colony of caged rhesus monkeys in Cambridge, England (Hinde, 1974; Rowell et al., 1964; Spencer-Booth, 1968), and have since been reported among free-ranging rhesus monkeys as well. In each case a disproportionate number of nulliparous females participated in aunting behavior. If the aunt was not related (that is, a sibling or a grandmother), subordination to the mother appeared to be a prerequisite for infant access among the rhesus monkeys, which have pronounced female hierarchies. For example, Rowell et al. (1964) report that among the caged rhesus females who were allowed to cuddle and carry the first five of seven infants born into the group, all were subordinate to the mother in rank.

Blaffer-Hrdy (1976) suggests that because the "cost" of permitting aunting may vary with the age and status of the aunt involved, one would expect the rhesus mother to discriminate on the basis of which female provides the most advantages (in terms of freedom for the mother to forage, socialization and protection of the infant, and adoption if the mother is sick and dies) with a minimum of the disadvantages (incompetence in care, kidnapping).

Adoption in this species has been observed under laboratory conditions, even to the extent of the production of apparently normal milk by non-pregnant, initially non-lactating females (Harlow et al., 1963; Hansen, 1966). In cases in which the infant's mother was temporarily removed, infant rhesus monkeys clung to a foster mother, a female group companion, during the period of separation (Spencer-Booth and Hinde, 1967). Instances have been reported in which grandmothers as well as siblings have assumed care for orphaned young. While adoption among siblings is more common among free-ranging rhesus monkeys, Breuggeman (1973) reported a case among captive animals in which a lactating grandmother rhesus adopted and reared an infant after its mother (her daughter) had died.

Although male care is relatively rare in free-ranging rhesus monkeys in the wild, males are attracted to newborns in distress. Koford (1963) reported that 1-year-old rhesus males may be especially attracted to their newborn siblings (although not as much as their sisters are), and Sade (1967) observed that an adolescent rhesus male had his 6-year-old brother as his most frequent companion after he was orphaned at age 4.

Langurs

The caregiving behavior of the common Indian, or Hanuman, langur has been studied in a variety of settings, both in the wild and in captivity. Such troops can be organized in one-male or multi-male patterns. Where Indian langurs are found in dry deciduous forests, with severe summer conditions and a high population density, they tend to form one-male/multi-female groups, with many extraneous males or all-male bachelor groups. In more temperate, less densely populated areas, they are organized in more homogenous multi-male/multi-female groups (Jay, 1965). Resident males are thought to be replaced by a new adult male who, along with a raiding band of bachelor males expels the old males. A systematic killing of the dependent offspring by the new resident adult males can accompany this replacement process in some, but not all langur troops (Blaffer-Hrdy, 1977).

Among the Indian langurs, many female individuals other than the mother deliver care and establish social relationships with an infant. This has been documented both in the wild and among colonies housed in research facilities. McKenna (1981) reports data based on some 1500 hours of observation collected on a colony of langurs housed in a research facility at the San Diego Zoo. Data show that even before the langur infants were 3 months old, they had extensive contact with female caregivers that varied in age and in their caregiving skills. Subadult nulliparous females (between the ages of 3 and 4.5 years) were involved in the greatest amount of allomothering, followed by multiparous and primiparous adult females. In the first week of life, when the biological mother more closely monitored the extramaternal caregiving of her infant, multiparous and presumable "experienced" females held the neonates longer on the average per allomothering episode than nulliparous ("inexperienced") females. By the time the langur infant was 1 week old, it spent as much as 57% of the time in the care of a female other than the mother. Dolhinow's (1978) study of mothering behavior among colony living langurs at the University of California, Berkeley Animal Research Station shows that mothers may vary with respect to their restrictiveness or permissiveness from one infant to the next. Research by Poirier (1977) suggests that old females without infants may play an important role in comforting yearlings as they are weaned, and the langur mothers turn their attention to new infants.

The constant activity of allomothering exposes the langur neonate, infant, and weanling to a wide variety of social contacts, which differ in age, parity, caregiving competence, and temperament. It is noteworthy that among langurs, subadult and adult males and females develop a nexus of social relationships quite separate and independent from the one established by the mother. Both laboratory and field studies (Blaffer-Hrdy, 1977; McKenna, 1981) have shown that langur social bonds depend less on matrilineal kinship ties than among the macaques.

McKenna (1981) speculates that relative to primate species with matrilineal hierarchies, competition for resources and the need to control access to food is reduced among the common langurs. Thus female-female behaviors are less influenced by status differential (that is, dominance), and more by integrating behaviors, most notably shared infant and child care. The reduction of competition for food coincides with close spatial feeding patterns, especially in captivity. In the wild, such alloparenting facilitates foraging by freeing the langur mother from carrying a cumbersome infant (Blaffer-Hrdy, 1977).

As with other non-human primates, allomothering also increases the chances of an infant's adoption, and therefore survival, should the langur mother die. Such adoptions have been observed in the field by a number of investigators (Boggess, 1976; Dolhinow, 1978; Jay, 1965).

Last, but not least, allomothering among the langurs, as among the other anthropoids, seems to lead to the acquisition of maternal skills among nulliparous females, which can aid them in the care and survival of their own infants. It also hastens the infant's socialization (Blaffer-Hrdy, 1977).

NEW WORLD MONKEYS

Marmosets and tamarins are New World monkeys about the size of a tree squirrel found in the tropical rain forests of the Amazon and in other parts of Central and South America. They are among the relatively small number of non-human primates who live in monogomous social units (Redican and Taub, 1981).

Care of infants by both males and females is seen in marmosets and tamarins to the greatest known extent among non-human primates. All marmoset and tamarin mothers characteristically give birth to twins and triplets. For the first 2 months adult males may carry infants on their backs throughout the day, except when the infant is nursing, and may continue to carry them even after weaning (Ingram, 1975).

However, father and mother are not the only active caregivers in such groups. All marmoset and tamarin group members old enough to do so have been seen to assist in caregiver activities (Epple, 1975; Ingram, 1975). Although the first set of marmoset infants is carried and cared for by their parents, the second and especially subsequent sets are cared for largely by older siblings (Hearn and Lunn, 1975; Vogt et al., 1978). Ingram (1975) reports that of all available siblings, 10- to 15-month-old subadults are most involved in caregiving, having had some experience in handling the last set of offspring.

The opportunity for subadult marmosets to participate in the care of younger siblings appears to be a crucial factor in producing parents who will successfully care for their own offspring. Early attempts to breed marmosets in captivity were unsuccessful because juveniles had been removed from the nest before they had a chance to interact with younger siblings. If left long enough in the nest to do so, they matured into prolific breeders, even in captivity (Hearn and Lunn, 1975).

THE ROLE OF ALLOPARENTS AMONG
HIGH-RISK OFFSPRING OF MONKEYS AND APES

Extraparental care among non-human primates seems to contribute to the survival of infants with physical deficits, to the prevention of child abuse, and to the amelioration of the trauma of maternal deprivation.

Fedigan and Fedigan (1977) reported on the social development of a severely and multiply handicapped infant in a free-living troop of Japanese monkeys. One of the male infants born into this group suffered from severe brain damage, evident at birth, that led to characteristics similar to those seen in human children with spastic cerebral palsy. He had poor vision, strabismus, serious motor deficits, and ataxia, with weak and poorly coordinated hind limbs and difficulties in grasping. Longitudinal observations and genealogical data were available on this infant through the first year of life. On the occasions when he could not locate his mother, he "hopped" to his grandmother and aunt, and attempted to follow and sit by them. Two of this handicapped monkey's peers were close relatives and among his most frequent companions. He also developed an enduring social bond with a female who was the offspring of his mother's closest companion. Unrelated members of his group (including the highest ranking males) were highly tolerant of his lack of socially appropriate behaviors. He was retrieved by non-relatives even more often than by kin, and received a large amount of comforting (gentle grooming, holding, and touching) that exceeded that directed at orphaned infants—almost always from young females. At the time of the report he had survived for 13 months until he disappeared. (For a similar report on a polio victim among the wild chimpanzees, see van Lawick-Goodall, 1971.)

Berkson (1977) has reviewed the available evidence on visually handicapped rhesus monkeys, both in the wild and in captive groups. He notes that in both conditions protection is provided by the group as a whole, but that such defective animals benefit from a special relationship and support from siblings and alloparents, especially when the animal is young. This "group care" compensates for the handicap (both partial and total loss of vision) early in development, but tends to diminish as the animal matures. Even totally blind infants survive, remain with the group; and live indefinitely when predators are absent and food is plentiful; but they tend to be somewhat more passive and subordinate in their social interactions.

Allomothers can apparently also be helpful in preventing child abuse among primate mothers. Nadler (1979, 1980), a psychologist at the Yerkes Regional Primate Center of Emory University in Atlanta, reported the unfortunate outcome of the center's first gorilla birth. The female infant, born to a 9-year-old, wild-born gorilla which had been captured as an infant, had to be separated from her mother 1 week after the birth because the mother pushed her from her breast, neglected her, and dragged her across the floor.

When the same gorilla mother gave birth to a second daughter and began rejecting her as well, another female gorilla, her former cage-mate, was moved into her cage, and the mother reared the infant from there on without any problems. Next, a social group of gorillas consisting of one male and three females was formed in an outdoor compound of the center's field station. Less than a year later, all three females gave birth to their infants. Surrounded by their companions, there was no sign of child abuse. Thus, the presence of another adult appears to facilitate competent mothering among higher primates, a fact noted by Rohner (1975) for humans in his cross-cultural survey of the antecedents of parental acceptance and rejection in over 100 societies (see Chapter 3, this volume).

Even monkeys who have been reared in an environment of maternal deprivation in infancy appear to profit from the presence of peer "therapists." Rosenblum (1971) raised rhesus monkeys individually from birth in single cages containing inanimate cloth "surrogate mothers," a rearing procedure that had consistently produced socially disturbed and inept individuals. He permitted the infants to interact in groups of four for 30 minutes, 5 days per week. They developed strong relationships to one another and acquired many of the social skills characteristic of normally reared rhesus monkeys. Hansen (1966), using a similar procedure, provided rhesus infants with continuous exposure to inanimate surrogate mothers, and 2 hours of peer interaction daily. His findings were similar to Rosenblum's. It seems that such "peer therapy" enables even monkeys who had been totally isolated from conspecifics for the first 6 or 12 months of their lives to obtain a substantial level of social competence, at least in captivity (Suomi, 1979).

Alloparental Care by Males

As evident by this selective review, allomaternal care is much more common than allopaternal care among the higher primates. However, male care for infants, especially in the laboratory setting, has received an increasing share of research interest in the past decade. The interested reader is referred to two excellent reviews that summarize recent data on this topic: Parke and Suomi (1981) and Redican and Taub (1981).

Redican and Taub (1981) suggest that the relatively high likelihood of female parental care in mammals is consonant with several biological considerations. First, her small number of large gametes represents a more extensive investment than the male's abundant number of small gametes. Second, there is certainty that the female's offspring bears the mother's genes, whereas paternity may be difficult to ascertain in most higher primate groups. Together, these factors predict a higher degree of parental investment by females (and their female relatives) in the caring for the young. A male's parental care appears to be highly and positively correlated with his genetic relatedness to offspring; thus, males in polygamous social systems appear less solicitous of young than those in monogamous systems (Redican and Taub, 1981).

The expression of male's caregiving potential appears to be affected by several variables. Among them are the abundance and seasonality of food supply, predation, sexual selection (male competition and female choice), and the relatedness of adult caregivers and infants, and of the caregivers themselves (Redican and Taub, 1981). There is accumulating evidence that male non-human primates may be a flexible and critical resource for child care "in reserve," that is, when the mother is absent for prolonged periods of time, is incapacitated, or has died or been removed from the social group. Under such circumstances, males can play a prominent caregiving role if their access to the infants is not restricted by other females (Redican and Taub, 1981).

For example, in Spencer-Booth and Hinde's (1967) colony of rhesus monkeys in Cambridge, England, when several mothers were removed from the group, there was an enhanced degree of male-infant interaction that included babysitting, carrying, grooming, and play. At the University of California at Davis, Redican (1975) and Redican and Mitchell (1974) gathered and analyzed longitudinal data on four pairs of adult males and infant monkeys housed in the absence of mothers and peers. All adults were born in the wild and fully mature at the beginning of data collection. Two infants of each gender were in each rearing condition. Comparable data for mother-infant dyads were also available.

In the absence of "restrictive mothers," adult males were seen to interact with infants in a highly affiliative manner very rarely observed among groups in the wild; however, there were some fundamental differences between the mother-infant and male-infant pairs in the pattern of contact. First, adult males were less likely than the mothers to maintain contact with the infants, but this difference was primarily evident in the early months. In this study, close interactions between mothers and infants took place primarily in the early part of the infants' lives, whereas adult males engaged infants more so in later months. Second, sex differences were consistently greater in adult-male infant pairs than in mother-infant pairs. Mothers interacted only slightly more positively with female than male infants, whereas adult males clearly did so with male infants.

From the point of view of the infant, adult males and females appeared to be equally suitable objects of attachment. Responses to separation from and reunion with their caregivers (vocalization, approach, locomotion, self-directed behavior) were similar in mother-reared and adult male-reared infants (Redican and Taub, 1981).

The Benefits and Costs of Alloparental Care

We have seen in this brief overview that there is a high frequency of alloparental care among the higher primates, a wide range of participants in such care, and different types of care that are extended. Most often, alloparents among primates are allomothers, either related females (older sisters, aunts, or grandmothers) or females who are in close spatial propinquity to the mother (especially among captive animals). In rank, alloparents tend to be subordinate to the mother, if there is a pronounced social hierarchy in the social unit, and if they are not related to the mother.

Such alloparents may carry the infant, protect it from predators, retrieve it, groom it, console it, play with it, and on occasion adopt it (when the mother dies) or act as a foster parent (when the infant is temporarily separated from the mother). They may also babysit with groups of primate infants while the mother forages for provisions.

Sociobiologists argue that parental care is ultimately subject to a cost/benefit analysis. If such behavior "pays" in terms of enhanced fitness of a species (that is, a proportionately larger contribution to the gene pools of future generations), it persists; otherwise it does not (Klopfer, 1981). But who benefits from alloparental care? Blaffer-Hrdy (1976), Harper (1981), and Swartz and Rosenblum (1981) have suggested a number of functions that alloparenting serves which benefits all three parties:

Alloparenting contributes to the survival of the *infant.* It protects the infant (especially if handicapped) from predators and provides a substitute caregiver if the mother is absent, incapacitated, or dead. Last, but not least, alloparents are a familiar set of social partners within the larger social unit which teach the young primate social skills important for adult development and sexual maturity.

Alloparental care benefits the *mother.* It ensures not only the survival of her offspring cared for by others, but also allows her to focus her parental care on younger infants after the older ones are weaned. It gives her the freedom to forage for food at a greater distance. It also creates coalitions between the mother and other females in the social group that are sources of support and protection when there are predators.

Alloparental care benefits the *alloparent,* both directly and indirectly. Nulliparous females, who provide the bulk of allomothering, learn the skills for effective care of their own offspring through "playmothering" (Lancaster, 1971). Alloparents also increase their inclusive fitness if they are related to the infant they care for (Hamilton, 1964).

On the negative side, alloparents may turn out to be incompetent caregivers if such care is extended by younger, inexperienced primates. Alloparents may also kidnap the infant if they have lost their own offspring, or they may exploit the infant and use it as a passport to gain access to others which have a higher rank in their social group (Blaffer-Hrdy, 1976; Harper, 1981).

Primate mothers appear to be able to discriminate on the basis of which alloparent(s) provides the most advantages with a minimum of disadvantages for her and her offspring (Blaffer-Hrdy, 1976). The mother controls the access of infants to other caregivers, but the availability of alloparents depends on the social system in which the primates and their offspring live. Such social systems, in turn, evolve in response to availability of food resources and predation pressure.

We shall see in the next chapter that similar parameters determine the context in which shared child care among human families take place. Mode of subsistence, social structure, kinship, and propinquity are all important factors that determine the availability and choice of alternate caregivers for the young in our own species as well as among non-human primates.

SUMMARY

Care of the young by individuals other than the genetic parents of the offspring is common among many avian and mammalian species. It is especially characteristic of the higher primates, both in captivity and in the wild. Examples of such alloparental care have been observed among Old World and New World monkeys and among the great apes, including the chimpanzees.

In each of these species, alloparents fulfill a variety of roles in the care of offspring other than their own. They carry, care for, groom, protect, play with, and at times foster or adopt young animals whose mothers are absent or have died. The frequency and quality of such extramaternal care among primates varies with the age and sex of the offspring as well as that of the alloparent. Subadult females tend to extend more alloparental care to primate infants of both sexes, and maintain more prolonged contact with them. Adult males tend to interact more often with older offspring and more positively with male than female young. There also appear to be individual characteristics in the young that tend to elicit such alloparental care.

Among primate groups for which long-term genealogical data are available, matrilineal kinship plays a major role in determining the access of an alloparent to the offspring of another primate mother. Most alloparents are female, and are either related to the mother, such as older (half) sisters, aunts, cousins, and grandmothers, or live in close propinquity (more common in captive groups). If the alloparent is unrelated, she tends to be subordinate to the mother in the dominance hierarchy of the social group, and the mother controls her access to the infant (and restricts it as well).

Males are less frequently involved in alloparental care among primates which live in multi-male/multi-female groups, although older brothers may on occasion care for and adopt younger siblings. Males are more involved in such care in one-male/multi-female or monogamous groups (where paternity is more certain) and in captivity when the mother has been removed and access to the infant is not restricted by other adult females. Primate infants become attached to both male and female alloparents.

Alloparental care appears to benefit the mother, the infant, and the alloparent. It contributes to their survival, reproductive success, and socialization. The potential benefits of alloparental care (protection of the infant from predators, freedom for the mother to forage, and creation of coalitions among members of the primate social group) tend to outweigh the occasional disadvantages (incompetent handling, kidnapping, and exploitation of the young).

Among key variables that determine the extent of alloparental care among primates are the accessibility of food supply and predation pressures, the social system that has evolved in response to these pressures, and the degree of relatedness or propinquity of potential alloparents in the social unit in which the primate mother and her offspring live.

REFERENCES

Alexander, B.K. 1970. Parental behavior of adult Japanese monkeys. Behaviour 36:270–285.

Berkson, G. 1977. The social ecology of defects in primates. In: S. Chevalier-Skolnikoff and F.E. Poirier (eds.), Primate Biosocial Development: Biological, Social and Ecological Determinants, pp. 189–204. Garland, New York.

Bertram, B.C.P. 1975. The social system of lions. Sci. Am. 23:54–65.

Blaffer-Hrdy, S. 1976. Care and exploitation of non-human primate infants by conspecifics other than the mother. In: J.S. Rosenblatt, R.A. Hinde, E. Shaw, and C. Beer (eds.), Advances in the Study of Behavior, Vol. 6, pp. 101–158. Academic Press, New York.

Blaffer-Hrdy, S. 1977. The Langurs of Abu: Female and Male Strategies of Reproduction. Harvard University Press, Cambridge, MA.

Boggess, J.E. 1976. Social behavior of the Himalayan langur (*Presbytis entellus*) in Eastern Nepal. Doctoral dissertation, University of California, Berkeley.

Breuggeman, J.A. 1973. Parental care in a group of free-ranging rhesus monkeys (*Macaca mulatta*). Folia Primat. 20:178.

Caldwell, R.C., and Caldwell, D.K. 1969. Epimeletic (caregiving) behavior in cetacea. In: K. Norris (ed.), Whales, Dolphins, and Porpoises. University of California Press, Berkeley.

Chevalier-Skolnikoff, S., and Poirier, F.E. (eds.). 1977. Primate Bio-Social Development: Biological, Social and Ecological Determinants. Garland, New York.

Clark, C.B. 1977. A preliminary report on weaning among chimpanzees of the Gombe National Park, Tanzania. In: S. Chevalier-Skolnikoff and F.E. Poirier, (eds.), Primate Biosocial Development: Biological, Social and Ecological Determinants, pp. 235–260. Garland, New York.

Clutton-Brock, T.H., and Harvey, P.H. 1978. Mammals, resources and reproductive strategies. Nature 273:191–195.

de Saint-Exupery, A. 1943. The Little Prince, trans. K. Woods. Harcourt, Brace, Jovanovich, New York.

Dolhinow, P. 1977. Caretaking patterns of the Indian langur monkey. Paper presented at the Annual Meeting of the American Association of Physical Anthropologists.

Dolhinow, P. 1978. Langur monkey mother loss and adoption: Commentary. Behav. Brain. Sci. 3:443–444.

Douglas-Hamilton, I., and Douglas-Hamilton, O. 1975. Among the Elephants. Viking Press, New York.

Epple, G. 1975. Parental behavior in *Saguinus fuscicollis* Spp. Callithricidae. Folia Primatol. 24:221–238.

Essapian, F.S. 1963. Observations on abnormalities of parturition in captive bottle-nosed dolphins (*Tursiops truncatus*) and concurrent behavior of other porpoises. J. Mammal. 44:405–414.

Fedigan, L.M., and Fedigan, L. 1977. The social development of a handicapped infant in a free living troup of Japanese monkeys. In: S. Chevalier-Skolnikoff and F.E. Poirier (eds.), Primate Biosocial Development: Biological, Social and Ecological Determinants, pp. 205–224. Garland, New York.

Fossey, D. 1979. Development of the Mountain Gorilla. In: D.A. Hamburg and E.R. McCown (eds.), The Great Apes. Benjamin Cummings, Menlo Park, CA.

Goodman, M., and Tashian, R. 1976. Molecular Anthropology. Plenum Press, New York.

Gubernick, D.J., and Klopfer, P.H. (eds.). 1981. Parental Care in Mammals. Plenum Press, New York.

Hall, R.L., and Sharp, H.S. 1978. Wolf and Man: Evolution in Parallel. Academic Press, New York.

Hamburg, D. 1971. Foreword. In: J. van Lawick-Goodall, In the Shadow of Man. Houghton-Mifflin, Boston.

Hamilton, W.D. 1964. The genetic evolution of social behavior. J. Theor. Biol. 7:1–16.

Hansen, E.W. 1966. The development of maternal and infant behavior in the rhesus monkey. Behaviour 27:107–149.

Harlow, H.F., Harlow, M.K., and Hansen, E.W. 1963. The maternal affectional system of rhesus monkeys. In: H. Rheingold (ed.), Maternal Behavior in Mammals. Wiley, New York.

Harper, L.V. 1981. Offspring effects upon parents. In: D.J. Gubernick and P.H. Klopfer (eds.), Parental Care in Mammals. Plenum Press, New York.

Hasegawa, T., and Hiraiwa, M. 1980. Social interaction of orphans observed in a free ranging troop of Japanese monkeys. Folia Primatol. 33:129–158.

Hearn, J.P., and Lunn, S.F. 1975. The reproductive biology of the marmoset monkey Callithrix jacchus. Lab. Anim. Handb. 6:191–204.

Hinde, R.A. 1974. Biological Bases of Human Social Behavior. McGraw-Hill, New York.

Ingram, J.C. 1977. Interaction between primates and infants and the development of independence in the common marmoset. Primates 18:61.

Itani, J. 1959. Paternal care in the wild Japanese monkey: Macaca fuscata fuscata. Primates 2:61–94.

Jay, P.C. 1965. The common langur of North India. In: I. DeVore (ed.), Primate Behavior Field Studies of Monkeys and Apes. Holt, Rinehart & Winston, New York.

Jolly, A. 1966. Lemur Behavior. University of Chicago Press, Chicago.

Kaufmann, J.H. 1966. Behavior of infant rhesus monkeys and their mothers in free-ranging band. Zoologica 51:17–29.

Kaufmann, I.C., and Rosenblum, L.A. 1969. The waning of the mother-infant bond in two species of macaque. In: B.N. Foss (ed.), Determinants of Infant Behavior, Vol. 4. Methuen, London.

Kawai, M. 1965. On the system of social ranks in a natural troup of Japanese monkeys. In: K. Imanishi and A. Altmann (eds.), Japanese Monkeys: A Collection of Translations, pp. 87-104. Emory University Press, Atlanta.

Kawamura, S. 1965. Matriarchal social ranks in the Minoo-B troop: A study of the rank system of Japanese monkeys. In: K. Imanishi and A. Altmann (eds.), Japanese Monkeys: A Collection of Translations, pp. 105–113. Emory University Press, Atlanta.

King, M.C., and Wilson, A.C. 1975. Evolution at two levels in humans and chimpanzees. Science 188:107–116.

Kleiman, D.G. 1968. Reproduction in the canidae. Int. Zoo. Yearb. 8:3–8.

Klopfer, P.H. 1981. Origins of parental care. In: D.J. Gubernik and P.H. Klopfer (eds.), Parental Care in Mammals. Plenum Press, New York.

Klopfer, P.H., and Dugard, J. 1976. Patterns of maternal care in lemurs, III. Lemur variegatus. Tierpsychologie 40:210.

Kuford, C.D. 1963. Rank of mothers and sons in bands of rhesus monkeys. Science 141:356–357.

Koyoma, N. 1967. On dominance rank and kinship of a wild Japanese monkey troop in Arashiyama. Primates 8:189–216.

Koyama, N. 1970. Changes in dominance rank and division of a wild Japanese monkey troop at Arashiyama. Primates 11:335–390.

Kurland, J.A. 1977. Kin selection in the Japanese monkey. Contrib. Primatol. 12:1–145.

Lancaster, J.R. 1971. Playmothering: The relations between juvenile females and young infants among free-ranging vervet monkeys. Folia Primat. 15:161–182.

Loy, J., and Loy, K. 1974. Behavior of an all-juvenile group of rhesus monkeys. Am. J. Physiol. Anthropol. 40:83–96.

MacDonald, D.W. 1979. "Helpers" in fox society. Nature. 282:69–85.

McKenna, J.J. 1981. Primate infant caregiving behavior: Origins, consequences, and variability with emphasis on the common Indian Langur Monkey. In: D.J. Gubernick and P.H. Klopfer (eds.), Parental Care in Mammals, pp. 389–415. Plenum Press, New York.

Mech, D.L. 1970. The Wolf: The Ecology and Behavior of an Endangered Species. Natural History Press, Garden City, NY.

Moehlman, P.O. 1979. Jackal helpers and pup survival. Nature. 277:382.

Nadler, R.D. 1980. Gorilla abuse. Child. Today. March-April:31. (Also published in Caring, Fall 1979, by National Committee for the Prevention of Child Abuse.)

Nicolson, N.A. 1977. Development in wild and captive chimpanzees. In: S. Chevalier-Skolnikoff and T.E. Poirier (eds.), Primate-Biosocial Development: Biological Social and Ecological Determinants, pp. 547–550. Garland, New York.

Parke, R.D., and Suomi, S.J. 1981. Adult male-infant relationships: Human and nonhuman primate evidence. In: K. Immelmann, C.W. Barlow, L. Petrinovitch, and M. Main (eds.), Behavioral Development. Cambridge Press, New York.

Poirier, F.E. 1977. Introduction in: S. Chevalier-Skolnikoff and F.E. Poirier (eds.), Primate Biosocial Development: Biological, Social and Ecological Determinants, pp. 1–37. Garland, New York.

Redican, W.K. 1975. A longitudinal study of behavioral interaction between adult male and infant rhesus monkeys (*Macaca mulatta*). Doctoral dissertaion, University of California, Davis.

Redican, W.K., and Mitchell, G. 1974. Play between adult male and infant rhesus monkeys. Am. Zool. 14:295–302.

Redican, W.K., and Taub, D.M. 1981. Male parental care in monkeys and apes. In: M.E. Lamb (ed.). The Role of the Father in Child Development, 2nd Ed., pp. 203–258. Wiley, New York.

Reynolds, V. 1968. Kinship and the family in monkeys, apes and man. Man 3:209–223.

Richard, A.F. 1976. Preliminary observations on the birth and development of propithecus verrauxi to the age of six months. Primates 17:357–366.

Rohner, R.P. 1975. They Love Me, They Love Me Not: A World-Wide Study of the Effect of Parental Acceptance and Rejection. Human Relations Area Files Press, New Haven, CT.

Rosenblum, L.A. 1971. The ontogeny of mother-infant relations in macaques. In: H. Moltz (ed.), The Ontogeny of Vertebrate Behavior. Academic Press, New York.

Rowell, T.E., Hinde, R.A., and Spencer-Booth, Y. 1964. Aunt-infant interaction in captive rhesus monkeys. Anim. Behav. 12:219–226.

Sade, D.S. 1965. Some aspects of parent-offspring and sibling relations in a group of rhesus monkeys, with a discussion of grooming. Am. J. Physiol. Anthropol. 23:1–18.

Sade, D.S. 1967. Determinants of dominance in a group of free ranging rhesus monkeys. In: S.A. Altman (ed.), Social Communications among Primates. University of Chicago Press, Chicago.

Sade, D.S. 1972. A longitudinal study of social behavior of rhesus monkeys. In: R.H. Tuttle (ed.), The Functional and Evolutionary Biology of Primates, pp. 378–398. Aldine-Atherton, Chicago.

Schaller, G.B. 1963. Mountain Gorilla: Ecology and Behavior. University of Chicago Press, Chicago.

Schaller, G.B. 1972. The Serengeti Lion: A Study of Predator-Prey Relations. University of Chicago Press, Chicago.

Spencer-Booth, Y. 1968. The behavior of group companions toward rhesus monkey infants. Anim. Behav. 16:541–577.

Spencer-Booth, Y. 1970. The relationship between mammalian young and conspecifics other than their mothers and peers: A review. In: D.S. Lehrman, R.A. Hinde, and E. Shaw (eds.), Advances in the Study of Behavior, Vol. 3, pp. 119–194. Academic Press, New York.

Spencer-Booth, Y., and Hinde, R.A. 1967. The effects of separating rhesus monkey infants from their mothers for six days. J. Child. Psychol. Psychiat. 7:179–197.

Suomi, S.J. 1979. Peers, play and primary prevention in primates. In: M.W. Kent and J.F. Rolf (eds.), Primary Prevention of Psychopathology, Vol. 3, pp. 127–149. University Press of New England, Hanover, NH.

Swartz, K.B., and Rosenblum, L.A. 1981. The social context of parental behavior: A perspective on primate socialization. In: D.J. Gubernik and P.H. Klopfer (eds.), Parental Care in Mammals. Plenum Press, New York.

Van Lawick-Goodall, H., and van Lawick-Goodall, J. 1971. Innocent Killers. Houghton-Mifflin, Boston.

Van Lawick-Goodall, J. 1965. Chimpanzees of the Gombe Stream Reserve. In: I. De Vore (ed.), Primate Behavior, pp. 425–473. Holt, Rinehart & Winston, New York.

Van Lawick-Goodall, J. 1967. Mother-offspring relationships in free ranging chimpanzees. In: D. Morris (ed.), Primate Ethology. Aldine, Chicago.

Van Lawick-Goodall, J. 1968. The behavior of free-living chimpanzees in the Gombe Stream area. Anim. Behav. Monogr. 1:161–311.

Van Lawick-Goodall, J. 1971. In the Shadow of Man. Houghton-Mifflin, Boston.

Van Lawick-Goodall, J., and Hamburg, D.A. 1975. Chimpanzee behavior as a model for the behavior of early man: New evidence on possible origins of human behavior. American Handbook of Psychiatry, 2nd Ed. Basic Books, New York.

Vogt, J.L., Carlson, H., and Menzel, E. 1978. Social behavior of a marmoset group: I. Parental care and infant development. Primates 19:712.

Wilson, E.O. 1975. Sociobiology: The New Synthesis. Harvard University Press, Cambridge, MA.

Yamada, M. 1963. A study of blood relationship in the natural society of the Japanese macaque. Primates 4:43–66.

CHAPTER **3**

Domestic Groups

A Perspective on the
Context of Shared Child Care

According to the materialist conception, the determining factor in history is, in the final instance, the production and reproduction of immediate life. This again is of a twofold character: On the one side, the production of the means of existence, of food, clothing and shelter, and the tools necessary for that production; on the other side, the production of human beings themselves, the procreation of the species. The social organization under which the people of a particular historical epoch and a particular country live is determined by both kinds of production.

Frederick Engels, *The Origins of the Family, Private Property and the State*

Among the oldest fossil finds of the genus *Homo* are the remains of some 13 individuals who were related. They include adult men and women and at least four children, two under the age of 5. They lived in one or two proximate domestic groups during the Pliocene Age, some 3 million years ago. A team of scientists led by Don Johanson, an American paleoanthropologist, and Maurice Taieb, a French geologist, unearthed the fossils in 1975 in East Africa at Hadar in the remote Afar region of Ethiopia. The dramatic story of the discovery of this "first family" is told in *Lucy: The Beginnings of Humankind* (Johanson and Edey, 1981).

In contrast to the great apes, these hominids and their successors, dating back more than 2 million years, were exclusively ground dwelling, walked upright, shared food, and made and used tools. They also pair-bonded, established families and a home base, and engaged in shared child care.

Since these prehistoric times, the caring and rearing of young children has taken many forms—among kin, neighbors, and, more recently, strangers. Cross-cultural studies provide us with a perspective across time and space. They enable us to see that the children and their caregivers who live in the context of modern industrialized societies as we know them are a select group and probably not representative of the human species in most other cultures and during most of human history (Lozoff, 1977).

Once we step outside the familiar world of our own childhood into other cultures, we note that exclusive nurturance of the young by their parents, especially their mothers, is the exception rather than the rule. In most traditional societies, there is no extreme role specialization of child care, such that it constitutes the major or exclusive task for a whole group of people—mothers (Minturn and Lambert, 1964).

The availability of alternate caregivers for young children in domestic groups is related to settlement patterns and population size, which, in turn, are tied to the technology and economy of a society (Berry and Annis, 1974). The composition of the household, the prevailing mode of subsistence and women's workload, put certain constraints on shared child care that offer different options for people living in traditional rather than in modern societies.

VARIATIONS IN DOMESTIC GROUPS

Let us first examine some of the variations in domestic groups that exist around the world. Table 2 gives a brief synopsis of the various social and kinship organizations that characterize domestic groups in simple, intermediate, and complex societies (Van den Berghe, 1979).

Although anthropologists commonly employ the terms *family* and *household* loosely to denote domestic groups that share the provision and consumption of food and the rearing of children, most recognize some sort of distinction between the two (Yanagisako, 1979). The family is a kinship unit that may or may not involve residential unity, while the household is a residential unit that may or may not be predicated on kinship. Often the two overlap, but there are societies in which families do not form households. There are even more numerous instances of households that are not composed of families, or in which a collection of kin and non-kin, such as boarders or servants, share a common residence.

Domestic groups define the number and age of persons with whom a young child interacts and the physical setting in which he or she is socialized. Although there is some variation in household structure in our society and a growing recognition of single-parent families and communal child care arrangements, most children in the U.S. are brought up in domestic groups that consist of a mother, father, and their unmarried sons and daughters—the monogamous nuclear family. This arrangement is by no means universal.

An examination of kinship organizations in several hundred societies, representing a sample of world cultures (Murdock, 1967), indicates that the nuclear family, considered the "norm" in most industrialized societies, is a rare arrangement worldwide. Only 5% of 858 societies in Murdock's *Ethnographic Atlas* (1967) chose that option. In the majority of the world's societies, children grow up in domestic groups that consist of extended or polygamous families.

The two most likely possibilities for establishing an extended family are for the bride to join her husband and his folks or, conversely, for the husband to join his bride and her kinsmen. In either case, this forms family groups that include more than two generations because children of one sex now stay put

Table 2. Evolutionary synopsis of social and kinship organization[a]

Variables		Overall level of complexity			
	Simplest	Low intermediate	High intermediate	Complex	Most complex
Social organization					
System of production	Hunting, fishing, gathering	Swidden horticulture	Advanced horticulture	Agrarian	Industrial
Population size	40–100	100–10,000	10,000–100,000	100,000–300,000,000	5,000,000–300,000,000
Population density per km	<1	1–2	20–100	50–500	50–500
Political system	Stateless	Incipient chieftainship	Small states	Bureaucratized states	Highly bureaucratized states
Stratification	Mostly by age and sex	Incipient status differences and slavery	Extensive class distinctions and slavery	Elaborate and rigid class order and slavery	Flexible class distinctions; no slavery
Kinship organization					
Type of family	Nuclear or limited extended	Extended	Extended	Extended or stem	Nuclear
Rule of residence	Flexible	Virilocal, less commonly uxorilocal	Virilocal, less commonly uxorilocal	Virilocal	Neolocal
Marriage type	Limited polygyny	Extensive polygyny	Extensive polygyny	Upper-class polygyny, peasant monogamy	Monogamy

[a] Reprinted by permission of the publisher from Human Family System: An Evolutionary View, p. 94, by P. Van den Berghe. Copyright 1979 by Elsevier Science Publishing Co., Inc., New York.

with their parents after marriage. When the men stay put with or near their father's family, the rule of residence is called *virilocality* (or *patrilocality*), when the women stay put with or near their mother's kin, it is called *uxorilocality* (or *matrilocality*). Together, these two rules of residence account for 86% of the 858 societies in the Murdock (1967) sample. Worldwide, over four times as many societies are virilocal as are uxorilocal (69% versus 17%).

An extended family may consist of domestic groups either linked together in a large compound (household) or living nearby in the same locality (Goody, 1972). Children are thus raised in the presence or propinquity of grandparents, uncles, aunts, siblings, and cousins, who assist in child care and take collective responsibility for the rearing of the young (Minturn, 1969).

For example, the Arunta of the central Australian desert live in *patrilocal* extended families. Here a boy learns that his paternal grandmother will serve him as mother as well, and that there are many men besides his biological father (his paternal grandfather, his uncles) who will care for him, protect him, and discipline him as his father does. In contrast, most of the West African Ashanti live with their mother's kin. Ashanti children learn that their mother's sisters (their aunts) are to be treated and responded to as their own mothers, and they are cared for regularly in infancy by their maternal grandmother (Williams, 1972).

Polygamous families are created through an extension of the marriage relationship. Quite common around the world are *polygynous* families where a man marries two or more wives. If a man marries sisters (sororal polygyny), all co-wives tend to live in the same household and share in the rearing of all children, as among the Kikuyu of East Africa. If a man marries women who are unrelated, each wife with her offspring has her own (mother-child) household and the husband may have a domicile of his own, as among the Central African Baganda. Societies that practice polyandrous marriages—the marriage of one woman to several husbands, usually brothers—are much rarer than polygyny, and this family structure has nearly vanished today (Peter, H.R.H., Prince of Denmark and Greece, 1963).

There are exceptions to the "ideal" family types in both complex and simpler societies. Not all families in the Western world consist of a father, mother, and joint offspring. Many children are raised without one parent, usually the father. Other families include other relatives, but not consistently one type of kin (that is, the husband's or wife's parents). In addition, there are many individuals who live by themselves or who establish households with others who are neither spouses nor children.

Simpler societies usually do not have such a wide range of family types as industrial societies, but a number of them allow for some variation. For example, in the case of *bi-local* societies, prevalent in about 9% of the world's ethnographic samples, a young couple may decide to join either the husband's or the wife's parents, depending on who is the most prosperous and can accommodate them.

MODE OF SUBSISTENCE AND DOMESTIC GROUPS

Economic factors are significantly related to family type and household structure. Thus, the composition of domestic groups tends to vary with the prevailing mode of subsistence and the labor requirements of the parents, especially the mother.

For millions of years all humankind lived in hunter-gatherer societies, the
prevailing mode of subsistence during more than 99% of our known history as
a species. Ten thousand years ago, they numbered about 10 million and included 100% of the earth's population. Today, a scant quarter of a million
hunters and gatherers are left—no more than 0.003% of the more than 4
billion people on the planet (Coon, 1971).

Hunters and gatherers are predominantly nomadic, with small population
units and small families, usually of the nuclear or limited extended type. The
need for mobility is great in such relatively simple cultures where people survive
by capturing wild animals and fish and by collecting nuts, berries, and edible
plants. Thus, we find nuclear families among the Stone Age tribe of the
Tasaday, who were discovered in 1971 in the mountains of the Philippine island
of Mindanao (Wernick, 1974).

With the advent of agriculture, some 10 thousand years or roughly 400
generations ago, other modes of subsistence were introduced to our planet.
Agrarian, horticultural, and pastoral societies are predominantly sedentary,
with larger population units and domestic groups. The majority of the children
of today's world (some four out of five) live in such preindustrial societies or in
societies in transition from an agrarian to an industrial way of life. In most of
these societies the nuclear family appears to be too small and inefficient, given
their labor requirements and technology.

Pasternak et al. (1976), using a sample of 60 societies of the world,
selected randomly from the Human Relations Area Files (HRAF) and Murdock's *Ethnographic Atlas* (1967), found that extended family households
tended to prevail in both agricultural and non-agricultural societies where there
were incompatible activity requirements that could not be met by a mother or
father in a one-family household. In the absence of hired or slave labor, extended families are found in societies where work done by the mother (such as
gathering, cultivating, or market activities and trade) make it difficult for her to
tend her children and/or perform her other regular time-consuming domestic
chores, or where the outside activities of the father (such as migratory wage
labor, trading trips, or distant warfare) make it difficult for him to perform his
subsistence work. Correlational evidence, however, is not necessarily proof of a
causal sequence because one cannot unequivocally demonstrate with these data
which of the two variables preceeded the other in time.

Generally we think that extended family households in our own past and
in developing countries today are of a large size. However, United Nations
surveys in the developing world have shown that the number of persons actually

Table 3. Economic development and demographic characteristics, selected countries, 1973–1977 [a]

Country	Development indices					Demographic indices		
	Per capita income in 1977 (U.S. $)	Population urban (%)	1973 per capita paper consumption (kg)	Population (%) literate	Annual population increase (%)	Life expectancy at birth (years)	Crude birth rates per 1000	Crude death rates per 1000
Industrial countries								
United States	7060	74	46.2	99	0.6	72	14.7	8.9
West Germany	6610	88	19.7	99	-0.2	71	9.7	12.1
France	5760	70	11.4	97	0.4	72	15.2	10.4
Japan	4460	72	19.9	98	1.1	74	18.6	6.5
Great Britain	3840	78	28.5	99	0.1	72	12.4	11.9
Semideveloped countries								
South Africa	1320	48	7.7	46	2.5	52	42.9	14.4
Brazil	1010	59	2.6	67	2.8	61	37.1	8.8
Turkey	860	43	1.7	55	2.7	57	39.6	12.5
Albania	600	34		70	2.5	67	33.3	8.1
North Korea	430	43	0.1	90	2.6	61	35.7	9.4
Poor countries								
Bolivia	320	34	0.9	38	2.6	47	43.7	18.0
Egypt	310	45	1.3	40	2.3	52	35.5	19.7
Nigeria	310	18	0.3	25	2.7	41	49.3	23.6
India	150	21	0.3	29	2.1	50	34.6	16.9
Bangladesh	110	9	0.2	25	2.7	47	49.5	20.5

[a] Data compiled from Population Reference Bureau (McHale and McHale, 1979) and United Nations (1973–1978).

living together in residence at any given point in time is less than we might imagine, and tends to vary from 3.5 to 6.5, with an average of five persons in units of production and consumption. This comes close to the average size household (4.75) recorded in Western Europe and the U.S. from the 16th to the 19th century (Goody, 1972; United Nations, 1976).

Industrial societies, where approximately one out of every five of the world's children live, have been in existence only since the 19th century, mostly in the Northern hemisphere. The complex technological societies of Northern America, Europe, Japan, Australia, and some of the more developed Latin American, African, and Asian countries are different from each other in many ways (see Table 3). However, all have developed domestic groups that can adapt quickly to rapid and radical changes in technology.[2]

To survive and prosper under the conditions of the modern industrial society the family unit has to be small, at least as a residence unit, if not necessarily as a network of cooperating kin. There are three ways in which a family can be made smaller, more movable, more flexible, and more responsive to outside changes (Van den Berghe, 1979):

1. It adapts neolocality as the main rule of residence, that is, the bride and groom leave their respective families and establish a household of their own.

2. It eliminates polygamy, at least de jure if not de facto.

3. It reduces its fertility to levels approaching zero population growth.

Thus, the prototype of the industrial family in complex, modern societies looks actually somewhat like the family in the simplest hunter-gatherer bands, the reasons being similar: to make the best of available resources given the prevailing level of technology and mode of subsistence, and to be prepared for repeated changes in residence and work locations for both men and women.

Although such domestic groups may sometimes seem isolated by criteria of geographic distance or economic autonomy, they still often function as modified extended families (Litwak and Szelenyi, 1969). Changes in means of transportation and communication have made it possible to keep in frequent contact with kin.

THE IMPACT OF MIGRATION AND
URBANIZATION ON CONTACT AMONG KIN

Until the advent of modern means of long-distance communication and mass transportation and in the absence of writing, one's interactions were largely

---

[2] Recent research in the history of the family has shown that in Western Europe and North America the nuclear family household already predominated some centuries *before* the onset of the Great Industrial Revolution, and may have been an active contributor to rapid technological change (Laslett, 1977).

limited to people who lived in walking distance of one another. Thus, *propinquity* became a key determinant of social relations, and for the mother with young children, of the opportunity for shared child care. Even today in complex industrialized societies, kin tend to be concentrated in areas in which frequent contact is possible. The contact is, however, easier to make and maintain because of the expansion of roads and means of transportation, whether by bicycle, motor scooter, bus, car, train, or plane. Whether or not they live close together, kith and kin can keep in touch by letter (as literacy expands around the globe) and/or by telephone.

In earlier generations, migrating family members often established themselves in places that did not include members of their own kin group. The likelihood that kin would be found in the destinations of the next generation of migrants, however, was increased by the fact that earlier migrations of family members had occurred. In both the 19th and the 20th century, migrants to and within the U.S., for example, chose their destinations, in part, because of the presence of relatives in the new area. This is true for the great wave of migrations from Europe in the 19th century, for the post-World War II migration of black Americans from the South to the Northern cities of the U.S., for the migration of Hispanic families in the Southwest and the Pacific and Eastern seaboards, and for recent immigrants from Southeast Asia to the U.S. It is a pattern that is also found in migrating populations from rural to urban areas in the developing world. Thus, migration under modern technological conditions does not necessarily reduce contact among kin, but makes it optional, that is, informal and voluntary.

SUBCULTURAL VARIATIONS IN DOMESTIC GROUPS: THE CASE OF THE U.S.

Complex societies that are stratified by class, caste, or ethnicity, such as the U.S. and Western Europe, contain a diversity of family systems. Thus, if we want to understand the role and impact of alternate caregivers on the lives of young children, we need to consider subcultural as well as cross-cultural variations in domestic groups. Suzanne H. Woolsey (1977) raises the sensible question why the principle method of child care used most by working mothers—within the household and the extended family—comes so little into the spotlight of public discussion. She surmises that one explanation for this odd phenomenon is that the spokespersons (men) are generally white and upper middle-class. They are the least likely group in the American society to have functioning extended families, and they may forget that the poor and the lower middle-classes do.

For example, often cited mobility figures (for example, the average American moves once every 5 years) mask important social class differences. The poor and the working classes move within the same area in the hope of finding better housing; long-range moves to new cities are relatively rare. The post-World War II migration of black Americans from the South to Northern cities largely followed kinship lines: They went where friends or relatives were already established. Another case in point is the Native American family in the American metropolitan society (Jorgenson, 1971). The lower the amount of income among American Indian families, the larger the household. Brothers or sisters of the husband and wife, nieces and nephews, all join together to pool their meager resources, and grandparents are actively involved in shared child care (Burgess, 1980).

In contrast, the probability of long-distance moves away from kin in the U.S. increases sharply with income and educational level. Those at the upper end of both scales are the least likely to live near a relative, the most likely to use and advocate organized day care—outside of a domestic group—and to be making public policy that affects families and children. Woolsey (1977) suggests that it is easy to forget that for those who live in South Boston or Harlem, a child's grandmother or aunt is more likely to be a few blocks rather than a continent away.

Thus, a visitor to the U.S. will find not one, but a multiplicity of marriage and kinship systems. If he or she came, for example, from a traditional matrilineal society there would be many facets in the family organizations of the Navajo, the largest Native American "tribe," numbering some 100,000 persons, that would be familiar to him or her. He or she would find that a number of Hispanic-Americans live in large extended families consisting of groups of nuclear households that are located close to each other and are "kin integrated." He or she would note that Asian-Americans such as the Chinese, the Hawaiians, the Japanese, the Filipino, and, more recently, the Vietnamese and Cambodian refugees to this country, maintain active kinship ties that stretch across several generations (Werner, 1982).

He or she might notice remnants of what has been referred to as a "matrifocal" system among black Americans. Today half of all the women in African American families do not have a resident husband and maintain the primary responsibility for raising their children. Some 40% of black children in the U.S., compared to 12% of white children, lived with their mothers as sole parent in 1976. There is also a black "extended family," usually with the oldest woman in the kin group as the dominant figure (Martin and Martin, 1978).

She might be told that among the Anglo-American majority the nuclear family is considered the norm.[3] Americans seem to take pride in their autonomy and independence, and stress the privacy of the husband-wife and parent-child bond. Formal kin obligations seem to be more diluted than in traditional

---

[3] In 1970 only 4.9% of the people in family units and 4.4% of all children under 18 lived in extended families—roughly one out of 20 families in the U.S. (U.S. Bureau of Census, 1973).

societies. Most forms of assistance among kin in the U.S. are informal and voluntary.

But if our visitor is an astute observer of the human condition, he or she will recognize a common bond between his or her people and ours: In case of disruption of the domestic unit (whether by death, desertion, divorce, or teenage pregnancy) and, when there is need for shared child care among working mothers of young children, most Americans turn to their kith and kin. It will come as no surprise to our visitor that most of the help extended comes from the relatives of the wife and mother, and among them, from the women of her kin.

FICTIVE KIN AND CHILD CARE RESPONSIBILITIES

A great many societies extend the fiction, and sometimes the privileges, of membership in the kin group to various non-kin. Among Native Americans, for example, an individual may become a namesake for a child through formal ritual and subsequently assume family obligations and responsibilities for child-rearing and role-modeling (Momaday, 1976).

A well-known form of ritual kinship in Spain and Hispanic America are the ties of godparenthood established on the rites of passage of the Catholic church (baptism, confirmation, marriage). Godparenthood, or *compadrazgo de bautismo*, is numerically and socially the most important form of ritual or fictive kinship in Latin countries and among Hispanic Americans (Pitt-Rivers, 1973). At Catholic baptism the biological parents choose one or more godparents. In case of death or disability, the godparent has the moral obligation to take over the economic maintenance of the godchild and to look out for his or her spiritual welfare as well. In some Catholic countries, such as France or Mexico, an actual kinsman is often chosen as a godparent (that is, brothers and sisters or parents or parents-in-law of the child's parents). In many Latin American countries, the usual choice falls on a non-kin with whom one already has ties of reciprocity or dependence. For instance, *peones* on the *hacienda* might choose the owner as godfather of their children (Van den Berghe, 1979). In the world of urban marginality, godparenthood can become a legitimation of a network of mutual assistance. For example, in all cases studied by Lomnitz (1977) in a Mexican shantytown, *compadres* were involved in a regular exchange of goods and services—and a majority of the instances of godparenthood were contracted between neighbors and friends.

NON-KIN AND SHARED CHILD CARE

Within the past decade some new perspectives on surrogate mothers have been provided by anthropologists and by family historians (Laslett and Wall, 1972;

de Mause, 1974). Motherhood, it turns out, is not everywhere and at all times construed in the same manner, and unequal access to the resources of complex societies (such as education and money) allows some women to acquire or buy full- or part-time mother surrogates who are not kin.

Even before the onset of the industrial revolution this seems to have been relatively common among the more affluent European families whose social history has been recorded (Aries, 1962) and whose household composition has been documented (Laslett, 1977). Between the 16th and the 18th century most children in Western Europe (that is, Denmark, England, France, Germany) had the experience of living with servants or of living as servants. Roughly one out of every five children under the age of 5 were members of domestic groups which contained servants; half of all children became servants themselves in their late teens or early 20s.

Later, during a period of unprecedented economic and population expansion that began with the onset of the industrial age in Europe, there arose, especially in British society, a peculiar surrogate mother: the "nanny" (of whom we shall hear more later). Nannydom flowered between the years 1850 and 1939, then virtually disappeared from England after World War II. However, nannies survive today among the wealthy families on the European continent, in Latin America, and among upper upper-class families in the U.S., and are beginning to make a comeback among the professional elite.

On her transatlantic journey, the nanny was also introduced into the plantation societies of the South and the West Indies (Drummond, 1978). While the children of well-off Southerners had black nurses or mammies, children north of the Mason-Dixon line also frequently lived with non-kin in their own homes. During the 19th century the proportion of urban households in the U.S. which at any particular time had boarders or lodgers was between 15% and 20% (Modell and Hareven, 1973) and was considerably higher than that of resident kin, other than members of the immediate nuclear family.

In contemporary Western Europe and North America we have contractual arrangements for the care of children by non-kin in domestic groups as well; they exceed by a wide margin the care of children in day care centers or nursery schools. Examples are the French "au pair girls," the British "childminders," and the American "babysitters" and providers of family day care. What distinguishes these nanny-type surrogates from a surrogate parent who is kin is a theme of separation from rather than inclusion in the family life of their charges.

DEMOGRAPHY AND THE
DEVELOPMENTAL CYCLE OF DOMESTIC GROUPS

So far we have discussed certain economic factors that put constraints on the availability of alternate caregivers for children within domestic groups. Now let us take a look at some biological factors that affect the developmental cycle of domestic groups. They are equally relevant in determining the availability of persons who are likely to share the care and rearing of the young.

Mortality

In the past, people generally did not live long enough for there to be a sizeable pool of older relatives with whom children could have contact. In the U.S., for example, in 1900, the expectation of life at birth for white males was 48.2 years and 51.1 years for females, comparable to those of the poorest countries in the world today—for example, Bangladesh. In 1970, these figures had risen to 68 years for white males, and 75.6 years for white females.

Infant mortality made a major contribution to death rates in industrial countries in the past, as it still does in the developing countries where most of today's children live. Nevertheless, higher mortality in the past affected adults as well as children. Thus, at age 20, the life expectancy of white males in the U.S. was 42.2 additional years in 1900, but 50.3 additional years in 1970; the comparable figures for white females were 43.8 additional years in 1900 and 57.8 additional years in 1970 (Laslett, 1979).

Data from the United Nations' *Demographic Yearbook* (1976) indicate that an increase in life expectancy is a worldwide trend, although it is more pronounced in industrialized countries, such as Japan, Western Europe, and North America than in less technically developed countries (see Figure 3). Thus, in contrast to the past, more parents and grandparents stay alive; and, in contrast to popular myths, more grandparents are available to participate in the socialization of their grandchildren. The opportunity for a meaningful overlap in the lives of grandparents and grandchildren is a phenomenon of the 20th century (Giraldo, 1980).

While the length of life of both sexes has increased throughout this century, the increase for women has been significantly greater than the increase for men. Contemporary sociological research has shown that women are more active than men in maintaining family ties. Thus, women's longevity may help to sustain contacts among related adults, be they siblings, children, grandchildren, nephews, or nieces (Adams, 1968).

Age at Marriage

The family cycle begins anew with each marriage. The age at which the creation of a new conjugal unit occurs varies from society to society as well as from generation to generation. During the 20th century there has been a general worldwide conversion on the early 20s as appropriate age for marriage. There have been some variations by generations in the U.S. For example, the generation that married between 1940 and 1950 married at an all-time low that persisted throughout the 1950s and 1960s. The median age of marriage in later decades is returning to pre-World War II levels. Thus, the rising age at mar-

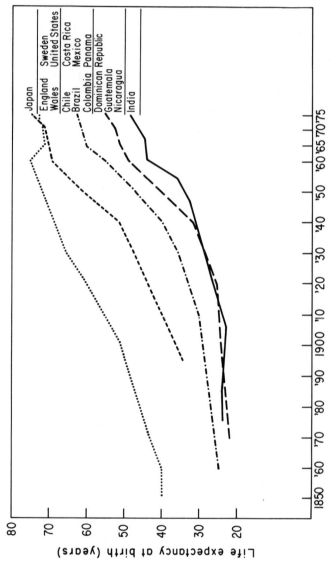

Figure 3. Trends in life expectancy; selected countries, 1850–1975. (Data compiled from Population Reference Bureau (McHale and McHale, 1979, p. 38.)

riage for contemporary females is more in accord with traditional patterns of American history from the end of the 19th century until the 1940s. It also makes the American pattern more consistent with the patterns in other industrialized countries (Giraldo, 1980).

Reproductive Phase

This phase of the family cycle begins with the birth of the first child and ends when the last child reaches adulthood. There are some distinct historical and cross-cultural differences in the length of this phase in family cycles around the world. In the U.S., in the 20th century, compared to the 19th century, children are born (and are more likely to survive) earlier in their parents' life-span. In general, the length of time devoted to produce children has steadily declined in the U.S. as women have had fewer children, but the spacing of these children has become increasingly constricted to the younger years. In most of the developing world, this reproductive phase is much more extended, as women bear and rear more children over a longer period of their life-span, although fewer of them are likely to survive.

Fertility

In general, in societies with low fertility and low mortality, older relatives are more available, younger relatives are less available. Thus, among the middle classes of the industrialized countries of the Northern hemisphere, such as Japan, North America, and Europe, and in the People's Republic of China (the most populous country on earth), we would expect a relatively large reservoir of grandparents and other adult kin to be available as potential caregivers and role models for young children (see Figure 4).

In contrast, under demographic conditions of higher mortality and higher fertility, which prevail in most of the developing countries of the Southern hemisphere and among the poor in the Western world, children will grow up with a larger number of other children, that is, siblings and cousins.

Under these conditions (which were also prevalent in the U.S. and Europe in the 19th century), older children will often take charge of their younger siblings. Sisters, especially, will carry a major share of responsibility for raising the younger siblings, and frequently act as surrogate mothers if the mother works outside the home, is incapacitated by illness, or dies (Hareven, 1977, 1978). In such a domestic circle, the oldest child has the greatest chance to overlap with grandparents, the youngest child the least. As the age configuration of the children in these families changes, the status of each child becomes different as well; after the oldest leaves home, the nest child becomes "the oldest" in the household and takes over new responsibilities as caregiver, counselor, and conciliator (Werner and Smith, 1982).

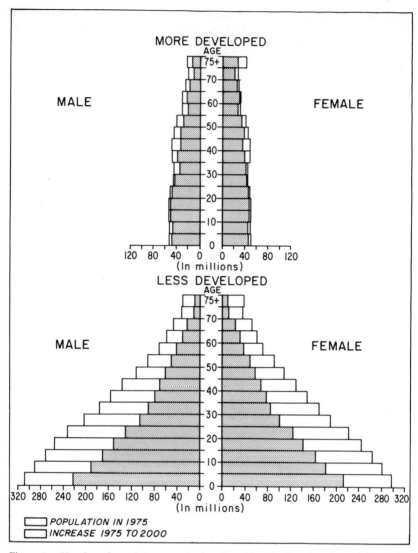

Figure 4. Number of people in more developed and less developed regions of the world, by age and sex, 1975 and 2000. (Data compiled from Council on Environmental Quality and Department of State, 1977.)

HOUSEHOLD COMPOSITION AND
PARENTAL ACCEPTANCE OF THEIR OFFSPRING

The importance of alternate caregivers in domestic circles is illustrated in a worldwide study of the effects of parental acceptance and rejection by Rohner (1975), based on an analysis of ethnographies from some 101 societies. Both acceptance and rejection were rated on a 5-point scale, ranging from the presence of a warm and accepting parent-child relationship, characterized by much fondling, cuddling, and demonstration of love and affection to the child by parental words and actions, to rejection that either took the form of indifference and lack of interest in the child's development or frequent and severe physical punishment and withdrawal of warmth and affection.

One of Rohner's principle hypotheses explaining the worldwide variability of parental acceptance-rejection relates to the intensity of interaction between parents and their children. Mothers or major caregivers are likely to reject their children whenever they are unable to break the intensity of continuous interactions with them.

Rohner (1975) found a significant worldwide relationship between parental behavior and household composition. Mothers who are alone all day with their children are more likely to reject them than mothers who have someone else in the domestic group, especially another adult, to share the burden of child care.

SUMMARY

Both biological variables, such as levels of fertility and mortality, and the onset and length of the reproductive cycle, as well as economic factors, such as mode of subsistence, level of technology, and labor requirements for mother and father, affect the size and structure of domestic groups. The relative impact of these economic and biological factors varies in different historical periods and across cultures and with it the context in which shared child care takes place. Generally they allow for fewer options, but for more continuity in child care among traditional than among modern societies. Worldwide, however, there seems to be a significant relationship between the availability of alternate caregivers in domestic groups and parental acceptance and responsiveness to the needs of young children.

REFERENCES

Adams, B. N. 1968. Kinship in an Urban Setting. Markham, Chicago.

Aries, P. 1962. Centuries of Childhood: A Social History of Family Life. Knopf, New York.

Berry, J.W., and Annis, R.C. 1974. Ecology, culture and psychological differentiation. Int. J. Psychol. 9:173–193.

Burgess, B. J. 1980. Parenting in the Native-American community. In: M.D. Fantini and R. Cardenas (eds.), Parenting in a Multi-cultural Society. Longman, New York.

Coon, C. S. 1971. The Hunting Peoples. Penguin Books, New York.

de Mause, L. (ed.). 1974. The History of Childhood. Psychohistory Press, New York.

Council on Environmental Quality and Department of State. 1977. The Global 2000 Report to the President, Vol. 1. U.S. Government Printing Office, Washington, DC.

Drummond, L. 1978. The transatlantic nanny: Notes on a comparative semiotics of the family in English-speaking societies. Am. Ethnol. 5:30–43.

Giraldo, Z. I. 1980. Public Policy and the Family: Wives and Mothers in the Labor Force. Heath, Lexington, MA.

Goody, J. 1972. The evolution of the family. In: P. Laslett and R. Wall (eds.), Household and Family in Past Times, pp. 103–124. Cambridge University Press, New York.

Hareven, T. K. 1977. Family time and historical time. Daedalus 106:57–70.

Hareven, T. K. (ed.). 1978. The Family and Life Course in Historical Perspecitve. Academic Press, New York.

Johanson, D., and Edey, M. 1981. Lucy: The Beginnings of Humankind. Simon and Schuster, New York.

Jorgenson, J. 1971. Indians and the metropolis. In: J.O. Waddell and O.M. Watson (eds.), The American Indian in Urban Society. Little, Brown, Boston.

Laslett, P. 1977. Characteristics of the western family considered over time. J. Fam. Hist. 2:89–115.

Laslett, P. 1979. The significance of family membership. In: V. Tufte and B. Myerhoff (eds.), Changing Images of the Family. Yale University Press, New Haven, CT.

Laslett, P., and Wall, R. (eds.). 1972. Household and Family in Past Times. Cambridge University Press, New York.

Litwak, E., and Szelenyi, I. 1969. Primary group structures and their functions: Kin, neighbors and friends. Am. Sociol. Rev. 34:465–481.

Lomnitz, L. A. 1977. Networks and Marginality: Life in a Mexican Shantytown. Academic Press, New York.

Lozoff, B. 1977. The sensitive period: An anthropological view. Paper presented at the Biennial Meeting of the Society for Research in Child Development, March 19, New Orleans.

Martin, E.P., and Martin, J.M. 1978. The Black Extended Family. The University of Chicago Press, Chicago.

McHale, M.C., and McHale, J. (with Streatfield, G.F.) 1979. Children in the World. Population Reference Bureau, Washington, DC.

Minturn, L. 1969. A survey of cultural differences in sex role training and identification. In: N. Kretschmer and D. Walcher (eds.), Environmental Influences on Genetic Expression. U.S. Government Printing Office, Washington, DC.

Minturn, L., and Lambert, W. 1964. Mothers of Six Cultures: Antecedents of Child-rearing. Wiley, New York.

Modell, J., and Hareven, T. K. 1973. Urbanization and the malleable household: An examination of boarding and lodging in American families. J. Mar. Fam. 35:467–479.

Momaday, N. S. 1976. The Names. Harper & Row, New York.

Murdock, G. P. 1967. Ethnographic Atlas. University of Pittsburgh Press, Pittsburgh.

Pasternak, B., Ember, C.R., and Ember, M. 1976. On the conditions favoring extended family households. J. Anthropol. Res. 32:109–123.

Peter, H.R.H., Prince of Greece and Denmark. 1963. A Study of Polyandry. Mouton, The Hague.

Pitt-Rivers, J. 1973. The kith and the kin. In: J. Goody (ed.), The Character of Kinship, pp. 89–105. Cambridge University Press, London.

Rohner, R. P. 1975. They Love Me, They Love Me Not: A World-wide Study of the Effect of Parental Acceptance and Rejection. HRAF Press, New Haven, CT.

United Nations. 1976. Demographic Yearbook, 1975. United Nations, New York.

United Nations Department of International Economic and Social Affairs. 1973-1978. Statistical Yearbook. United Nations, New York.

U.S. Bureau of the Census. 1973. Washington, DC.

Van den Berghe, P. 1979. Human Family Systems: An Evolutionary View. Elsevier, New York.

Werner, E. E. 1982. Sources of support for high risk children. In: N.J. Anastasiow, W.K. Frankenburg, and A.W. Fandal (eds.), Identifying the Developmentally Delayed Child, pp. 13–30. University Park Press, Baltimore.

Werner, E. E., and Smith, R. S. 1982. Vulnerable, but Invincible: A Longitudinal Study of Resilient Children and Youth. McGraw-Hill, New York.

Wernick, R. 1974. The Family. Time-Life Books, New York.

Williams, T. R. 1972. Introduction to Socialization. Mosby, St. Louis, MO.

Woolsey, S. H. 1977. Pied piper politics and the child-care debate. Daedelus 106:127–146.

Yanagisako, S. J. 1979. Family and household: The analysis of domestic groups. In: B.J. Siegel, A.R. Beals, and S.A. Tyler (eds.), Annual Review of Anthropology, Vol. 8, pp. 161–206. Annual Reviews, Palo Alto, CA.

CHAPTER **4**

Sibling Caregivers

By any standard, my older sister was an unusual person, and for me she was a shining example, my dearest friend and my mentor. Even late in life, when we were both grown women, grandmothers, in fact, Sheyna was the one person whose praise and approval—when I won them—which was not easy—meant most to me.

Golda Meir, *From My Life*

Among human relationships, the sibling relationship tends to be of the longest duration and may persist for 80 to 90 years, outlasting the bonds between parent and child or husband and wife. Yet we know relatively little about the consequences of being cared for or caring for one's brother or sister.

What cross-cultural evidence we can find indicates that the care of children by other children, be they siblings, cousins or child nurses, is a significant phenomenon in most societies of the world (Barry and Paxson, 1971; Weisner and Gallimore, 1977). In our own country, as well, studies of working mothers reveal that following fathers and grandparents, siblings most often assume the care of younger brothers and sisters in the mother's absence (Medrich et al., 1982; Smith, 1980; Westinghouse Learning Corporation, 1971).

It needs to be kept in mind that such sib care takes place within the context of the family, and that family structures in the industrialized world differ from those in traditional societies because of differential fertility and mortality rates and differences in the length of the reproductive cycle.

Under conditions of high infant mortality and high fertility, which are prevalent in most of the developing countries and among the poor in the industrialized world, children will grow up with a larger number of siblings, but see some of them die before they reach adulthood. In contrast, under conditions of low fertility and low mortality prevalent in the U.S., children will grow up with fewer siblings, but these siblings will with few exceptions reach an advanced old age.

These demographic conditions create different contexts for sibling relationships in a large versus a small family. For example, in a family with eight children, the first-born enters a unit of only three members that expands to ten, while the youngest child enters a very large unit, which then contracts in size as the older siblings leave the household.

Also, the ages of the parents and the ages and number of siblings available at different stages of childhood will vary more in a large family than in a small family with closely spaced births (Uhlenberg, 1979). A child in a small family will not experience as many changes in the domestic unit unless his or her parents divorce, remarry, and start a reconstituted family with their own offspring and stepchildren.

Thus, the declining fertility rate in the industrialized world, especially in the present child-bearing generation, has sharply reduced the number of children with more than two siblings and has increased the number of children in low birth order positions, especially first- and second-born.

Child development research has not yet begun to consider seriously the social and psychological implications of these demographic changes, but it stands to reason that they will have a significant effect on the nature of the relationship between brothers and sisters, both as caregivers and as recipients of sib care.

These differences in the context of sib care are reflected in the report of investigators from different disciplines. For example, recent reviews of American studies by Bank and Kahn (1982), Bryant (1982), and Furman and Buhrmester (1982) focus on psychological and sociological studies of the consequences of sib care on the affective, cognitive, and social development of the individual siblings or the sibling dyad. In contrast, cross-cultural data directly focused on brothers and sisters are scarce. Weisner (1982) points out that anthropological studies of siblings are more often found under topics that show how they function in the context of service to their family and kin. In many traditional societies, cousins and other kin (nieces and nephews) frequently are grouped in the same categories as are siblings, and sibling terminology may emphasize age and birth order as much as gender (Kronenfeld, 1974; Nerlove and Romney, 1967).

RANGE OF SIB CARE ACTIVITIES

Weisner and Gallimore (1977) note that sib caregiving represents a wide range of activities, from the performance of specific tasks for another child under the supervision of adults or other (older) children to complete and full-time care of a child by an older sibling. Caregiving can include verbal and nonverbal training and supervision of a child's behavior as well as "keeping an eye out" for younger brothers and sisters.

In single-parent families, the oldest sibling's responsibilities may be considerable, and may include *surrogate* parenting. But more widespread worldwide is a variety of forms of *supplementary* parenting (Furman and Buhrmester, 1982). Most common in the world is informal child and sibing care that is part of the daily routine of children within the family, which is carried out without formalized organizational rules. Under these circumstances child caregivers are frequently operating under two simultaneous sets of pressures: one from their small charges, the other from their parents (Weisner and Gallimore, 1977).

PREVALENCE OF SIB CAREGIVING

In an ethnographic survey of 186 societies, Barry and Paxson (1971) found that in the majority of the world's cultures, children assisted in caregiving, both of infants and young children, and that in approximately 25% of the societies, older children were the principal companions and caregivers (see Table 4).

In the U.S. a study by Medrich et al. (1982) conducted among 764 sixth graders in Oakland, California, reported that two-thirds of all boys and girls with younger brothers and sisters had child care responsibilities. Frequent child

Table 4. Importance of the roles of mother versus other caregivers and companions as rated from ethnographic sources on 186 sampled societies[a]

	Summary (N)	Rating (%)
During infancy		
1. Almost exclusively the mother	5	2.7
2. Principally mother, others have minor roles	81	43.5
3. Principally mother, others have important roles	63	33.9
4. Mother provides half or less of care	10	5.4
5. Mother's role is significant but less than all others combined	2	1.1
6. Most care except nursing is by others	1	0.5
7. Practically all care, including nursing, is by others	0	0
Could not be coded	24	12.9
Total	186	100.0
During early childhood		
1. Almost exclusively the mother	0	0
2. Principally the mother, but others have important roles	36	19.4
3. Child spends half or less of the time with mother	60	32.3
4. Majority of time is spent away from mother	38	20.4
5. Practically all the time is spent away from mother	2	1.1
Could not be coded	50	26.9
Total	186	100.0

[a] Adapted from Barry and Paxson (1971, pp. 474–480, Table 1, column 13).

care (four to five times a week) was more common when the mother had outside employment (in both two-parent and single-parent families).

Sib caregiving is also fairly frequent among Hawaiian children. More than 70% of Hawaiian mothers interviewed in Honolulu reported that their 5- to 8-year-old children performed caregiving chores for their younger sibs (Weisner, 1978). In such settings, where two or more siblings were present together, observers noted that sib caregiving occurred over three-fourths of the time (Weisner et al., 1981). And Bryant (1982) found in a non-metropolitan area of Northern California that 78% of first and fourth graders had an older sibling who would help them with their homework.

Older sisters most commonly take on the role of sib caregiver, both cross-culturally (Whiting and Whiting, 1975; Weisner and Gallimore, 1977) as well as in the U.S. (Bossard and Boll, 1956; Koch, 1960; Sutton-Smith and Rosenberg, 1970). However, there have been recent changes toward a greater involvement of boys in child care responsibilities, especially in families with working mothers (Medrich et al., 1982). The consequences of these changes need to be systematically documented.

CROSS-CULTURAL VARIATIONS OF SIB CARE

The percentage of societies using children as caregivers of infants and young children is smaller in the oldest and most basic human subsistence types than for other subsistence economies. Among hunters and gatherers, there is a great deal of *contact* with siblings, but less sib care than in agricultural and pastoral societies (Konner, 1975).

Most of this non-maternal contact takes place in multi-age play groups made up of siblings and cousins of both sexes, as for example among the Kung San (Bushmen) of the Kalahari Desert (Konner, 1977). These play groups provide incidentally protection, care, and teaching of infants and young children by older siblings, but children are not expected to be regular caregivers of infants.

Parental efforts to induce children to care for younger siblings is greater in societies whose economics involve more accumulation (Barry et al., 1959). The "farming out" of the actual care of infants and young children to "child nurses," often only 4 years older than their small charges, is more common in intermediate-level horticultural societies where women's work load is heavy. This type of child care gives an older sibling responsiblity for her younger sibling for longer stretches of time, while the mother is farther away than in the hunter-gatherer societies (Konner, 1981). Typically an older sister or, if not available, an older brother, is designated as a regular caregiver for the infant born second or third after her (Ember, 1973; Rosenblatt and Skoogberg, 1974).

For example, among the Kikuyu, an East African agriculturist tribe studied by Leiderman and Leiderman (1974a, 1974b, 1977), infant care is *polymatric* rather than *monomatric*. The Kikuyu mother, on the average, spends only about half of her daytime activities with her infant after the baby reaches 5 months. A considerable portion of daytime care is undertaken by a child caregiver, usually an older sister between the ages of 6 and 12 years, who carries the infant, attends to his or her needs, and provides most of the social interaction. In modernizing communities the caregiver may have completed between 2 and 5 years of primary school, finishing by age 11 or 12. She would be old enough to know the responsibilities of the household, yet young enough to want to be included in children's activities.

Most but not all caregiving of children by other children is done within the child's own domestic group, but there are also instances of extrafamilial child caregiving. Some societies use hired child nurses, or exchange young children between households in order to provide for caregiving. Specific kin of the mother (such as a younger sister or female cousin) are often preferred (Weisner and Gallimore, 1977).

Rogoff et al., (1975) made a cross-cultural survey of the age of assignment of roles and responsibilities to children, based on ethnographies of 50 cultures from the HRAF files. They find pancultural trends in the age of assignment of child care roles for girls centering on the 5- to 7-year period. This is the same age when Western bureaucracies introduce formal schooling, a phenomenon that is spreading in the developing countries.

The process of modernization may bring about some unexpected side effects in infant care that are created by the greater educational opportunities for older children, especially for girls in the developing world. For example, Leiderman and Leiderman (1977), in their study of an East African agricultural community, noted that families who send their children to school lose the services of an important infant caregiver of the requisite age for at least part of the day. Some families with sufficient economic resources can pay both the school fees and hire a non-familial caregiver. Less affluent families who send their daughters to school quite likely have the disadvantage of a less mature infant caregiver, often a preschool child as young as 4 (Whiting, 1977).

Because the stimulation of a more mature caregiver seems to contribute to higher performance on scales of infant development, the decrease in age of infant caregivers under the impact of schooling has important implications for a modernizing society.

In summary, caregiving of children by older children seems to be most common in societies where women make a substantial contribution to the subsistence economy, where the work takes the mother away from home and/ or is difficult to interrupt, and where circumstances of residence, birth order, and family size make such alternative caregivers available (Minturn and Lambert, 1964).

SUBCULTURAL VARIATIONS IN SIB CARE IN THE U.S.

Among the different subcultures in a pluralistic society, such as the U.S., there are differences in prevalence of sib care that are related to the same factors which lead to sib caregiving in other parts of the world: a large family; maternal employment outside of the household; disruption of the family unit by death, divorce, desertion, or incarceration of the major breadwinner; and the presence of a handicapped or ill family member. All these stressful life events occur more frequently among the poor; hence, sib caregiving is more prevalent and extensive in lower-class than middle- and upper-class families in the U.S.

Ethnic differences in the extent of sib care were noted by Medrich et al. (1982) in their study of sixth graders in Oakland, California. A higher proportion of black children than any other ethnic group were involved in sib care. Ethnic differences in sib care responsibilities increased when the mother worked, in both two-parent and single-parent families, with a higher proportion of black and a lower proportion of Asian than white children involved in sib care. Reliance on child care by siblings was also one of the major survival strategies for Mexican-American female heads of household in the single-parent families studied by Wagner and Schaeffer (1980) in San José, California.

The most extensive studies of sib care among American ethnic groups have been conducted in urban and rural Hawaii, on the islands of Oahu and Kauai (Gallimore et al., 1974; Weisner, 1978; Weisner et al., 1981; Werner and Smith, 1977; 1982). Among Hawaiians, as among Native Americans, sib caregiving is a functional adaptation of low-income families that allows them flexibility in coping with crises and increases the number of resource contributors (Jorgenson, 1971).

As infants, children in most Hawaiian and Polynesian families are largely under the direct care of adults (Jordan and Tharp, 1979). Babies, however receive a good deal of attention from older children as well. By the time Hawaiian children reach age 1 or 2, they begin to spend a high proportion of time in the company of other children as the charge of an older child, usually a sibling. Most children will be full-fledged members of such sib care groups by age 3 or 4.

There seems to be a gradual shift from children being cared for by other children, but not being caregivers themselves (ages 5 to 7 years) to a period when many Hawaiian children experience both roles (ages 8 or 9 and older). Thus, children learn to be both recipients and providers of sib care (Weisner, 1982).

Here are some examples from the records of the Kauai Longitudinal Study which show the importance of sib caregiving among large rural Hawaiian families whose economic status is marginal:

> ***Martin*** was the oldest of eight children in a family where socio-economic status was rated low, but where educational stimulation and emotional support were consid-

ered adequate. His father was a heavy equipment operator for one of the plantations on the island, and his mother worked part-time (summers) at a pineapple cannery. Although neither parent had graduated from high school, they supported the children's education. Their goal for Martin was placement in Kamehameha School—a private school on Oahu for Hawaiian and part-Hawaiian children.

Martin had regular daily chores and shared in the responsibility for his younger siblings. The family was quite close-knit . . . "almost everything we do, we do as a family, hunting, picnicing, family gatherings." The mother described 10-year-old Martin as a youngster of whom she was proud. She especially liked the way he took care of his siblings and showed concern for them.

Born prematurely, **Ellen** and **Darlene,** high-risk twin daughters of a 24-year-old mother and 35-year-old father, remained in the hospital for their first weeks of life. The other children were disappointed when the mother came home without the babies. The oldest child, a daughter of 9, was considered particularly helpful in the care of the infants and other household tasks when the twins came home.

The socioeconomic status of the family continued to be below average during the twins' childhood, but emotional support within the family was judged satisfactory. The father worked steadily for the sugar plantations during the next decade and the mother worked intermittently until the girls were 7 and then went to work on a full-time basis. In her absence an older sister had the responsibility for the primary care of the children. Not only was the older sister important in the twins' world, but the older brothers helped with their homework as well and participated in activities with them. The siblings not only provided support but also the opportunity for the girls to draw on their own skills and resources—"they usually can do most of their school work by themselves; they can cook their own food and do occasionally; they help clean house and wash dishes—they know I work, so they'll help" (mother of twins at age 10).

Their life events during this period provided little out of the ordinary and chiefly involved the day-to-day existence of home, school, and outings in a rural community. But the emotional support they received from their older siblings and the model of a gainfully employed mother seems to have contributed to their independence, competence and autonomy—characteristics the twins shared with the other resilient children in our study (Werner and Smith, 1982, pp. 74–76).

SIB CAREGIVING STYLES

Both styles and effects of sib caregiving are influenced by the number of children in the family, and by their birth order, ages, age spacing, and gender (Cicirelli, 1976b).

Among the rural families on Kauai (Hawaii) we noted a style of child care that was quite similar to the one described by adult siblings from large families on the U.S. mainland (Bossard and Boll, 1956) and found among the urban *Families of the Slums* (Minuchin et al., 1967).

In such large families, with marginal incomes, sib caregivers depended on goodwill, counsel, and appeals for cooperation to maintain their order, and were often involved in "rescue missions." The discipline of older siblings was usually seen by the younger ones as fair and sometimes more appropriate than that of their parents (who were more apt to rely on physical punishment). This sib caregiving style that includes "benevolent authoritarianism," interdependence, and shared functioning (Gallimore et al., 1974) also characterizes many traditional families in the developing world (Werner, 1979).

Observations of the interactions of sib caregivers in such families show, however, that the behavior of child caregivers varies with the age of their small charges. Whiting and Whiting (1975), in their *Six Cultures Study*, noted that sib caregivers of infants were predominantly nurturant and responsive in their behavior. In contrast, sib caregivers of 2- to 4-year-old brothers and sisters were more apt to reprimand, criticize, and punish their small charges.

Empirical data on sib caregiving in middle childhood come predominantly from middle-class families in the U.S., where there are fewer but more closely spaced children than in the non-Western world (Bryant, 1979, 1981, 1982; Bryant and Crockenberg, 1980; Cicirelli, 1976a; Sutton-Smith and Rosenberg, 1969, 1970). Sib caregiving in middle childhood, among such middle-class families seems to take two distinct forms: one stressing *nurturance*, the other *principled discipline* (Bryant, 1982).

Sutton-Smith and Rosenberg (1968) reported the results of an interview questionnaire administered to elementary school children, asking them about the tactics they used for getting their siblings to do what they wanted them to do. Responses varied by sex and birth order. Both first-born and same-sex children used more "power-oriented" tactics than did later-born siblings and siblings of the opposite sex. Boys used attack and offense more often, girls tried reasoning, defense, and making the sibling feel obligated. First-born children were more likely to boss, interfere, ignore, or bribe their younger siblings; second-born children were more likely to attack their sibling's property, or to plead or reason with their older siblings. Bossy, being offensive, sulking, and teasing were more often used with same sex siblings; being defensive and "making up" were more often used with opposite sex siblings.

Sib caregiving styles also tend to differ from parental caregiving styles, at least in American middle-class families in which comparisons between parent and child generations have been made (Bryant, 1982; Bryant and Crockenberg, 1980; Cicirelli, 1976a).

In such families, mothers tend to give more explanation and feedback to a child than do older siblings. Children, in turn, respond to their mothers more with help seeking and accepting behaviors than they do in response to sib caregiving (Cicirelli, 1976a, 1976b). For example, Bryant and Crockenberg (1980) found that older female siblings (mean age, 10.5) did not seem to adopt the style of their mothers when they acted as helpers to their later born sisters who were 2 or 3 years younger. For the older girls, "giving help" correlated positively with disparagement, instead, and seemed to involve more control and bossiness. In turn, help by the older sister correlated with anger expressed by the younger child. However, if the younger sibling did not get a response from her mother, she often turned to her older sister for help and received it from her.

Seven- to 10-year-old children who responded to the Cornell Parent Behavior Questionnaire in a study by Bryant (1979) saw their *parents* generally more active on five of six caregiving dimensions—nurturance, instrumental companionship, achievement demands, control, and principled discipline—but they saw their *siblings* more active in physical punishment when they took on a caregiving role.

In contrast to the parent generation, older siblings were perceived as providing nurturance and principled discipline to an equal degree for both 7- and 10-year-old siblings, and their achievement demands were perceived as similar by both brothers and sisters. However, children accept help and establish a dependency relationship more often with a sibling 4 years older than with a sibling only 2 years older, and more often with an older sister than with an older brother (Cicirelli, 1973; 1976b). The resolution of "dependency problems" may create greater ambivalence in families with a few closely spaced children (who have greater equity in power) than in large families where there is a wider age range between the providers and recipients of child care.

CONSEQUENCES OF SIB CAREGIVING

There is a great need for additional data that show the effects on a child of either providing or receiving child care. Most of the observations on the social and personality correlates of sib care come from cross-cultural studies, with relatively large families and a wide age range between siblings (Weisner and Gallimore, 1977; Weisner, 1982). There are hardly any data on the consequences of sib caregiving in contemporary American families. The few data available deal mostly with the effects of such care in middle childhood and adolescence (Bryant, 1982; Gallimore et al., 1974; Simeonsson and McHale, 1981; Werner and Smith, 1982).

Attachment

When an older sibling is substantially involved in the caregiving of an infant, the baby develops a strong attachment to both the mother and the sib caregiver. This has been documented repeatedly in cross-sectional and longitudinal studies among polymatric East African households where mothers share the care of an infant with older siblings.

For example, Ainsworth (1967) in her longitudinal study of Baganda babies in Uganda (whom she followed from 2 to 15 months), observed that nearly all the infants who became attached to their mothers also became attached to other persons who shared in the routine care of the baby, usually older sisters. Differential responses of the infant to the mother were followed fairly rapidly by differential responses to the child caregiver. Actual attachment to other caregivers emerged in the third quarter of the first year, in the same period in which the first clear-cut attachment to the mother was observed.

In neighboring Kenya, Leiderman and Leiderman (1974b) monitored the responses of Kikuyu infants to the mother, to child caregivers, and to strangers. As measured by their positive affective responses, 7- to 8-month-old and 10- to 12-month-old infants reacted similarly to their mothers and to child caregivers, but the babies were more wary of strangers and reacted more negatively toward their approach in polymatric than in monomatric (exclusively mothered) households. Reed and Leiderman (1981) observed similar age-related changes in attachment behavior among the Gussi, where infant care is also shared by mothers and child caregivers. There were peaks in the infants' display of attachment behavior to both the mother and the child caregiver around 9 to 11 months, and again around 20 to 22 months, suggesting two periods of formation and consolidation of attachment bonds (see Figure 5).

Canadian investigators who monitored sibling interactions in the home report that during the second year of life (mean age, 20 months), infants increasingly directed their social behavior toward their siblings, and that most of these behaviors were positive in nature (Abramovitch et al., 1979). Older siblings tended to reciprocate in kind, but older sisters (2.5 to 4 years older)

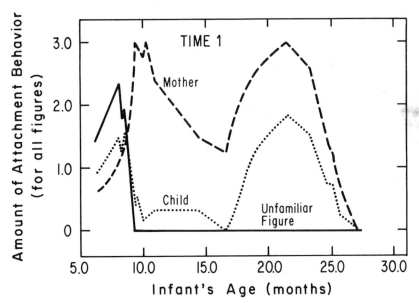

Figure 5. Attachment behavior to mother, child, and unfamiliar figures (Adapted from Reed and Leiderman, 1981. Reprinted with permission from Lawrence Earlbaum Associates, Inc., Hillsdale, NJ.)

were more likely to engage in positive behavior with the infants (acting as "little mothers") than older brothers or more closely spaced siblings (1 to 2 years older) of either sex. The infants tended to imitate the behavior of their older siblings. In a follow-up study 18 months later, when the younger siblings were about 38 months old, this pattern of sibling interactions had remained quite stable (Pepler et al., 1981). Older siblings initiated prosocial and agonistic behavior more often, while the younger siblings imitated more. Over time there was a marked increase in prosocial behavior by both the older and younger siblings (see also Lamb, 1978a, 1978b).

PROSOCIAL BEHAVIOR: NURTURANCE AND RESPONSIBILITY

In many traditional societies of the developing world, sib care is expected from children in the age range between 5 to 7 years, the age of the older siblings in the Canadian study. Whiting and Whiting (1973, 1975), in their *Six Cultures Study*, found that such sib caregivers of infants were more nurturant, responsible, and altruistic than children who did not take care of infants. Sixty-nine percent of the mothers from the East African highlands, 41% of the mothers from the Mexican barrio, and 25% of the Filipino mothers reported having been helped in infant care by an older sibling, usually a sister. These societies ranked also highest in the nurturant behavior of their children, higher than the Indian, Okinawan, and New England communities in which infant care by older siblings was less common.

Caudill and Plath (1966), in a study of sleeping arrangements of urban Japanese families, were impressed with the role of siblings in the care and instruction of the younger babies, and how this responsibility for parenting seemed to diminish any sibling rivalry and to create close bonding between brother and sisters. They ascribed the strong affectionate bond and interdependence between members of the Japanese family to the sleeping arrangements. When the baby is new, he or she sleeps with the mother; when another baby comes, the child sleeps with an older brother or sister. This phenomenon of sleeping with another member of the family apparently strengthens family bonds and contributes to a strong nurturant family life.

A similar strong bond between siblings was noted in both urban and rural Hawaiian families (Gallimore et al., 1974; Werner and Smith, 1977). In such households, mothers tended to turn over the care of young children to older sisters. In the case of permanent father absence because of death, desertion, or divorce, such sib caregiving seemed to be a special "protective" factor for the girls: It pushed them into the direction of earlier social maturity in childhood and contributed to a more pronounced sense of social responsibility than was typical of their age peers in adolescence (Werner and Smith, 1982).

In a like vein, studies of the effects of sib caregiving on the brothers and sisters of handicapped children report that such siblings are generally characterized by greater emotional maturity and social responsibility than is commonly found in American youth (Simeonsson and McHale, 1981).

In one of the most comprehensive inquiries in this area, Grossman (1972) interviewed college-age siblings of a handicapped child and found that some 45% were judged to have benefited from their experience. The benefits included an increase in altruistic concerns and tolerance toward other persons, as well as an increase in idealism and an orientation toward humanitarian interests. The extent to which such an experience affects the actual career choice of adults was assessed by Cleveland and Miller (1977). The oldest female siblings (who had the heaviest caregiving responsibilities for the handicapped child) were the most likely to pursue the helping professions and to put into practice their caring and concern for the welfare of others.

SEX ROLE TRAINING

In both traditional and modern societies, child caregiving seems to provide earlier and stronger sex role differentiated training for girls because girls are given this task more often than boys and are usually preferred over boys when both sexes are available (Minturn, 1979; Rogoff et al., 1975).

In all six cultures studied by Whiting and Whiting and among the horticultural Kikuyu of Kenya as well, older girls (ages 7 to 11) offered help and support to others more often than did boys (Whiting and Edwards, 1973). There were no such sex differences for children aged 3 to 6. The authors interpret the increased nurturance of the older girls as due to the assignment of increased child-rearing duties, especially infant caregiving.

Ember (1973) observed Luo boys in Kenya who were expected to perform child caregiving chores usually assigned to girls, because there were no older sisters available in the household. Such boys displayed more nurturant, "feminine" social behaviors than boys not needed for such tasks. Thus, it seems that sex differences in nurturance may only occur at particular ages and may not be uniform across all cultures. The critical factor for the development of nurturant behavior seems to be the demand for child care tasks within the home. It would be interesting to see whether similar findings could be replicated in the U.S. as sex role expectations change in the wake of a more egalitarian type of child-rearing.

We have a hint from our findings in the Kauai Longitudinal Study that involvement of males in child care responsibilities may lead to more nurturant and socially responsible behavior in our own country as well (Werner and Smith, 1982). Among a birth cohort of 698 Japanese-, Hawaiian-, and Filipino-American children whom we followed for more than two decades (from 1955 to 1980), there were some 72 resilient youth (42 females, 30 males) who grew into autonomous and competent young adults, in spite of constitutional vulnerabilities, chronic poverty, and parental psychopathology. Most of these youngsters were either first- or second-born. Involvement in sib care, either as providers or recipients, proved to be one of the major protective factors in their stressful lives.

At 17 or 18, both men and women in this resilient group scored significantly higher than their same sex peers on the following dimensions of the California Personality Inventory (CPI): Achievement via Conformance, Responsibility, Socialization, and Femininity. The latter scale identifies persons with emotional responsiveness, social perceptiveness, and sensitivity. The interests and activities of these youth were consistently less sex typed than that of their peers.

The greater involvement of both boys and girls in child care responsibilities in families of working mothers (which are on the increase in the U.S.) may have some desirable consequences for both recipients and providers of child care in the present and the next generation. First grade boys and girls seem to respond to their older sibs' caregiving with greater acceptance of individual differences in their peers (Bryant, 1982). Helping rear younger siblings, in turn, tends to make children more competent parents of their own offspring and increases their interest in joining groups to learn better ways of "parenting" (Essman, 1977; Essman and Deutsch, 1979).

AFFILIATION VERSUS ACHIEVEMENT MOTIVATION

In the African, Asian, Latin American, and Polynesian societies in which child caregiving has been studied, there is usually a more or less gradual transition between the maternal or shared care for infants and the sib care for toddlers and young children. A study of Kikuyu children illustrates this shift (Carlebach, 1967). After the infant is given a great deal of maternal attention during the first 1 or 2 years of life—attention that fosters strong attachment—the mother begins to refuse help and redirects the child to his or her siblings when she is pregnant again.

This shift from adult to sib care can occur without the toddler having learned self-help skills, thus imposing a rather strong burden on the sibling who is the caregiver. The provider of sib care usually is about at the age when schooling is introduced in modern societies (6 to 8) and when achievement motivation begins to crystallize. In societies or families where sib caregiving is prevalent, such achievement motivation may therefore be sacrificed for the sake of affiliation (Weisner and Gallimore, 1977).

Reliance on sib care as a factor in the development of affiliation motivation has been suggested by studies of Hawaiian-Americans (Gallimore et al., 1974). The pattern of being interdependent and affiliating with others is a significant feature of Hawaiian life and may cause problems in the classroom. Hawaiian children are inclined to attend to peers rather than teachers and individual work—behavior that is often interpreted by teachers in terms of attentional or motivational deficits.

On the positive side, MacDonald and Gallimore (1971) found in a number of classroom studies that Hawaiian-American students perform at high levels if they are allowed to interact or affiliate with peers in team work or in the sharing of earned privileges. Whether such peer interaction is also more motivating for those from high sib care families in other cultures is a question that has not been adequately answered.

SIBLINGS AS CHANGE AGENTS:
THE CHILD-TO-CHILD PROGRAMME

Four out of every five children in the world live in the developing countries of Africa, Latin America, Asia, and Oceania—regions in which few children have access to the nutritional, health, and educational services that most of the industrialized world takes for granted (Werner, 1979). Many children in the developing world are involved in some form of sib care, with older sisters and brothers acting as supplementary or surrogate parents.

In 1977, the Institute of Child Health at the University of London began the Child-to-Child programme, which addresses itself to the needs of these children (Figure 6).[4] Initiated by David Morley, a pediatrician at the Institute's Tropical Child Health Unit, this is an international program of vast potential that sets out to teach and encourage older children to take an active role in improving the health and development of their younger brothers and sisters (Morley, 1979).

Since 1979—the International Year of the Child—the Child-to-Child programme has prepared activity sheets on such topics as nutrition; sanitation, health habits, and hygiene; accident prevention and provision of a safe environment; care for the sick child; and simple home-made games that stimulate the intellectual and social development of young children. These activity sheets and an illustrated book, *Child-to-Child* (Aarons et al., 1979), have been translated into all of the major languages of the world (English, French, Spanish, Portuguese, Arabic, Kiswahili, Hindi, and Indonesian).

---

[4] Interested readers can address inquiries about the program to Dr. Duncan Guthrie, Director, Child-to-Child programme, c/o Institute of Child Health, University of London, 30 Guilford Street, London, WCIN EH, England.

You too can teach in a CHILD-to-CHILD programme

Figure 6.

The Child-to-Child programme also publishes a newsletter that reports on projects for school-age children and their teachers in some 100 countries. Many of these preventive and curative activities are applicable for children in our own country as well, especially those who are at risk because of poverty or physical handicaps.

An evaluation of the program's effectiveness should have high priority among the participating countries and sponsoring international agencies, such as the United Nations Children's Fund (UNICEF). Some outcome criteria expected in a successful Child-to-Child programme might be relatively easy to assess, such as a decline in childhood accidents or cases of dehydration. Others, such as the positive effects of early stimulation by siblings through play, are more difficult to evaluate, but some methods used in the evaluation of early intervention programs in Western countries could be adopted (see Brown, 1978).

SIBLINGS AS TUTORS

In the U.S. academic tutoring is a frequently practiced form of sib caregiving, at least in middle-class families (Bryant, 1982). Several investigators have looked at the effectiveness of siblings in their role as teachers (Cicirelli, 1972, 1973, 1975, 1976a, 1976b; Steward and Steward, 1976), and some innovative education programs have introduced features distinctive of the sib caregiving system (MacDonald and Gallimore, 1971; Jordan and Tharp, 1979).

Margaret and David Steward (1976) have published one of the few studies that compare the teaching styles employed with young preoperational children (age 2 to 5 years) by their first-born siblings who are either concrete thinkers (ages 6 to 11 years) or formal operational thinkers (12 years old) and by their mothers. Half of the sibling pairs were boys, the other half were girls. In all dyads, a Piagetian sorting game was taught by the examiner to either the mother or the first-born sibling, who was then asked to teach the young child. Sibling teachers gave their preschool-age brothers and sisters significantly more total feedback, and in that total feedback more positive reinforcement, than did the mothers. In turn, the young learners accepted the task presented by the siblings' instructions significantly more often than they did when the mothers were teachers.

Cicirelli (1976a) studied the relative effectiveness of older brothers and sisters in teaching first grade children concept-learning and object-sorting tasks. He found that older siblings have a significant effect on their younger siblings' performance on cognitive tasks, but that this effect depends on the sibling status position, and especially on the sex of the sibling teacher.

Older sisters were more effective than older brothers when teaching younger siblings. Looking at four sibling dyads, highest average concept attainment scores were found for boys taught by older sisters, followed by girls taught by older sisters, and boys taught by older brothers; poorest scores were made by girls taught by older brothers (Cicirelli, 1972). Girls teaching their siblings used the deductive method more often than other teachers; boys teaching their siblings used the inductive method more often than other teachers.

Not only did older siblings vary in their teaching styles, but younger siblings responded differently to the gender of the sibling tutor. Cicirelli (1974) found that the younger sibling was more likely to work independently when the teacher/tutor was an older brother, and more likely to accept non-verbal directions when the teacher/tutor was an older sister.

The relative efficacy of older sisters as tutors is thought to be the result of two factors (Cicirelli, 1976b): First, role theory would hypothesize that older sisters are more ready to assume a teaching role because they identify more easily with their mothers and female school teachers (Koch, 1960; Sutton-Smith and Rosenberg, 1970), and they practice the role of sib caregiver more often. Second, older brothers tend to bring more competitiveness to the situation, especially when they are closely spaced. Such sibling rivalry could lead younger siblings to be defensive and resist learning from an older brother in a formal teaching situation, but it could also challenge the younger siblings' intellectual development in informal or incidental learning situations (Cicirelli, 1975).

Thus, if sibling teaching programs were instituted in schools, certain dyads might be especially effective in peer tutoring, for example, widely spaced siblings and older sisters who explain, provide verbal labels, and question their younger brother or sister.

Tutoring programs that use children as tutors for other children in the school system have been critically evaluated by Feldman et al. (1976). Although anecdotal reports of the effects of peer tutoring have been promising, empirical studies of its effects have yielded mixed results. Children acting as tutors often show positive gains in both achievement and attitudes toward school, but only a few studies have shown lasting academic gains by tutees. Gallimore, et al. (1978) found a significant correlation between attentiveness to a peer tutor and the degree to which male siblings assumed child care responsibilities among urban Hawaiians; and Fukuda (1975) reported similar results from a rural Hawaiian school: Males from families reporting high sib care were more attentive tutees.

One promising approach to education that incorporates features of the sib caregiving system is the Kamehameha Early Education Program (KEEP) in Honolulu. KEEP is a laboratory and demonstration school for Hawaiian and part Hawaiian children from kindergarten through grade three, and has a multidisciplinary research and development program involving anthropologists, educators, linguists, and psychologists (Weisner et al., 1981). It incorporates into its classroom system organization and curriculum several features of the Hawaiian sib caregiving that have profound importance educationally, that is, affiliation motivation and peer orientation. The outcome of KEEP's work at the time of the last report is a school situation that has resulted in greatly increased academic achievement on the part of the children. By the fourth grade, statewide testing places the means of schools with predominantly Hawaiian populations in the first and lowest stanine of national norms in reading, but KEEP children are achieving at levels considerably above national norms, especially in reading (Jordan and Tharp, 1979, pp. 276–277).

SIBLINGS AS THERAPISTS AND BEHAVIOR MODIFIERS

Among clinical psychologists and psychiatrists, the "family systems" approach to clinical intervention has recently gained increasing recognition. Within this framework, siblings have been considered as potentially valuable contributors to both the diagnosis and the resolution of the problems of other family members, be they parents or child clients. Most of the observations on the role of siblings have been based on clinical impressions, however, and there is an urgent need for some systematic evaluation of their contributions to the therapeutic process.

Greenbaum (1965), who used a joint sibling interview as diagnostic procedure, reports that siblings can offer valuable feedback to a child client regarding negative evaluations of his behavior, and that this feedback seems more tolerable for the child than the same evaluation offered by an adult. Older siblings may also be able to "verbalize" a child client's difficulties better, and offer emotional support during therapy. They seem to be able to reduce the inhibition of some children to engage in direct interaction with the therapist.

Bank and Kahn (1975, 1982) make siblings an important focus in family therapy, especially during childhood and in the teenage years. They stress the importance of obtaining thorough diagnostic information on sibling relationships and utilize brothers and sisters considered "helpful" by their client as consultants at different stages of the therapy process: 1) to move the therapy in certain strategic directions; 2) to assist the client(s) in rehearsing more constructive interaction patterns; and 3) to foster encouragement, support, and candor through "sibling rallies."

Studies that document systematically the effectiveness of a sibling as an adjunct in behavior therapy are rare. Lavigueur (1976) found that having both siblings and parents take on therapists' roles successfully modified a child's disruptive behaviors at home when these behaviors had a history of sibling reinforcement. Siblings' consistent use of behavior modification procedures leads to an increase in the frequency of positive interactions between the sibling therapist and the "troubled child" and seems to benefit both children (Milner and Cantwell, 1976).

Behavior modification also seems to be a helpful tool for siblings of mentally retarded children. Weinrott (1974) established a summer program for retarded children, their 10- to 18-year-old siblings, and their parents. The siblings were taught the basic principles of learning theory and observed the application of operant techniques by camp counselors. They were then given the opportunity to use these techniques with both their own retarded brother or sister and with other handicapped children.

Follow-up data based on retrospective parental reports indicated that the quality of the sibling relationship seemed to change markedly in two respects: 1) siblings began to focus on adaptive behaviors of the retarded child and to reinforce these behaviors rather than deviant ones; and 2) sibling interactions began to involve teaching rather than custodial care of the mentally retarded child. Since the parents were receiving training in behavior modification at the same time as the siblings, however, it is unclear how much of an effect the sibling intervention per se actually had. The use of siblings as behavior modifiers for mentally ill and retarded children seems to be a promising tool that needs to be examined more systematically.

PARENTAL SUPPORT FOR SIB CAREGIVING

The attitudes of parents, especially mothers, probably make a significant impact on the quality and effect of sib caregiving, but they have not been extensively studied. Cross-culturally, in households in which the mother shares the daytime care of her infants with others, she is more likely to retain the primary caregiving role herself if the baby is male, and male babies seem to receive more maternal attention and physical stimulation than female infants. Mothers are likely to delegate the daytime care of their infant daughters to someone else, usually an older sister (Super, 1977).

Weisner (1982) asked urban Hawaiian and urban and rural mothers in Kenya about their views of sib caregiving. Mothers in both cultures felt that it was important for children to be responsible for the care of younger siblings in the family circle, and had specific task obligations for them, which varied with the size of the domestic group and the birth order of the children. The African mothers, however, believed more strongly that they were "in charge" or "control," whereas among the Hawaiian mothers there was more emphasis on the "sharing" of child care responsibilities and family decisions between parents and the sib caregivers.

SIB CARE: SUPPLEMENTARY VERSUS SUBSTITUTE PARENTING

Sibling caregiving tends to be more effective if it is *supplementary* rather than *substitute* parenting (Furman and Buhrmester, 1982). But under some traumatic circumstances (for example, in abusive homes or during wars, notably among the survivors of the Holocaust), children have served as surrogate parents for each other (Bank and Kahn, 1982). A classic example were the "six orphans of Terezin" (Freud and Dunn, 1951), who had lost their parents as infants in a concentration camp and were shifted from one camp to another during the first 3 years of their life.

When they were brought to a therapeutic nursery in England at the end of World War II, they did not trust any adult, but they had developed strong attachments to each other and looked out for each other with fierce loyalty and without any "sibling rivalry." They provided emotional support for each other, were sensitive of each other's needs, and resisted any effort to be separated. As children, they seemed to be remarkably resilient, and they have remained so as adults (Moskovitz, 1983).

On the other hand, both Bossard and Boll (1956) and Bank and Kahn (1982) report from their extensive interviews with adult siblings that being saddled with the major responsibility of tending a younger sibling or looking out for each other in a "Hansel and Gretel" fashion may have a detrimental effect on the social life and emotional growth of the older child.

The *availability of supplemental adult resources* for organizing sib caregiving seems to be a crucial determinant of whether the caregiver helps or hurts a sibling in the long run (Bank and Kahn, 1982). Among the "vulnerable, but invincible children" of Kauai, we noted that in the absence of parents or in the presence of severe parental psychopathology, other concerned adults, such as grandparents or relatives, acted as parent substitutes and shared the burden of child care with the older siblings in the family (Werner and Smith, 1977, 1982). The role of such kith and kin as alternate caregivers is discussed in subsequent chapters.

NEEDED RESEARCH

The study of sib caregiving is still in its infancy. On the most general level, there is a need for some unifying perspectives that would make sense out of bits and pieces of isolated data provided by anthropologists, child development researchers, educators, family specialists, psychologists, and psychiatrists.

Some theoretical perspectives have gained recognition in the past decade (Sutton-Smith and Rosenberg, 1970). Among the most popular are social learning theory and systems theory. The former stresses the role of siblings as models for each other, the latter emphasizes the synergism between parental and child caregiving styles (Furman and Buhrmester, 1982). Another challenging perspective is sociobiology (Freedman, 1979). Sociobiologists hypothesize that those who share a greater proportion of genes are more likely to be involved in all kinds of caring relationships that promote the survival of close relatives and their offspring. Full siblings share an average of 50% of the genes in which the parents differ, and seem to be involved everywhere in the world in interdependent relationships that appear to promote altruistic behavior. Borden, (1975), at the University of Chicago, developed a test for such "selective altruism" and gave it to 93 high school students. The respondents were asked to assess their chances of their putting themselves in jeopardy for someone else. The degree of relationship between the subject and the person he or she was supposed to help varied. Borden found that brothers might be helped when cousins might not be, and sisters before girlfriends.

Regardless of the theoretical perspective that might be adopted by individual researchers, there is a strong methodological challenge in doing research on sib caregiving. There are a number of "structural" variables, that is, sibling and family indicators that are needed to describe the general context in which sibling relationships develop and that seem to interact in complex ways (Bryant, 1982). Among them are the age and age spacing of the siblings, their birth order and gender, and the size and type of family (large versus small, nuclear versus extended, two-parent versus single-parent).

There are very few longitudinal studies that examine changes in sibling relationships. The few existing ones (for example, by Lamb, 1978a, 1978b; Leiderman, 1974a, 1974b; and Pepler et al., 1981) have dealt with sibling relationships in infancy and the preschool years, but none have directly monitored changes in the quality and effectiveness of sib caregiving, especially common in middle childhood and adolescence.

Particularly scarce is research on the effects of siblings on the parent-child relationship in a caregiving situation (for a rare example, see Kendrick and Dunn, 1980). Only Bryant (1982) reports some recent analysis of second-order effects of sib caregiving in middle childhood, with due consideration of both parental and sib caregiving styles.

Most importantly, the broader cultural context in which sib caregiving takes place needs to be considered in future research. This context differs dramatically for most families and societies in the traditional world in comparison with middle-class American families. The socialization goal of most societies and families in which sib caregiving has been observed cross-culturally is the integration of the child into the social context rather than the independence and individual achievement, stressed in contemporary U.S. society. It may be that sib caregiving fosters certain psychological and behavioral characteristics in children that are *more* adaptive in some settings and circumstances (with peers, at play, within the family, when survival is at stake) but *less* adaptive in other settings and circumstances (in the competitive world of school and work, under conditions of relative affluence). In short, the behavior of recipients and providers of sib care needs to be observed in a wider range of contexts than has been done so far.

SUMMARY

The role of children in child care has received little attention in studies of child development, although cross-cultural research indicates that caregiving of children by siblings, cousins, and child nurses is a significant phenomenon in the developing world. In the U.S. siblings often assume the care of younger brothers and sisters when the mother has outside employment.

Cross-cultural surveys find a pancultural trend in the age of assignment of child care roles, especially for girls, which coincides with the introduction of formal schooling in the Western world. Sib and child caregiving are most common in societies and families in which women make significant contributions to the economy, work takes the mother away from home, and household composition makes such alternative caregivers available.

Child caregiving seems to be an important antecedent of prosocial, nurturant, and responsible behavior in both sexes and tends to foster affiliation and interdependence among siblings. It also significantly affects their parenting skills with their own children.

The care of younger siblings by older brothers and sisters is on the increase in the U.S., with the increase of working mothers in both two-parent and single-parent families. It is the one out of school activity for children that provides them with a meaningful domestic role and productive responsibilities. There is an urgent need to document the consequences of such sib care, as they affect the children (as providers and recipients) and the parents and the family system as well. Major attention needs to be paid in future studies to the role of child caregivers as change agents, that is, as transmitters of new social values and as links between the family and a rapidly changing social world.

REFERENCES

Aarons, A., Hawes , H., and Gayton, J. 1979. Child-to-Child. The MacMillan Press, Ltd., London.

Abramovitch, R., Corter, C., and Lando, B. 1979. Sibling interactions in the home. Child Dev. 50:997–1003.

Ainsworth, M.D.S. 1967. Infancy in Uganda: Infant Care and the Growth of Love. Johns Hopkins Press, Baltimore.

Allan, V.L. 1976. Children as Teachers: Theory and Research on Tutoring. Academic Press, New York.

Bank, S., and Kahn, M.D. 1975. Sisterhood-brotherhood is powerful: Sibling subsystems and family therapy. Fam. Process. 14(3):311–331.

Bank, S.P., and Kahn, M.D. 1982. The Sibling Bond. Basic Books, New York.

Barry, H.A., and Paxson, L.N. 1971. Infancy and early childhood: Cross-cultural codes. Ethnology 10:466–500.

Barry, H.A., Child, I.L., and Baxon, M.K. 1959. Relations of child training to subsistence economy. Am. Anthropol. 6:51–63.

Borden, T. 1975. Altruism in two perspectives. Unpublished master's thesis, University of Chicago, Chicago.

Bossard, J., and Boll, E. 1956. The Large Family System: An Original Study in the Sociology of Family Behavior./ University of Pennsylvania Press, Philadelphia.

Bossard, J., and Boll, E. 1960. The Sociology of Child Development. Harper & Row, New York.

Brown, B. (Ed.). 1978. Found: Long-term Gains from Early Intervention. Westview Press, Boulder, CO.

Bryant, B.K. 1979. Siblings as caretakers. Paper presented at the Annual Meeting of the American Psychological Association, as part of a symposium entitled Lifespan Perspectives on Sibling Socialization, September, New York.

Bryant, B.K. 1981. Developmental Perspective on Sources of Support and Psychological Well-Being. Final Report to the Foundation for Child Development. Department of Applied Behavioral Sciences, University of California at Davis.

Bryant, B.K. 1982. Sibling relationships in middle childhood. In: M. Lamb and B. Sutton-Smith (eds.), Sibling Relationships: Their Nature and Significance across the Lifespan. Erlbaum, Hillsdale, N.J.

Bryant, B.K., and Crockenberg, S.B. 1980. Correlates and dimensions of prosocial behavior: A study of female siblings with their mothers. Child Dev. 51:529–544.

Carlebach, J.I. 1967. Family relationships of deprived and non-deprived Kikuyu children from polygamous marriages. J. Trop. Pediatr. 13:186–200.

Caudill, W., and Plath, D.W. 1966. Who sleeps by whom? Parent-child involvement in urban Japanese families. Psychiatry 29:344–366.

Cicirelli, V.G. 1972. The effect of sibling relationship on concept learning of young children taught by child teachers. Child Dev. 43:282–287.

Cicirelli, V.G. 1973. Effects of sibling structure and interaction on children's categorization style. Dev. Psychol. 9:132–139.

Cicirelli, V.G. 1974. Relationship of sibling structure and interaction to younger siblings' conceptual style. J. Genet. Psychol. 125:37–49.

Cicirelli, V.G. 1975. Effects of mother and older siblings on the problem-solving behavior of the younger child. Dev. Psychol. 11:749–756.

Cicirelli, V.G. 1976a. Mother-child and sibling-sibling interaction on a problem-solving task. Child. Dev. 46:588–596.

Cicirelli, V.G. 1976b. Siblings teaching siblings. In: V.L. Allen (ed.), Children as Teachers: Theory and Research on Tutoring, pp. 99–111. Academic Press, New York.

Cleveland, D., and Miller, N. 1977. Attitudes and life commitments of older siblings of mentally retarded adults: An exploratory study. Ment. Retard. 38–41.

Ember, C.R. 1973. Female task assignment and social behavior of boys. Ethos 1:424–439.

Essman, C.S. 1977. Sibling relations as socialization for parenthood. Fam. Coord. 26(3)259–262.

Essman, C.S., and Deutsch, F. 1979. Siblings as babysitters: Responses of adolescents to younger siblings in problem situations. Adolescence 14(54): 411–426.

Feldman, R.S., Devin-Sheehan, L., and Allan, V.L. 1976. Children tutoring children: A critical review of research. In: V.L. Allan (ed.), Children as Teachers: Theory and Research on Tutoring, pp. 236–252. Academic Press, New York.

Freedman, D.G. 1979. Human Sociobiology: A Holistic Approach. The Free Press, New York.

Freud, A., and Dunn, S. 1951. An experiment in group upbringing. In: R.S. Eisler (ed.), The Psychoanalytic Study of the Child, Vol. VI. International Universities Press, New York.

Fukuda, N. 1975. A study of classroom attending behavior among ethnic Hawaiian children. Unpublished manuscript.

Furman, W., and Buhrmester, D. 1982. Parenting by siblings and peers. In: N.J. Rostelnik and H. Fitzgerald (eds), Patterns of Supplementary Parenting. Plenum Press, New York.

Gallimore, R., Boggs, J.W., and Jordan, C.E. 1974. Culture, Behavior and Education: A Study of Hawaiian–Americans. Sage, Beverly Hills, CA.

Gallimore, R., Tharp, R.G., and Speidel, G.E. 1978. The relationship of sib caretaking and attentiveness to a peer tutor. Am. Educ. Res. J. 15(2):267–273.

Greenbaum, M. 1965. Joint sibling interview as a diagnostic procedure. J. Child Psychol. Psychiatry 6:227–232.

Grossman, F.K. 1972. Brothers and Sisters of Retarded Children. Syracuse University Press, Syracuse.

Jordan, C., and Tharp, R.G. 1979. Culture and education. In: A.J. Marcella, R.G. Tharp, and R.J. Ciborowski (eds.), Perspectives in Cross-Cultural Psychology, pp. 265–286. Academic Press, New York.

Jorgenson, J. 1971. Indians and the Metropolis. In: J.O. Waddell and O.M. Watson (eds.), The American Indian in Urban Society. Little, Brown, Boston.

Kendrick, C., and Dunn, J. 1980. Caring for a second baby: Effects on interaction between mother and firstborn. Dev. Psychol. 16:303–311.

Koch, H.L. 1960. The relations of certain formal attributes of siblings to attitudes held toward each other and toward their parents. Monogr. Soc. Res. Child Dev. 25(4):No. 78.

Konner, M.J. 1975. Relations among infants and juveniles in comparative perspective. In: M. Lewis and L.A. Rosenblum (eds.), Friendship and Peer Relations, pp. 99–129. Wiley, New York.

Konner, M.J. 1977. Infancy among the Kalahari Desert San. In: P.H. Leiderman, S.R. Tulkin and A. Rosenfeld (eds.), Culture and Infancy: Variations in the Human Experience, pp. 287–328. Academic Press, New York.

Konner, M.J. 1981. Evolution of human behavior development. In: R.H. Munroe, R.L. Munroe, and B.B. Whiting (eds.), Handbook of Cross-Cultural Human Development, pp.3-52. Garland Press, New York.

Kronenfeld, D.B. 1974. Sibling typology: Beyond Nerlove and Romney. Am. Ethnol. 1(3):489–506.

Lamb, M.E. 1978a. Interactions between eighteen-month-olds and their preschool aged siblings. Child Dev. 49:51–59.

Lamb, M.E. 1978b. The development of sibling relationships in infancy: A short-term longitudinal study. Child Dev. 49:1189–1196.

Lamb, M.E., and Sutton-Smith, B. (eds.). 1982. Sibling Relationships: Their Nature and Significance Across the Lifespan. Earlbaum, Hillsdale, N.J.

Lavigueur, H. 1976. The use of siblings as an adjunct to the behavioral treatment of children in the home with parents as therapists. Behav. Ther. 7:602–613.

Leiderman, P.H., and Leiderman, G.F. 1974a. Familial influences on infant development in an East African agricultural community. In: E.J. Anthony and C. Koupernik (eds), The Child in His Family, Vol. 3, pp. 305–330. Wiley, New York.

Leiderman, P.H., and Leiderman, G.F. 1974b. Affective and cognitive consequences of polymatric infant care in the East African highlands. In: A.D. Pick (ed.), Minnesota Symposia on Child Psychology, Vol. 8, pp. 87–110. University of Minnesota Press, Minneapolis.

Leiderman, P.H., and Leiderman, G.F. 1977. Economic change and infant care in an East African agricultural community. In: P.H. Leiderman, S.R. Tulkin and A. Rosenfeld (eds.), Culture and Infancy: Variations in the Human Experience, pp. 405–438. Academic Press, New York.

Levy, R.I. 1968. Child management structure and its implications in a Tahitian family. In: E. Vogel and N. Bell (eds.), A Modern Introduction to the Family, pp. 590–598.

Free Press, New York.

MacDonald, S., and Gallimore, R. 1971. Battle in the Classroom: Innovations in Class-room Techniques. Intext, Scranton.

Medrich, E.A., Roizen, J., Rubin, V., and Buckley, S. 1982. The Serious Business of Growing Up: A Study of Children's Lives Outside School. University of California Press, Berkeley.

Meier, G. 1975. From My Life. G.P. Putnam's Sons, New York.

Miller, N.B., and Cantwell, D.P. 1976. Siblings as therapists: A behavioral approach. Am. J. Psychiatry. 133(4)447–450.

Minuchen, S., Montalvo, B., et al. 1967. Families of the Slums. Basic Books, Inc., New York.

Minturn, L. 1969. A survey of cultural differences in sex-role training and identification. In: N. Kretschmer and D. Walcher (eds.), Environmental Influences on Genetic Expression. U.S. Government Printing Office, Washington, DC.

Minturn, L., and Lambert, W. 1964. Mothers of Six Cultures. Wiley, New York.

Morley, D. 1979. The Child-to-Child programme. Assign. Child. 47/48:171–185.

Moskovitz, S. 1983. Love despite Hate: Child Survivors of the Holocaust and Their Adult Lives. Schocken Books, New York.

Nerlove, S., and Romney, A.D. 1967. Sibling terminology and cross-sex behavior. Am. Anthropol. 69:179–187.

Pepler, D.J., Abramovitch, R., and Corter, C. 1981. Sibling interaction in the home: A longitudinal study. Child Dev. 52:1344-1347.

Reed, G., and Leiderman, P.H. 1981. Age related changes in attachment behavior in polymatrically reared infants: The Kenyan Gusii. In: T. Field, P.H. Leiderman, et. al. (eds.), Culture and Infant Interaction. Earlbaum, Hillsdale, NJ.

Rogoff, B., Sellers, M.J., Piorrata, S., Fox, N., and White, S. 1975. Age of assignment of roles and responsibilities to children: A cross-cultural survey. Hum. Dev. 18:353–369.

Rosenblatt, P.G., and Skoogberg, E. 1974. Birthorder in cross-cultural perspective. Dev. Psychol. 10:49-54.

Simeonsson, R.J., and McHale, S.M. 1981. Review: Research on handicapped children: Sibling relationships. Child Care Health Dev. 7(3):153–171.

Smith, P.K. 1980. Shared care of young children: Alternative models to monotropism. Merrill–Palmer Q. 26:371–389.

Steward, M., and Steward, D. 1976. Parents and siblings as teachers. In: E.J. Mash, L.C. Handy, and L.A. Hamerlynek (eds.), Behavior Modification Approaches to Parenting, pp. 193–206. Brunner/Mazel, New York.

Super, C.M. 1977. Differences in the care of male and female infants: Data from non-American samples. (Mimeograph) Clark University, Worcester, MA.

Sutton-Smith, B., and Rosenberg, B.G. 1968. Sibling consensus on power tactics. J. Genet. Psychol. 112:63–72.

Sutton-Smith, B., and Rosenberg, B.G. 1970. The Sibling. Holt, Rinehart & Winston, New York.

Uhlenberg, P. 1979. Changing configurations of the life course. In: T. Hareven (ed.), Transitions: The Family and the Life Course in Historical Perspective, pp. 65–97. Academic Press, New York.

Wagner, R.M., and Schaeffer, D.M. 1980. Social networks and survival strategies: An exploratory study of Mexican American, Black and Anglo female family heads in San José, California. In: M. Melville (ed.), Twice a Minority: Mexican-American Women, pp. 173–190. Mosby, St. Louis, MO.

Weinrott, M.R. 1974. A training program in behavior modification for siblings of the retarded. Am. J. Orthopsychiatry. 44:362–375.

Weisner, T.S. 1978. The Hawaiian-American cultural and familial context: What can it tell us? In: C. Jordan, R.G. Tharp, K.H. Au, et al. (eds.), A Multidisciplinary Approach to Research in Education: The Kamehameha Early Education Program. Technical Report No. 81. The Kamehameha Schools, Honolulu.

Weisner, T.S. 1982. Sibling interdependence and child caretaking: a cross-cultural view. In: M. Lamb and B. Sutton-Smith (eds.), Sibling Relationships: Their Nature and Significance across the Lifespan, pp. 303–325. Earlbaum, Hillsdale, NJ.

Weisner, T.S., and Gallimore, R. 1977. My brother's keeper: Child and sibling caretaking. Curr. Anthropol. 18(2):169–190.

Weisner, T.S., Gallimore, R., and Tharp, R.G. 1977. Sibling caretaking in an urban Hawaiian setting. Paper presented at the Society for Cross-Cultural Research, East Lansing, MI.

Weisner, T.S., Jordan, C., Gallimore, R., and Tharp, R.G. 1981. Cultural homogeneity, familial variability and educational adaptability: Sibling caretaking among urban Hawaiians. Unpublished manuscript.

Werner, E.E. 1979. Cross-Cultural Child Development: A View from the Planet Earth. Brooks/Cole, Monterey, CA.

Werner, E.E., and Smith, R.S. 1977. Kauai's Children Come of Age. University Press of Hawaii, Honolulu.

Werner, E.E., and Smith, R.S. 1982. Vulnerable, but Invincible: A Longitudinal Study of Resilient Children and Youth. McGraw-Hill, New York.

Westinghouse Learning Corporation, Westat Research Inc. 1971. Day Care Survey 1970: Summary Report and Basic Analysis. Washington, DC.

Whiting, B.B. 1977. Changing life styles in Kenya. Daedelus 106:211–216.

Whiting, B.B., and Edwards, C.A. 1973. A cross-cultural analysis of sex differences in the behavior of children aged three through eleven. J. Soc. Psychol. 91:171–188.

Whiting, B.B., and Whiting, J.W.M. 1975. Children of Six Cultures: A Psycho-Cultural Analysis. Harvard University Press, Cambridge. MA.

Whiting, J.W.M., and Whiting, B.B. 1973. Altruistic and egoistic behavior in six cultures. In: L. Nader and T. Maretzki (eds.), Cultural Illness and Health (Anthropological Studies No. 9). American Anthropological Association, Washington, DC.

CHAPTER 5

Grandparents as Alternate Caregivers

*Everyone needs to have access both to grandparents and grand-
children in order to be a full human being.*

Margaret Mead
Blackberry Winter: My Earlier Years

In her autobiography Margaret Mead suggests that we speak a great deal about a human scale of things, but that we also need a human unit in which to think about time. Her friend Ralph Blum defined such a unit of time as "the space between a grandfather's memory of his own childhood and a grandson's knowledge of those memories as he heard about them" (1972, p.284).

Contrary to popular assumptions, this time span is on the increase today, thanks to the increased longevity of grandparents and the earlier birth of their grandchildren in the reproductive cycle of parents.

The most dramatic changes in the family cycle may well be those that have taken place since the 19th century in the lives of the "average" American woman. By the time she and her husband are in their 40's, with just over 20 years of marriage behind her, she has completed the bearing and rearing of her children and launched them into young adulthood. Even 10 years earlier she would have no preschool children in the home during the day, since the spacing of her few children has become increasingly constricted to her younger years.

By the time her children are launched into young adult life, the couple, however, is not yet halfway through married life and the woman has on the average another 30 to 35 years of life ahead of her. If husband and wife stay together until death, they have another quarter of a century of married life ahead of them before one of the spouses (usually the husband) dies. Approximately half of their married life is then spent without resident children in the home (Giraldo, 1980).

We might contrast this life cycle of contemporary women with the one prevalent before the turn of the century, as it has been documented by family historians: Before 1900, only about 40% of all women went through the cycle of marrying, bearing children, and surviving to age 50 with the first marriage still intact. The remainder either never married, never reached marriageable age, died before or in childbirth, or were widowed while their offspring were still young children (Uhlenberg, 1974).

There is a certain irony in the fact that just when more and more people in the West are surviving to become grandparents and even greatgrandparents, the role of grandparent threatens to become largely a symbolic one—at least among the affluent members of Western societies. In tribal and peasant societies grandparents still play significant and culturally defined roles in the care and education of their grandchildren. They either assist the mother as subsidiary caregivers of infants and young children or share fairly equally child-care with a few other stable figures in the household (that is, the parents and older siblings).

In the majority of the world's traditional societies, grandparents are also the principal portrayers of the "ethos" and the cultural history of a society (Williams, 1972). Grandparents teach skills, socialize their grandchildren, and enculturate them into their society, especially in places where change is still slow enough so that children see their own futures as they observe their grandparents (Mead, 1974).

In transitional and modern societies the role of grandparents as educators and transmitters of cultural history to older children tends to be progressively reduced, as schools and the mass media take over; but in these societies grandparents still actively participate in shared child care, especially care of infants and young children, and in meeting their social-emotional as well as material needs.

THE ROLE OF GRANDPARENTS
IN TRADITIONAL AND TRANSITIONAL SOCIETIES

Let us first take a look at some of the cross-cultural literature to see what anthropologists and ethnographers tell us about the *roles* of grandparents in traditional societies and in societies that are in transition from a traditional to a modern way of life.

Simmons' (1945) ambitious cross-cultural study of the aged in primitive societies suggests that marked sex differences obtain in these roles. Because of the fragmentary ethnographic data on which his study is based, Simmons suggests caution in the interpretation of his findings. No demographic data are reported, hence we do not know if the life expectancy in these societies varied by sex (as it does in contemporary societies).

Simmons investigated, among a variety of aspects of aging, the relationship of the aged to their families, and found that one outstanding activity of aged women in all types of traditional societies is the practice of midwifery and care of infants and young children. Aged men seemed more likely to perform services related to childbirth and child care in matriarchical forms of family organizations than under the patriarchical type of family organization (which is more prevalent around the world). Story-telling was a universal opportunity afforded both aged men and women for holding their place in the social life of their group and among their grandchildren.

In nomadic hunter-gatherer and in settled agricultural societies, older women actively participate in the care of infants. Among contemporary African hunter-gatherers, such as the G/wi bushmen (Silberbauer, 1972) and the Mbuti pygmies (Turnbull, 1965), infants are often passed around amongst older women in the band. The mother gathering plant food can carry her infant with her; but in many agricultural and peasant communities, subsistence activities are sufficiently arduous that this is not easy for her. Shared care with grandparents, usually maternal grandmothers, is particularly common in such societies.

An examination of the social structure of grandparenthood, based on some 75 societies, the majority of which were contained in the HRAF files, found that in traditional societies, an indulgent, close, and warm relationship with the grandchildren is fostered by the dissociation of grandparents from family authority. A grandmother who is titular head of a household is likely to function more as a disciplinarian, whereas one with less status is more likely to function in a nurturant caregiving role (Apple, 1956).

For example, among the Hausa of Nigeria (LeVine and Price-Williams, 1974; Marvin et al., 1977), children live with their paternal grandparents in a patrilocal extended household. The maternal grandmother, however, is frequently involved in the weaning of the child from his or her mother's breast. The traditional ideal is for a woman to deliver her first-born at her mother's compound, to remain there until the child is ready for weaning (around age 2), and to return without the child to her husband's compound. Such first-born children grow up with the maternal grandmother as the *primary* caregiver. For the other grandchildren, the maternal grandmother is also a particularly nurturant person, associated with uninhibited affection.

By contrast, Hausa children are taught to respect the *paternal* grandmother, and many grow up thinking of her as representative of the paternal authority. As in many patrilineal societies, father's kin come to symbolize authority and discipline, mother's kin affection and indulgence (LeVine and Price-Williams, 1974).

Minturn and Lambert (1964), in their statistical analyses of the Whitings' *Six Cultures* study, found a strong tendency for children to receive more warmth in societies (such as Mexico, the Philippines, and Okinawa) where a set of grandparents live with the parents and children than in nuclear family households where parents live alone with their children. They conclude that the presence of grandparents, particularly the grandmother, reduces the isolation of the mother, provides an alternate caregiver, and therefore allows the mother to express more affection for her children than where she is their sole caregiver.

Similar findings are reported from societies in transition to a modern way of life, such as Taiwan (Olsen, 1976) and the People's Republic of China (Kessen, 1975). Olsen (1976) conducted interviews with 49 three-generation families, most of whom lived in and around Taipei, the capital of Taiwan. Grandmothers in her study seemed to adhere to traditional child-rearing attitudes (for example with regard to aggression control and behavioral conformity), but made relatively few demands (of obedience and self-reliance) on their young grandchildren. The likelihood that a grandmother acted as a source of nurturance (rather than discipline) was higher if she was widowed. Grandmothers were not likely to play a dominant role in the rearing of school-age children, but were actively involved in shared child care of infants and preschool-age children.

Grandparents play also an important role as supplementary caregivers in the largest of the developing nations, the People's Republic of China, where more than 1 billion people live. Even today the majority of Chinese children under the age of 7 (the age of school entry) are cared for by grandmothers and other relatives rather than in collective institutions, especialy in the rural areas where more than 80% of the mainland Chinese live. According to Kessen (1975) a number of factors continue to place Chinese grandparents, and especially grandmothers, in a prominent position as caregivers.

1. Mothers and fathers are expected to work full-time, but places in nurseries and kindergartens are in short supply, especially in rural areas.

2. Although both men and women work, there are different retirement ages for the sexes. Grandmothers retire in their early 50's just at the point when their sons and daughters have young children in need of care.

3. Grandparents have acquired status and prestige as victims of prerevolutionary "bitterness" and as teachers of the history of Maoist revolution.

In spite of the "official" Marxist line of complete social and economic equality between the sexes, grandmothers, like their daughters, carry a larger share of the household chores and child care than the men. American visitors found them to be generally nurturant toward their grandchildren. Both parents and teachers described the grandparents as "indulgent," and the emotional attachment between grandmother and grandchild seemed to be quite strong (Kessen, 1975).

Cross-cultural studies from traditional tribal and peasant societies and from societies in transition from a preindustrial to a modern way of life indicate that children are given a fair amount of nurturance when grandparents are significant child-rearing agents. This same trend is apparent in the industrialized societies of the West, that is, Europe and North America.

THE ROLE OF GRANDPARENTS IN WESTERN SOCIETIES

A number of reviews (Campbell and Buholz, 1982; Troll et al., 1979; Wood and Robertson, 1976) have addressed the significance of grandparenthood in contemporary U.S. Some cross-national studies on aging in Western societies (Burgess, 1960; Shanas, 1973; Shanas and Streib, 1965) have also compared the relationship between generations in the U.S. with those in European countries (such as Denmark, England, West Germany, France, The Netherlands, Yugoslavia, Poland, and Israel).

According to a 1975 study prepared by Harris et al. on the basis of a probability sample of U.S. households, about three-fourths of all Americans age 65 and over have living grandchildren. The proportions of Europeans in the same age range who have living grandchildren are similar, ranging from 68% to 70% (Burgess, 1960).

The average age of becoming a grandparent in these surveys was the mid-40s in the U.S. and early to mid-50s in Europe. In the future, Americans will have their first grandchildren probably at an age approximating that of Europeans, since the "model" age at which American women marry is advancing and becoming more consistent with the pattern in other industrialized societies (Bianchi and Farley, 1979; Giraldo, 1980).

Both American and European surveys report that most elderly people live in close distance (within a half-hour of transportation in the U.S.; within 1 hour of transportation in Europe) from at least one of their children and have regular contact with them and their offspring (Shanas, 1973; Troll et al., 1979). However, across all social strata parents are more likely to visit with an adult daughter and her children than a son.

Table 5. Contact with friends and family[a]

Population having friends or relatives (age)		Within last day or so (including live with)	Within last week or two	A month ago	Two to three months ago	Longer ago than 2–3 month
		When last seen (%)				
Close friends						
Public (18 to 64)	97	64	30	3	1	2
Public (65 and over)	94	60	31	5	2	2
Children						
Public (18 to 64)	73	87	8	2	1	2
Public (65 and over)	81	55	26	8	3	8
Brothers and sisters						
Public (18 to 64)	91	31	31	12	6	20
Public (65 and over)	79	22	22	15	10	31
Parents						
Public (18 to 64)	70	48	24	9	5	14
Public (65 and over)	4	32	23	8	11	26
Grandchildren						
Public (65 and over)	75	46	28	10	5	11
Grandparents						
Public (18 to 64)	30	24	20	18	8	30

[a] Reprinted with permission from National Council of Aging (Harris et al., 1975).

Among grandparents about three-fourths see their grandchildren at least every week or two, and nearly half of all Americans see a grandchild every day (Harris et al., 1975) (Table 5).

In 1975, 7 of every 10 older Americans reported giving help to their children; the same proportion gave help to grandchildren (Shanas, 1980). For people over 65, the proportion of elderly people who reported that they "were able to do something" for their grandchildren was higher in the U.S. than in Western European countries, like Denmark and Great Britain, where the government has a greater involvement in social services (Stehouwer, 1965).

The type of services rendered for their grandchildren seem to be similar for grandparents in the U.S. and Western Europe and include babysitting, looking after them when their parents go to work, and occasionally being the main charge for the grandchild (Robertson, 1977; Townsend, 1957). However, the proportion of grandparents who teach skills and family history and give advice on work and religion is much smaller than that engaged in babysitting and "entertaining" their grandchildren. Grandparent services tend to reach their peak during the preschool years of their grandchildren (Adams, 1968).

GRANDPARENTS' PERCEPTION OF THEIR ROLES

The grandparents' own perspective on their role tends to vary with age, education, and social status. One of the first typologies of grandparent roles was provided by Neugarten and Weinstein (1964), who studied 70 grandmother-grandfather pairs in middle-class families in Chicago, in the age range from the early 50s to the late 60s. The most common source of significance and meaning for the grandparent role among these persons came from seeing it as a means of biological renewal, continuity, and emotional fulfillment that parenthood had not given them. In this group the perception of the grandparents' role was found to vary from formal to fun-seeking, from parent surrogate and reservoir of family wisdom to that of a relatively distant figure. These grandparent styles represented different levels of involvement with grandchildren and tended to vary with the age of the grandparent.

The *formal* grandparents tended to be older; the majority was over 65. They enjoyed treating their grandchildren and served as occasional babysitters, but were careful not to offer advice and separated the role of grandparent from that of parenting. The role of *surrogate* parent only occurred among (a minority of) grandmothers, and was usually assumed after the young parents requested help when the mother was working. Only a few grandfathers were considered reservoirs of family wisdom and maintained an air of authority. *Fun-seekers* among the grandparents were generally younger. Major emphasis in this group was on companionable relationships and mutuality of satisfaction with their grandchildren. A minority of grandparents (some 20% of the grandmothers and 30% of the grandfathers) seemed to be *distant figures* who were not involved in the daily lives of their grandchildren, but had contact with them only on holidays and birthdays when they enjoyed providing gifts for them. They tended to be younger than the other groups.

Neugarten and Weinstein (1964) suggest that the fun-seekers and distant figures represented new grandparent roles that were emerging at that time. They reflected the younger ages at which grandparenthood was occurring, more independent and healthy lives of older persons, and secular changes in values, expectations, and socialization.

A decade later, the meaning of grandparenthood was examined by Wood and Robertson (1976) in an area sample of 257 grandparents (125 grandmothers, 132 grandfathers), from skilled or semiskilled working-class backgrounds in Madison, Wisconsin. The average age at which these persons had become grandparents for the first time was 46. Nine percent of the group were in their 40s, 53% in their 50s and 60s, and 38% were age 70 or over.

Grandparents who were labeled the individualized type had the least involvement with community and friends and high involvement with their grandchildren. They derived great personal satisfaction from their grandparenthood. Grandparents who were labeled the apportioned type were highly involved with their grandchildren as well as with community and friends. Grandparents from the individualized and apportioned groups were older and less well educated, had more grandchildren, and engaged in a greater number of activities with them than the other two types.

Among the younger grandparents was a symbolic type who placed less emphasis on personal satisfaction with their grandchildren, but was more concerned with what was morally good or right for them. This group was the youngest, had the highest educational level, was highly involved with community and friends, and was second lowest in activities engaged in with grandchildren. A minority (some 28%) of grandparents were in the remote group. They placed little emphasis on either social or personal aspects of grandparenthood, and were not very involved with their grandchildren or with friends or community.

Claven (1978) suggested that the grandparent role differs by degree of "functional centrality" in middle and lower socioeconomic status families. For the middle class the role is more "ideological" than real, in the sense that, although there is a kinship position of grandparent, there are no normative rights and obligations attached to this position in contemporary societies (as they are in traditional societies). Becoming a valued grandparent thus becomes an earned and acquired status rather than an ascribed one. It is an option open to the grandparent which he or she may or may not choose to take and usually involves only supplementary parenting (Boyd, 1969b).

In poor families, on the other hand, the grandparent, especially the grandmother, is more integrated into family life and performs many valued and needed parenting activities. Here the grandparent is more often essential in family life and at times serves as a true parent surrogate and the grandparent role becomes more "real."

In modern societies, with rapidly changing economic and occupational roles, a functional role for grandfathers may be more difficult to develop than one for grandmothers. This may help explain the neglect of grandfathers in studies of family life in the U.S. and why the grandparent role in the form of supplementary or surrogate parenting is so often a grandmothering role in American families.

SUPPLEMENTAL PARENTING BY GRANDPARENTS

In studies of American families in which the third generation is included, the most frequent help extended by grandparents is babysitting. This seems to be true regardless of geographical location, social class status, and ethnicity. For example, Hill et al. (1970), in a study of kin contacts among 312 white families in the metropolitan Minneapolis/St. Paul area, found that the most frequent kind of help given by elders was child care. Seventy-eight percent (78%) of the parents received this help, 50% of the grandparents and 16% of the great-grandparents provided it.

Wood and Robertson (1976) and Robertson (1977) studied the behavior of 125 white grandmothers from a stable blue-collar background in Madison, Wisconsin, and reported that 92% engaged in babysitting with grandchildren, 55.2% with high frequency.

Jackson (1971), in a study of sex and social class variations in black, aged parent-parent-child relationships among 83 families in the South, found that 80% of the offspring of black middle-class elders and 92% of the offspring of black manual workers reported getting help in child care from grandparents.

Seña-Rivera (1979) undertook intensive case studies of 293 persons in four clans of three-generation Mexican-American working-class families in the Midwest (Michigan, Indiana, Illinois). All families mentioned frequent babysitting and assistance in child care by grandmothers and mothers-in-law. Gilbert (personal communication, 1981) reported similar findings in her study of 107 Mexican-American and white couples of working class and middle-class backgrounds in Santa Barbara, California.

The involvement of grandparents in child care is very high among Native Americans. Grandparents have a voice in child-rearing, and, in the absence of a natural grandparent, children and parents may adopt an unrelated elder into the family. Red Horse et al. (1979) reported on a Native American community in the Southwest where 92% of the elderly fulfilled traditional family roles on a daily basis for their children, grandchildren, and great-grandchildren; and Bachtold (1982), in her study of preschoolers, found a high incidence of child care by grandparents among the Hupa in Northern California.

Kitano and Kikumura (1976) reported that many Japanese Americans absorb grandparents into the household, and Huang (1976) found that most Chinese-American children grow up in the midst of adults, including grandparents who act as babysitters. In our own longitudinal study of Chinese, Japanese, Hawaiian, and Filipino families on the island of Kauai, Hawaii, grandparents made a significant contribution to child care, especially among working mothers and in cases of disruption of the family unit through death, desertion, divorce, or mental illness (Werner and Smith, 1982).

In all studies in which the relationship and sex of the grandparent were identified, shared child care was engaged in more frequently by grandmothers than grandfathers and more frequently by the maternal grandmother than the paternal one. Kahana and Kahana (1970), in a small sample study, reported that maternal grandmothers show closeness and warmth toward their grandchildren, view them as if they were their own children, and approve of their upbringing. In contrast, maternal grandfathers and paternal grandmothers expressed more negative attitudes.

Although much of the literature on grandparenthood does not differentiate child care by ethnic or socioeconomic status, the few studies that do tend to show variations in the involvement of grandparents in the care of their grandchildren. Regularity of contact and amount of responsibility assumed for the grandchild vary from occasional babysitting and entertaining of grandchildren when they visit or stay overnight among the more affluent, to regular child care while mothers are engaged in outside employment among working-class families, to informal adoption and/or full-time fostering of a grandchild in the absence of one or both parents among lower-class families.

SURROGATE PARENTING BY GRANDPARENTS

The grandparent role, especially the role of the grandmother, becomes essential for the survival of the family in poor and/or female-headed households. The single-parent family headed by a woman is the fastest growing household type in the U.S. and more than half of the female-headed families subsist below the poverty level (Bianchi and Farley, 1979). Black, Native American, and Puerto Rican families have especially high rates of female-headed households, and among these families the proportion of children under age 18 who live below the poverty level ranges from 66% to 69% (U.S. Bureau of the Census, 1979) (See Figure 7).

In such households grandparents often act as surrogate rather than sup-

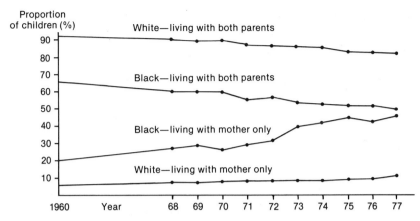

Figure 7.   Proportion of children under age 18 living with both parents or living with their mother only; 1960–1977. (U.S. Bureau of the Census, 1979).

plementary parents. For example, one of the key roles black grandparents have played is in informal adoption or foster care of grandchildren. Such crisis and voluntary type of kinship fostering is also prevalent in a number of West African societies from which many black Americans descended (Goody, 1970). Although this practice has declined somewhat in recent years, it is still common (Bianchi and Farley, 1979).

In 1976, 50% of black births were to unmarried women, many of them teenagers. Black children born out of wedlock are much less likely than white children to be given up for adoption. In 9 out of 10 cases they are retained by the extended family and often reared by grandparents (Hill, 1977).

Children are also informally adopted by grandparents in cases of divorce, separation, death, or illness of one or both parents, or to allow the parents to go to work or school. Of the 3 million children in the U.S. in the mid-1970s who lived with relatives, over half were black. Of these children one-half did not have either parent present. Over half of the black children living with relatives without their parents present were being reared by persons who were without mates. In most cases these were grandmothers. Three-fifths of all black children living in homes without either parent present were grandchildren or great-grandchildren of their caregivers (Campbell and Buholz, 1982). Younger children are more likely to live with their grandparents than older children (Hill, 1977). Several reasons have accounted for this practice.

Martin and Martin (1978) who have studied the black extended family network assert that it is important for blacks to develop a sense of family and obligations to their kin. Persons who take in relatives' children are showing their concern for the family. Some feel an obligation because they were cared for by relatives themselves when they were young children. Love and concern for their grandchildren are other motives.

Although black families have the highest rates of female-headed households in the U.S., female-headed households are on the increase among Native Americans as well. Miller (1979), herself part Indian and a grandmother, has studied 120 Native American families living in the Greater San Francisco/Oakland area and found that one-third of the households are female headed (and two-thirds are poor).

Social welfare professionals are often reluctant to legitimate grandparents as alternate or surrogate caregivers even though they play an important role in the kin network of Native Americans. Red Horse et al. (1978) cited an example of what happened to a family of Ojibway Indians in Minnesota:

> Nancy was an 18-year-old mother identified as mentally retarded and epileptic by the department of welfare officials. Although retardation was subsequently disproved, the department assumed control and custody of Nancy's infant child in a foster home.
>
> Nancy's parents insisted that the family network was available for assistance, if necessary. The welfare staff, however, considered this offer untenable. The grandparents were deemed senile and unable to care for an infant. They were in their early fifties.
>
> The staff ignored the fact that the grandparents had just finished caring for three other young and active grandchildren without dependence on institutional social intervention. The placement orders were eventually overruled in Nancy's case, but not without legal intervention.

Fosterage or informal adoption by grandparents has also been common in Polynesian island societies (Carroll, 1971). Our research among modern Hawaiians demonstrates that it is still prevalent today. Grandparents "hanai" grandchildren after their own children have grown up, especially if one of their daughters bears an out-of-wedlock child or her family unit is disrupted by death, desertion, or divorce (Werner and Smith, 1977, 1982).

Prospective adopters among Hawaiian-Americans are rarely denied the privilege of adoption because of economic circumstances, old age, or ill health. On the other hand, natural parents, such as unwed mothers who give up their children, are not stigmatized. There seems to be little effort to sever legal and social relations between a child and his or her natural parents, especially the mother. Thus, such adoptions must be thought of more as creating an additional parental relationship for the adopted child rather than replacing the bond between parents and their natural children.

Emphasis on the positive aspects of the grandparent's role as surrogate parent should not obscure the fact that there may also be occasionally undesirable consequences. Davis (1968) has suggested that role strain and conflict between mothers and grandmothers in such a setting may be resolved by the young mother by relinquishing her maternal role and behaving as an older sister. Dell and Applebaum (1977) have used the term *trigenerational emmesh-*

ment to describe the conflict that can result as single parents play overlapping roles of parent and child. The child of the young parent may have difficulty in differentiating between parent and grandparent (Bemis et al., 1976) as one might note in this example of a married teenage mother who was interviewed at age 18 in the Kauai Longitudinal Study (Werner and Smith, 1977).

> Actually when I was born, my mother wasn't married to my father, so I was adopted by my grandparents, my mother's parents. Then my mother got married to a guy. We all lived in a 3-bedroom house, 3 families living in one house . . . I lived with them till I was about 10. Then my mother got married to this other guy and she and my brothers and sisters moved to Honolulu . . . and I stayed on Kauai, and my stepfather and my cousins and me, we moved to another house. When I was much younger I used to have fights with my brothers and sisters, and my real mother would feel bad because they were my brothers and sisters and I shouldn't do that. But then my grandparents used to spank me, and she would feel bad and she would say she shouldn't have put me up for adoption, and if she didn't, I would be in Honolulu with her right now. I don't know, I guess she felt bad . . . When I was about 12 years old, I found out I was adopted. Then I remembered when I was small, there was this guy that would come over and be with them, and he was my father, and my grandmother would call me in the house and ask me what he was telling me, and I would tell her that he was my father . . . Then after I got married my godmother told me he was going back to the Philippine Islands. So I tried to find out where he lived and saw him the day before he left and he cried. He didn't really want to go . . . I wrote to him for a couple of months, and the last time I wrote to him, he didn't answer. *(Q. You've had so many parents and parent substitutes, how do you feel about it?)* I feel that all my life I've been moved here and moved there, and I guess I'll never really be able to understand it all. Guess I'll never be able to settle down. Even now. (pp. 116-117).

THE EFFECTS OF GRANDPARENTS ON THEIR GRANDCHILDREN

Only relatively few investigations have examined the meaning and significance of the grandparent for the grandchild. Most of these studies have shown that grandparents can have a significant positive effect on the socioemotional and cognitive development of their grandchildren.

A few studies have taken a cross-cultural perspective, but the majority were conducted in the U.S. The American studies include data from children of different socioeconomic and ethnic groups, that is, from Anglo-, black, Hispanic-, and Asian-American samples in different regions of the country.

Infants

Ainsworth (1967), in her cross-cultural longitudinal study on the *attachment behavior* of infants among the Baganda in East Africa, was one of the first to demonstrate that infants become attached to grandparents who care for them. These attachments were formed to persons who shared in the routine care of the infant in the household. Differential responses to such caregivers emerged in the third quarter of the first year, the same quarter in which the first clear-cut attachment behaviors to the mother were displayed. The more caregivers there were in the household, the less exclusively attached to the mother was the infant. In a study by Marvin et al. (1977) the same trend was found among the Hausa in Nigeria: In their spontaneous behavior in the family compound most babies demonstrated attachment to three or four people, especially to the maternal grandmother, who plays a significant role in weaning the children from their mother in this culture.

Young Children

Rohner (1975), in a cross-cultural survey of some 101 traditional societies, found a significant relationship between parental behavior and the presence of a grandparent in a domestic unit. Children tended to be more accepted and less often rejected if a grandmother was present to help assume or share the burden of child care. Accepted children, in turn, tended to be more self-reliant than rejected children and to draw on their own skills and resources to meet their physical and emotional needs. They also formed warmer and less hostile peer relations than rejected children.

Minturn and Lambert (1964), in their analyses of parental care extended to young children in *Mothers of Six Cultures*, found a strong tendency for them to receive more warmth in Mexican, Filipino, and Okinawan families where grandparents lived in the same household.

Furstenberg (1976) conducted a rare longitudinal study of low-income, predominantly black teenage mothers who had kept their babies. The cognitive development of their offspring was assessed at age 3 to 4 years with a preschool inventory. The children of these unmarried teenagers tended to have higher scores if they were cared for by more than one adult, either by the father of the child or the grandmother.

School-Age Children

Scott (1974) studied 302 children (mean age, 5 years 10 months) who were entering the first grade in a predominantly white, middle-class, suburban school district near Seattle. She found a significant interaction effect between grandparent contact, birth order, and the child's degree of competence in meeting the demands of school. Scores of later-born children with frequent grandparent contact on the Metropolitan Readiness Test (MRT) were higher than those of later-borns with infrequent grandparent contact. Among children without grandparent contact, first-borns scored significantly higher than later-borns, but there was little difference between the MRT scores of first- and later-born children with frequent grandparent contact. Scott's findings suggest that frequent contact with grandparents may ameliorate some of the negative correlates of being later-born that may result from less parental attention.

Kellam et al. (1977) found a similar trend among poor blacks in Woodlawn, a suburb of Chicago. Mother/grandmother families were nearly as effective as mother/father families in contributing to a positive adaptation of the child in the first and third grade in school and his psychologic well-being in the third grade. Positive social adaptation in grades 1 and 3 included successful relations with peers and with the teacher, paying attention in the classroom, and achieving up to ability in the elementary grades. Children from mother/grandmother families also showed fewer psychiatric symptoms and reported less sadness and nervousness than children in mother only or mother/stepfather families. Kellam et al. concluded that both intact mother/father families and mother/grandmother families seem to offer considerable protection against social maladaptation, especially for boys. Girls in this study were more likely to adapt to the demands of elementary school than boys, regardless of the household type in which they grew up.

School-age children themselves report that grandparents are a significant source of support and psychological well-being. In a study of Hispanic children, ages 7 to 13, growing up in an urban barrio in Houston, Goodman and Beman (1971) found that the children considered their grandparents to be important figures in their lives. They were more likely to be perceived as warm and affectionate rather than as authority figures, a trend that has also been reported in ethnographies by anthropologists who studied traditional cultures.

Bryant (1981) explored the access of two middle childhood groups to various sources of support in their families and communities. One hundred and sixty-eight families participated in this project. All resided in nonmetropolitan and rural northern California and tended to be predominantly middle-class and white. Seventy-two of the families had a target child just finishing the first grade (mean age, 7 years 3 months) and 96 had a target child just finishing the fourth grade (mean age, 10 years 3 months). Within each age group, there were equal numbers of male and female target children from equal numbers of large families (three or more children) and small families (two children), with equal numbers of older brothers and sisters.

More 10 year olds than 7 year olds among these later-born children reported parent and grandparent generation persons as among the 10 most important individuals in their lives. More males than females knew and interacted with the adult generations, and children from larger families had more intimate talks with the grandparent generation than children from smaller families. In large families a significant positive relationship was found between children's report of intimate talks with persons in the grandparent generation and a measure of empathy.

Extensive and intensive involvement with the grandparent generation was positively related to the social perspective taking skill of boys and negatively related to this skill in girls. Extensive involvement with the grandparent generation was related to increased expression of empathy among boys and decreased empathy among girls. Intensive involvement with the grandparent generation, on the other hand, was positively linked to increased expression of empathy among the girls but not the boys in this study. In sum, not only did the boys and girls seem to differ in the extent to which they sought out, responded, and reported extensive and intensive relationships with the grandparent's generation, but these experiences also seemed to have different developmental outcomes for boys and girls in middle childhood.

Adolescents

Grandparents were a stabilizing factor in the lives of black and white adolescents from delinquency-prone homes in metropolitan St. Louis. In a series of studies of three generations of families, half of whom were either unskilled or unemployed, Robins et al. (1975) examined the relationship between the arrest records of grandparents and their grandchildren. Delinquency records were lowest for white males by age 17, when neither grandparent had been in trouble, and second lowest for black males and females by age 17 when neither grandparent had been arrested. Robins and her associates conclude that the extended family in the person of law-abiding grandparents can be a protective factor keeping their grandchildren from delinquency, even if one or both parents have a record of arrests.

Access to, nurturance by, and advice from grandparents contributed significantly to the stress resistance of a cohort of 698 Japanese, Filipino, and Hawaiian youth who live on the rural island of Kauai and were followed longitudinally from birth to young adulthood (Werner and Smith, 1982). Most of these youngsters were born and reared in poverty among semi- and unskilled plantation workers, and were exposed to higher than average rates of prematurity, perinatal stress, and parental psychopathology. In interviews at age 18, many of the resilient youth (some 10% of the total cohort) gave credit to their grandparents for the nurturance they had received in childhood and the structure and guidance they had provided for them in adolescence. The presence and support of caring grandparents seemed to be a significant factor in their lives that tipped the balance from vulnerability to resiliency.

In summary, grandparents can have a positive effect on the development of their grandchildren at different stages of life, in infancy, in young childhood, during the school years, and even in "troubled" adolescence. The impact of grandparents may be especially significant for children who are more vulnerable or "at risk" for social maladaptation because of lack or scarcity of parental attention: children of teenage mothers; children with absent fathers; offspring of the poor, the mentally ill, and delinquency prone; and later-born children who must share their parents' attention with other children in large families. More attention needs to be paid in future studies to the differential outcome of relationships with grandparents for boys and girls at different stages of the life cycle.

THE EFFECTS OF FOSTER
GRANDPARENTS ON INSTITUTIONALIZED CHILDREN

Children who are in hospitals or institutions because of physical, mental, and/ or emotional handicaps seem to benefit from the care and commitment of foster grandparents as well (Ashby, 1981).

Since 1965, the *Foster Grandparent Program* has offered older low-income men and women opportunities to provide companionship and care for children in many different settings. Some work in hospitals and residential institutions for children who are physically, mentally, or emotionally handicapped. Some work in programs for children who come from single-parent, low-income homes, which have been established in public schools. Foster grandparents, after initial training and orientation, work about 20 hours per week with these children and play a family-type role of "special" friend or substitute grandparent. They are encouraged to develop close relationships with the children to whom they are assigned. As of 1982, some 18,000 foster grandparents worked with more than 54,000 children in the U.S., Puerto Rico, and the Virgin Islands (Reagan, 1982).

Several evaluation studies of the Foster Grandparent Program have documented positive effects on the foster grandchildren. In a series of studies by Saltz (1967, 1971) the effect of a foster grandparent program was assessed in a home in which children had been placed because of financial and/or emotional deprivation in their own families. Such deprivation included mother absence, child abuse, neglect, alcoholic or imprisoned parents, and mental illness. The children ranged in age from newborn to 6 years. All children with foster grandparents were matched with children without foster grandparents who resided in a similar institution. Positive effects were noted at several age levels.

During a 2-week timed observation study of 24 infants, from 1 to 7 weeks old, the infants with foster grandparents vocalized more and showed less irritability (whimpering and crying) than did the infants with no grandparents. Other results showed improved motor and social development of the children who were in the 4-month to 2-year age range. After 6 months with foster grandparents, these children showed a significant increase in social competence as measured by the Vineland Social Maturity Scale. In the age range from 2 to 6 years institutionalized children with supplementary foster grandparent care made significant progress in cognitive development and in social competence. The progress was greatest for those who received part-time mothering by elderly institutional aids for a period of up to 4 years.

Supporting the results of the Saltz study are findings by Gray and Kasteler (1967) and Hammond (1968), who found significant improvement in language development and social competence among institutionalized mentally retarded children (mean chronological age, 11) who had been assigned foster grandparents for a minimum of 12 months.

Saltz (1971) found several predictive factors that were associated with measures of later successful performance as a foster grandparent:

1. A readiness on the part of a prospective foster grandparent to express the feeling that children need to be loved and wanted

2. A positive approach to life circumstances

3. A high value placed on young children

4. A relatively good ability to abstract or generalize.

Neither chronological age nor relative health status was predictive of foster grandparent performance on any of the measures used in her study. Foster grandparent work experience was associated with improved life satisfaction and was also conducive to maintenance of health and vigor in many participants. The mutually beneficial impact of the Foster Grandparent Program on both the children and the older persons suggests that there may be a special compatibility between aging persons and parentally deprived children.

CHILDREN'S PERCEPTIONS OF THEIR GRANDPARENTS

A handful of cross-sectional studies in the U.S. and Europe have examined the meaning of the grandparent's role from the perspective of the grandchild. Children's perceptions of their grandparents vary from early childhood to young adulthood, with their relative stage of cognitive and psychosocial development. Thus, the grandparent role must be understood in the context of the changing needs of the developing grandchild as well as those of the grandparent.

One of the pioneer studies of developmental changes in children's views of their grandparents was conducted by Kahana and Kahana (1970), who examined the views of three groups of children, aged 4 to 5, 8 to 9, and 11 to 12 years. More frequent contact was reported by all three age groups with maternal rather than paternal grandparents. The maternal grandmother was the most frequently favored by all grandchildren. Children's views of their grandparents ranged from emphasis on concrete physical characteristics by the youngest children, to functional views of their behavior by the middle group, to the emergence of an abstract interpersonal orientation among the oldest children—closely paralleling the Piagetian stages of preoperational, concrete operational and formal operational thinking.

The youngest group, ages 4 to 5, valued their grandparents mainly for their indulgent qualities, that is, on the basis of what grandparents give in love, food, and presents. The middle group, ages 8 to 9, focused on mutuality and shared experiences, and preferred active, fun-sharing grandparents. The oldest group, ages 11 to 12, focused on abstract, interpersonal qualities of their grandparents ("She is nice, kind, etc.").

The youngest children in this study favored older grandparents, while older children preferred younger grandparents. Thus, the needs of the young child seemed most congruent with the affectional needs of the elderly grandparent (as we also saw in the Foster Grandparent Program), whereas older children may have more in common with the more active younger grandparent. There may be an optimistic note for grandparenthood in middle age rather than old age; at least in the Western world, the potential of sharing activities in a one-to-one relationship between grandparents and grandchildren (and young great-grandchildren) should increase.

The findings by Kahana and Kahana were extended by Schultz (1980), who investigated the grandchild-grandparent bond from the perspective of Kohlberg's cognitive developmental theory of attachment. The youngest group in his study (mean age, 4.6 years) was selected to represent the *preoperational* stage of cognitive development, the middle group (mean age, 9.3 years) corresponded to the *concrete* operational stage, and the youth among the oldest group (mean age, 19.2 years) were assumed to be capable of *formal operational* thought.

Children in the middle group and youth in the oldest group used a greater variety and proportion of abstract descriptions for the grandparent with whom they interacted the most in a reciprocal relationship. The middle and oldest group also attributed greater perspective taking (less egocentrism, more empathy) and greater feelings of attachment to that grandparent. The youngest group, however, had the highest attachment scores for both sets of grandparents.

These preschool-age children expressed warmth and strong feelings of attachment to all their grandparents, regardless of the amount of contact they had with them. Schultz (1980) concluded from his findings that early attachments to grandparents, as evidenced by the preschool children in his study, are qualitatively different from later ones and have a stronger *affective* (emotional) basis than later attachments, which are based on more adult-like *cognitive* functions and role transactions. Among the oldest group in this study, the female youth all chose a female grandparent as the one with whom they had the most reciprocal social interactions.

Van der Straeten (1971) in a study at the Catholic University of Louvain in Belgium found age changes in the perception of grandparents among European children and youth in the age range of 10 to 20. The youngest children in the Belgian study, ages 10 to 12 years, valued their grandparents for their concrete share of affection and as playmates. The 13 to 15 year olds considered their grandparents as more personally important. The desirability of a good relationship was more significant to them than material advantages. The 16 to 18 year olds pronounced more differentiated judgments and stressed certain character traits of their grandparents. The oldest group, the 19 year olds, expressed their respect for the kind of grandparent who was a good role model, who knew about life and had wisdom.

In general, the European findings, although complementary to the American studies, show a greater emphasis on the affectionate relationship between grandchild and grandparent throughout the first decade of life. Europeans generally become grandparents about a decade later than the contemporary generation of Americans, and we know from the Kahana study that older grandparents are valued for their affectionate, indulgent qualities by their grandchildren.

An American study by Robertson (1976) assessed the significance of grandparents in the lives of young adults from a stable working class background. They ranged in age from 18 to 26, with a model age from 21 to 23, and the majority were still unmarried. Robertson found that: 1) grandparents are not seen as old-fashioned or out of touch, and are considered an important source of influence on these young adults; and 2) adult grandchildren feel definite responsibility toward their grandparents, especially in providing them with emotional support and tangible help when needed.

CHILDREN'S PERCEPTION OF
THEIR GRANDPARENTS VIS-À-VIS THE ELDERLY

The amount and quality of contact that grandchildren have with their grandparents may also affect their attitude toward the elderly and aging in general. This is a topic that has just begun to be explored and should be given increased attention in child development research, in view of the increasing number of older persons in our society.

Phenice (1981) examined the perceptions of grandparents and elderly persons held by 44 preschoolers in day care centers in Michigan and found that children who had the most contact with grandparents mentioned more things they could do with and for elderly persons than children who had the least contact. Contact with real grandparents had more influence on young children's perceptions of older persons than did involvement with foster grandparents or other elderly persons.

A Belgian study of 114 second, fourth, and sixth graders who attended a Catholic school in Antwerp and came from a wide socioeconomic range analyzed children's drawings of aged persons and grandparents (Marcoen, 1979). These 7- to 11-year-old European children clearly differentiated between their grandparents and aged persons in general and viewed their grandparents more favorably. They pictured their grandparents with fewer deficit characteristics than aged persons in general. They drew more stereotypical pictures (wrinkles, cane, and hat for both old men and women; beard and pipe for old men; bun and long clothes for old women) for the aged, and more realistic images of their grandparents that were embedded in a positive affective context. However, the "old age stereotypes" that were present among elementary school-age children became more differentiated across the age span, with fourth and sixth grade children drawing fewer deficit characteristics for the elderly than second graders.

Bekker and Taylor (1966) explored the influence that the number of generations in a young person's own family has on his or her perception of old people. Their findings suggest that young people with grandparents and great-grandparents have fewer age prejudices than those who grow up without great-grandparents. Youngsters who had living great-grandparents perceived their grandparents as having fewer characteristics of old age than did young people who had no living great-grandparents. There was no significant difference in the ages of the grandparents in the two comparison groups.

In summary, the perception of grandparenthood and aging must be understood in the context of the changing needs of grandchildren (and grandparents as well). In general, the image of grandparenthood and the elderly is less negative and more differentiated among children and youth than one might expect from popular stereotypes. It also seems that young people who have grandparents and great-grandparents tend to have less "age prejudice" than those who do not.

PARENTAL ATTITUDES AND
GRANDPARENT-GRANDCHILD RELATIONSHIPS

Parental attitudes are important influences on grandparent-grandchild relationships (Troll et al., 1979). The middle generation serves as a lineage bridge between grandparent and grandchild, with the women in that generation more prominent in this function than their husbands (Hill et al., 1970). When good relationships exist between the adult generations, especially between the adult daughter and her mother, and where attitudes and values are consonant, interactions with grandparents serve as a positive and stabilizing influence on grandchildren's development.

In traditional societies that stress interdependence, caregivers in both the older and the younger generations have a common set of socialization goals and a common set of practices in relation to the rearing of children (Werner, 1979). In modern and transitional societies undergoing rapid social change, such attitudes and practices may vary between the generations. The amount of harmony in shared child care thus tends to depend on the balance between autonomy from and dependence on each other that parents and grandparents have achieved. This seems to be especially true for the mother-grandmother relationship, and particularly so within working-class families in which mothers of young children are likely to maintain close ties with their own mothers (Cohler and Grunebaum, 1981).

In intensive interviews with a group of working-class wives, Komarovsky (1962) found that the majority (more than 60%) of the daughters report close and harmonious relationships with their mothers. But Neugarten and Weinstein (1964) reported that in the one-third of middle-class grandparents who felt discomfort with their role, the major issue was that of being asked to assume continuing responsibility for child care.

Cohler and Grunebaum (1981) commented on the potential for ambivalence in the relationship between mothers of young children and their own late middle-aged mothers living in modified extended urban families. They noted that from earliest childhood, the daughters in these families were socialized into an interdependent relationship with their own mothers that continued into adulthood as the daughters became mothers themselves. As a result of the developmental changes in personality across adulthood (which in part may be cohort related), requests by the adult daughter for continued support and assistance, especially in matters of child care, were responded to by some late middle-aged mothers with great discomfort. They conclude that such interdependence across generations becomes a source of conflict only when the mother of the child has not resolved her own problem of identity (in the Eriksonian sense). On the other hand, continued involvement in a multigenerational family also can provide an important source of ego strength which fosters adjustment.

Within our contemporary society, findings reported by Boyd (1969b) suggest that the best relationship between the generations is that in which the grandparent generation is willing to provide help and assistance while recognizing the needs of the parent generation for autonomy and independence.

Studies of the child care behaviors most frequently engaged in by grandparents (such as babysitting, home entertainment, and drop-in visits of grandchildren) suggest that such activities are initiated more frequently by parents and children than by grandparents; thus, parents *tend to control* the frequency of such interactions between grandparents and grandchildren (Wood and Robertson, 1976). This becomes an important issue when parents divorce and/or remarry.

INTERGENERATIONAL SIMILARITIES AND
DIFFERENCES IN ATTITUDES TOWARD CHILD CARE

Most earlier studies of child care attitudes of mothers and grandmothers were based on groups of upper middle-class women (who are probably the least frequently involved in shared child care in our society). When differences were found between the child care attitudes of the two generations, the studies did not consider the greater degree of formal education of the daughters that may have accounted for generational differences, independent of other effects.

Staples and Smith (1954), for example, reported a significant relationship between mothers and their own mothers on a scale of authoritarian-democratic attitudes toward control of the child's expression of autonomy. There was less of a difference between the two generations when they lived apart than when they shared a common residence, however. Kell and Aldous (1960) found a significant relationship between the attitudes of the two generations regarding discipline, but not regarding display of affection.

A comprehensive recent assessment of child care attitudes of mothers and grandmothers has been reported by Cohler and Grunebaum (1981). They studied 90 mother-grandmother pairs in each of which the mother had at least one child below the age of 5. Their sample was drawn primarily from the blue-collar or working-class strata (where ties between mothers and grandmothers tend to be strong). The age of the mothers ranged from 20 to 40 years, with a mean of 24.5 years. Their mean educational level was 12.5 years of schooling, and the median number of children in the mother's household was 2. The age of the grandmothers ranged from 51 to 75 years, with a median age of 58. Their median level of schooling was 10 years, and the median number of children in their own families was 3.

All participants were administered the Maternal Attitude Scale (MAS), a 233 item Likert-type instrument developed to measure attitudes regarding several issues with which a mother is confronted sequentially in the care of her infant or young child. Significant positive intergenerational relationships were found for three of the five factor scores derived from this instrument: appropriate control, encouragement of reciprocity, and competence in meeting the baby's needs. Feelings of being able to channel the child's expression of angry feelings, of being able to respond to the baby's demand for a social relationship, and being competent to interpret the baby's cues regarding physical needs among the mothers were all related to the attitude their own mothers (the grandmothers) had regarding these issues. On the other hand, maternal attitudes toward self-sacrifice for the baby and differentiating a mother's needs from those of a child, together with attitudes reflecting more ambivalence regarding child care, were less closely related to the attitudes of one's own mother.

Grandmothers expressed significantly fewer adaptive attitudes than mothers regarding the control of aggressive feelings in young children, but more adaptive attitudes toward meeting the needs of babies. Older grandmothers (above age 60) expressed more ambivalent attitudes regarding the care of young children than the younger ones (below age 60). Mothers and grandmothers who shared a common residence had less adaptive attitudes than did mothers and grandmothers living apart.

Among families in which mothers and grandmothers live together, there is the potential for a greater degree of conflict, vacillation, and ambiguity both in the relationship between mother and grandmother and in the relationship of each with the child than among families where mothers and grandmothers live apart. This is an issue that deserves more attention by researchers because the number of female-headed households that include a grandmother is increasing among both whites and non-whites in the U.S. We know, for example, very little about the children of unmarried adolescents who were raised in households where the single parent plays overlapping roles of parent and child. We also know very little about the role of a grandparent, usually a grandmother, as a way station for the custodial parent and her child after divorce.

DIVORCE AND RELATED CHANGES
IN GRANDPARENT-GRANDCHILD RELATIONSHIPS

The majority of all divorces in the U.S. involve at least one child (U.S. Department of Commerce, 1977). About three out of four persons who divorce eventually remarry, thus increasing numbers of children experience both a dissolution and reconstitution of the family. Do these events deprive children of their contacts with grandparents?

Given the large number of children affected, there is a great need to document changes in the involvement of grandparents in parenting and child care in the wake of divorce and their effects on the grandchild. A longitudinal study by Furstenberg et al. (1980) provides us with some information on intergenerational ties between grandparents and grandchildren following divorce and remarriage. This study began in 1977 and included 210 persons in a central Pennsylvania county who had either filed for separation or obtained a divorce in the previous 26 months. In 1979, 181 persons—some 86% of the original sample—were reinterviewed. Information on children's contacts with grandparents was obtained from 104 respondents who had a child under the age of 18, living either with the respondent or the former spouse, and from 25 remarried couples, all of whom had children from their previous marriages.

Children were reported to have more frequent contact with grandparents on the custodial parent's side than those on the non-custodial parent's side. Nearly 40% of the former saw grandparents at least once a week, while only

4% of the latter saw their grandparents that often. However, about one-third saw the other set of grandparents at least once or twice a month. The amount of contact between parents and between the child and the non-custodial parent appeared to influence relationships with grandparents on that side. The fate of grandparent-grandchild relations following divorce was linked to the parent-child relations which evolved, and was also affected by physical proximity, especially for grandparents on the non-custodial side. This trend is similar to that reported for grandparent-grandchild relationships in intact families.

Information from respondents who had remarried or were living with a partner revealed that in most cases relationships between children and their new step-grandparents were readily established. Remarriage following divorce may actually result in augmentation and expansion of kin for most children. Frequent contact was maintained with biological grandparents on the custodial parent's side. In the overwhelming majority of cases this was the mother and her kin, but non-custodial fathers also tended to rely on their parents for child care assistance, a trend also reported in Australia by Katz (1979). Thus, some contact was maintained with biological grandparents on the non-custodial parent's side, and relatively frequent contact was established with step-grand-parents.

In recent years there has been some political action by "Grandparents' Rights" groups that have influenced the majority of state legislatures in the U.S. to pass some form of visitation rights legislation. Grandparents who believed that they were denied opportunities to see their grandchildren were instrumental in getting this legislation passed. [The state of California has extended judicially enforceable visitation rights not only to grandparents, but also to great-grandparents and the children's brothers and sisters as well (West, 1982).]

The purpose of the visitation rights statutes is to offer the grandparents an independent right of action that is not contingent on the rights already given to the child's parents. Grandparents can now utilize state habeas corpus proceedings to force an impartial evaluation of their request for visitation privileges with their grandchild. The decision making power of determining "the best interests of the child" is thus shifted from the parents to the courts. The policy sought to be furthered is the continued relationship between blood relatives (Borzi, 1977).

There seems to be a growing legal consensus that in the majority of cases, a grandchild will profit greatly from continued contact with his or her grandparents after the dissolution of his or her parents' marriage (Allen, 1977). An often cited opinion is that by the New Jersey appellate court in the case of *Mimkon vs. Ford* (1975):

> [We] can only say that it is proper that in the unfortunate case of parental separation or death, grandparents should sometimes have privileges of visitation even over the objections of parents. It is not only the ordinary devotion to the grandchild that

merits the grandparents' continued right to be with him but also the fact that in such cases the continuous love and attention of grandparents may mitigate the feelings of guilt or rejection which a child may feel at the death of or separation from a parent and ease the painful transition.

So far, we have little research evidence to sustain this assumption. There is an urgent need to evaluate the impact of the grandparents' rights legislation on the families involved, especially on the grandchildren "in whose best interests" the courts proceed.

THE IMPACT OF SOCIAL CHANGE
ON THE GRANDPARENT GENERATION

The fact that more and more men and women are spending a greater number of years in the completion phase of the family cycle is one of the most radical changes experienced by the family in the 20th century. Today the overwhelming proportion of parents survive to see not only their own children reach adulthood, but in many cases their grandchildren. It is quite possible that with the extended life expectancy of families and the low birth rate in the Western world, the majority of families in the U.S. will be living in the completed phase by the end of this century (Giraldo, 1980).

For most people, however, the phase of family completion comes in their mid-40s or early 50s, not at the age of retirement. At this stage in life they are still highly productive and capable. Their willingness to help their children and grandchildren has been amply illustrated. The awareness of the potential that they have for assistance of younger families is gradually increasing—but not fast enough yet to keep pace with rising rates of divorce, teenage pregnancies, and female-headed and single-parent households, and the increasing number of women who enter the labor market and need care for their young children.

For years the tax structure in the U.S. has made it difficult for parents in need of child care to rely on other family members for such services. In other industrialized nations, for example in West Germany (Weatherford, 1977), there is a well-articulated concept of state support for family members who assist each other. The establishment of three-generational households is encouraged. Often a grandmother who has completed her own child-rearing will assist in the rearing of her grandchildren, so that both parents can work outside of the home.

Until the so-called "anti-grandmother" provision in the income tax deduction for child care was eliminated in the Tax Reform Bill of the mid-1970s, families who employed a relative closer than a cousin to provide child care were disallowed child care costs in the U.S. This policy has changed.

A taxpayer can now consider amounts paid to *any* relative for child care as qualifying expense if the relative is not a dependent or a child of the taxpayer who is under 19 years of age at the close of the tax year. The care of the child by a grandparent qualifies the taxpayer for child care credit, as long as the grandparent is not a dependent of the taxpayer. The deductible amount allowed for child care has been increased in the 1981 Tax Reform legislation.

In addition, S. 1378, the Family Protection Act, was introduced in the 97th Congress (Jepsen and Smith, 1981). It would allow tax credits or tax exemption for each household that includes a dependent person age 65 or older, and establish a parental care trust under which taxpayers can save for the support of an aged person (or handicapped relative).

These changes in American family and tax law are so recent that we do not yet know whether they will substantially increase the involvement of grandparents in supplementary parenting. The role of grandparents and other relatives may well become more functional if it is recognized and rewarded by public policy. Given the numbers, vigor, and longevity of American grandparents, it should not come as a surprise if in the future we will see their increasing impact on public as well as domestic life.

THEORETICAL AND RESEARCH PERSPECTIVES ON GRANDPARENTHOOD

Kahana and Kahana (1971) have provided a useful theoretical and research perspective on grandparenthood that gives some organization to the knowledge we have so far and some direction to research that is needed:

1. First, grandparenthood may be viewed (as it has been in most studies so far) as a *social role* involving ascribed status and expectations of role performance, vis-à-vis the family or the society at large. Most anthropological studies of grandparenthood in traditional societies and most sociological studies among contemporary middle- and lower-class groups have followed this approach.
2. At the opposite end, grandparenthood may be viewed as an *emotional state* or *intrapsychic* experience, part of the *individual's* developmental career, largely independent of society at large. This view emerges predominantly in psychological studies of the perspective of grandparents and grandchildren in modern industrialized societies.
3. Third is the view of grandparenthood as *transaction* between child, adolescent, or young adult and an older person, involving reciprocity and mutual influences. Studies of this process are exceedingly rare and need to be undertaken.
4. Fourth is the consideration of grandparenthood as a *group process within the family*, involving relationships and interactions between three or four generations. A few recent studies by psychologists and psychiatrists have addressed this issue.
5. Lastly, grandparenthood may be considered as a *symbol*. It may be a reflection of aging, of continuity, and of potency, or it may indicate financial independence and usefulness to society.

Future research needs to consider a number of theoretical, methodological, and topical issues that come to mind as one reviews existing studies on grandparents and their relationships to their grandchildren.

Among the *theoretical* issues noted was a relative absence of any viewpoint other than role theory. Alternative or complementary hypotheses could be derived from other perspectives, such as sociobiology, Eriksen's stages of psychosocial development, systems theory, and Whiting's psychocultural model.

The *methodological* approach of most studies of grandparenthood tends to neglect the interaction of a number of important variables: They include the age, sex, educational, and employment (socioeconomic) status of the grandparent, and the age, sex, and birth order of the grandchild. Relatively little attention has been paid to subcultural differences in the role of grandparents in a pluralistic society, such as the U.S., and to their changing needs as they move from middle age to old age. Most "developmental" studies are cross-sectional; thus, hypothesized age changes may often be due to cohort or generational effects. There is need for a few well-executed longitudinal studies that look at changes in the reciprocal impact of grandparents on their children and grandchildren as they move through the later part of the family cycle.

Among important *intragenerational* differences that need exploring are the relative roles and effects of grandfathers versus grandmothers, of maternal versus paternal grandparents, of middle aged (45 and over) versus older grandparents (65 and over), and the role that retirement and widowhood plays in the involvement of grandparents in the lives of their grandchildren.

Additional research is needed to establish whether grandparents influence their grandchildren directly or whether their influence is largely indirect, through the middle generation, that is, the mothers.

We urgently need to evaluate the effect of important social changes on the role and impact on grandparents. They include the surrogate parenting of teenage mothers, the supplementary parenting of children of working mothers, and the effects of grandparent visitation rights legislation on children and their parents and step-parents after dissolution and reconstitution of a marriage.

Finally, we also need to examine the needs of elderly persons without grandchildren—some 20 to 25% of older people in our society. Do they become adopted grandparents? Who becomes the adopted grandchild? Do they come from available kinfolk or their friends? How reciprocal are the needs that are met in such a relationship? A small beginning in that direction has been made in the evaluation of the Foster Grandparent Program.

SUMMARY

A worldwide increase in life expectancy, providing for a considerable overlap in the life-span of grandparents and grandchildren, is a relatively recent phenomenon in human history. This trend is more pronounced in the industrialized world than in the developing countries.

In modern societies the role of grandparents as transmittors of skills essential for survival and of a cultural "ethos" tends to be progressively reduced as educational institutions and mass media spread around the world. This seems to affect the "traditional" roles of grandfathers more than grandmothers. But even in industrialized societies, most grandparents, but especially maternal grandmothers, actively participate in the care of young grandchildren and in meeting their emotional as well as material needs.

In such societies, the grandparent role may become merely symbolic among the affluent and involves usually only supplementary parenting; but among poor and working-class families the grandparent role is functional and involves surrogate parenting as well.

Grandparents seem to be important sources of support for high-risk children, that is, those with emotional, mental, or physical handicaps; the children of teenage mothers, of the poor, and of the mentally ill; the children of divorce and the delinquency prone; and later-born children in large families. The effects of grandparent-grandchild relationships differ with the sex and stage of life cycle of the participants and depend also on the attitudes of the parents, especially the mother or custodial parent in case of divorce.

In contemporary U.S., the involvement of grandparents in shared child care is increasing as is the recognition of their legal rights. More interdisciplinary research on the roles and effects of grandparents in the domestic and public spheres is needed that can be translated into an effective family policy and just family laws.

REFERENCES

Adams, B.N. 1968. Kinship in an Urban Setting, pp. 17–28. Markham, Chicago.

Ainsworth, M.D.S. 1967. Infancy in Uganda: Infant Care and the Growth of Love. The Johns Hopkins Press, Baltimore.

Allen, M. 1967-77. Visitation rights of a grandparent over the objection of a parent: The best interests of the child. J. Fam. Law 15:51–76.

Apple, D. 1956. The social structure of grandparenthood. Am. Anthropol. 58:656–663.

Ashby, V.R. 1981. Foster grandparents teach Indian lore and language. Child. Today 10:17.

Bachtold, L.M. 1982. Children's social interaction and parental attitudes among Hupa Indians and Anglo-Americans. J. Soc. Psychol. 116:9–17.

Bekker, L.D., and Taylor, C. 1966. Attitudes toward aging in a multi-generational sample. J. Gerontol. 21:115–118.

Bemis, J., Diers, E., and Sharpe, R. 1976. The teenage single mother. Child Welfare 55:309–318.

Bianchi, S., and Farley, R. 1979. Racial differences in family living arrangements and economic well-being: An analysis of recent trends. J. Mar. Fam. 41:537–551.

Borzi, P.C. 1977. Statutory visitation rights of grandparents: One step closer to the best interests of the child. Catholic Univ. Law Rev. 26(2):387–401.

Boyd, R. 1969a. Emerging roles of the four generation family. In: R.R. Boyd and C.G. Oakes (eds.), Foundations of Practical Gerontology. University of South Carolina Press, Columbia.

Boyd, R. 1969b. The valued grandparent: A changing social role. In: W. Donahue (ed.), Living in the Multigeneration Family, pp. 90-106. Institute of Gerontology, Ann Arbor, MI.

Bryant, B.K. 1981. Developmental Perspectives on Sources of Support and Psychological Well-Being, p. 78. Final Report to the Foundation for Child Development. Department of Applied Behavioral Sciences, University of California at Davis.

Burgess, E. 1960. Family structure and relationships. In: E. Burgess (ed.), Aging in Western Societies, pp. 285–287. University of Chicago Press, Chicago.

Campbell, V., and Buholz, M. 1982. Parenting by related adults. In: M.J. Kostelnik and H.J. Fitzgerald (eds.), Patterns of Supplementary Parenting, Vol. II. Plenum Press, New York.

Carroll, V. 1971. Adoption in Eastern Oceania. University of Hawaii Press, Honolulu.

Clavan, S. 1978. The impact of social class and social trends on the role of grandparents. Fam. Coord. 27:351–358.

Cohler, B.J., and Grunebaum, H.U. (with the assistance of D.M. Robbins). 1981. Mothers, Grandmothers, and Daughters: Personality and Child Care in Three Generation Families. Wiley, New York.

Davis, E. 1968. The American Negro: From family membership to personal and social identity. J.A.M.A. 60:92–99.

Dell, P., and Applebaum, A. 1977. Trigenerational enmeshment: Unresolved ties of single parents to family of origins. Am. J. Orthopsychiatry 47:52–59.

Furstenberg, F.G. 1976. Unplanned Parenthood: The Social Consequences of Teenage Child-bearing. The Free Press, New York.

Furstenberg, F.G., Spanier, G., and Crawford, A. 1980. Marital dissolution and generational ties. Unpublished paper.

Giraldo, Z.I. 1980. Public Policy and the Family: Wives and Mothers in the Labor Force. D.C. Heath, Lexington, MA.

Goodman, M.E., and Beman, A. 1971. Child's-eye views of life in an urban barrio. In: N. Wagner and M. Haug (eds.), Chicanos: Social and Psychological Perspectives. Mosby, St. Louis, MO.

Goody, E. 1970. Kinship fostering in Gonja: Deprivation or advantage. In: P. Mayer (ed.), Socialization: The Approach from Social Anthropology, pp. 51-74. Tavistock Publishers Ltd., London.

Gray, R.M., and Kasteler, J.M. 1967. Foster grandparents and retarded children: A research report of the Utah Foster Grandparent Project. Utah Council on Aging, Utah State Welfare Department and the Utah State Training School, Salt Lake City.

Hammond, M.A. 1968. Effects of the Foster Grandparent Project upon the oral language development of institutionalized mentally retardates. Unpublished doctoral dissertation, North Texas State University, Denton.

Harris, L., et al. 1975. The Myth and Reality of Aging in America. National Council on Aging, Washington, DC.

Hill, R. 1977. Informal Adoption among Black Families. National Urban League, New York.

Hill, R., Foote, N., Aldous, J., and MacDonald, R. 1970. Family Development in Three Generations. Schenkman Publishing, Cambridge, MA.

Huang, L.J. 1976. The Chinese American family. In: C. Mindel and R. Haberstein (eds.), Ethnic Families in America. Elsevier, New York.

Jackson, J.J. 1971. Sex and social class variations in Black aged parent-adult child relationships. Aging Hum. Dev. 2:96–107.

Jepson, R.W., and Smith, A.L. 1981. S.1378 The Family Protection Act. June 17, U.S.

Senate, 97th Congress, First Session. Congress. Rec. 127(92).

Kahana, B., and Kahana, E. 1970. Grandparenthood from the perspective of the developing grandchild. Dev. Psychol. 3:98–105.

Kahana, E., and Kahana, B. 1971. Theoretical and research perspectives on grandparenthood. Aging Hum. Dev. 2:261–268.

Katz, A. 1979. Lone fathers: Perspectives and implications for family policy. Fam. Coord. 28:521–528.

Kell, L., and Aldous, J. 1960. Trends in child care over three generations. Mar. Fam. Living 22:176–177.

Kellam, S.G., Ensminger, M.E., and Turner, R.J. 1977. Family structure and the mental health of children. Arch. Gen. Psychiatry 34:1012–1022.

Kessen, W. 1975. Childhood in China. Yale University Press, New Haven, CT.

Kitano, H.H., and Kikumura, A. 1976. The Japanese American family. In: C. Mindel and R. Haberstein (eds.), Ethnic Families in America. Elsevier, New York.

Komarovsky, M. 1962. Blue-Collar Marriage. Random House, New York.

LeVine, R.A., and Price-Williams, D. 1974. Children's kinship concepts: Cognitive development and early experience among the Hausa. Ethnology 13:25–44.

Marcoen, J. 1979. Children's perception of aged persons and grandparents. Int. J. Behav. Dev. 2:87–105.

Marvin, R.S., Van De Vender, T.L., Iwanaga, M.I., LeVine, S., and LeVine, R.A. 1977. Infant-caregiver attachment among the Hausa of Nigeria. In: H. McGurk (ed.), Ecological Factors in Human Development. North Holland Publishing, Amsterdam.

Martin, E.P., and Martin, J.M. 1978. The Black Extended Family. The University of Chicago Press, Chicago.

Mead, M. 1972. Blackberry Winter: My Earlier Years. William Morrow, New York.

Mead, M. 1974. Grandparents as educators. Teachers Coll. Rec. 76(2):240–249.

Miller, D. 1979. The Native American family: The urban way. In: E. Corfman (ed.), Families Today, pp. 441-484, Vol. I. U.S. Government Printing Office, Washington, DC.

Mimkon vs. Ford. 1975. 66 N.J. 426, 332 A.2d 199, 204.

Minturn, L., and Lambert, W. 1964. Mothers of Six Cultures: Antecedents of Child-Rearing. Wiley, New York.

Neugarten, B., and Weinstein, K. 1964. The changing American grandparent. J. Mar. Fam. 26:197–205.

Olsen, N.J. 1976. The role of grandmothers in Taiwanese family socialization. J. Mar. Fam. 38:363–372.

Phenice, L.A. 1981. Children's Perceptions of Elderly Persons. Century Twenty-One Publishing, Saratoga, CA.

Reagan, N. (with Wilke, J.) 1982. To Love a Child. Bobbs-Merrill, Indianapolis.

Red Horse, J.G., Lewis, R., and Feit, H. 1978. Family behavior of urban American Indians. Soc. Casework 59:67–72.

Red Horse, J.G., Lewis, R., Feit, M., and Decker, J. 1979. American Indian elders: Needs and aspirations in institutional and home health care. Unpublished manuscript, Arizona State University, Tempe.

Robertson, J.F. 1976. Significance of grandparents: Perceptions of young adult grandchildren. Gerontologist 16:137–140.

Robertson, J.F. 1977. Grandmotherhood: A study of role conceptions. J. Mar. Fam. 39:165–174.

Robins, L.N., West, P.A., and Herjanic, B.L. 1975. Arrests and delinquency in two generations: A study of Black urban families and their children. J. Child Psychol. Psychiatry 16:125–140.

Rohner, R.P. 1975. They Love Me, They Love Me Not: A World-wide Study of the Effect of Parental Acceptance and Rejection. HRAF Press, New Haven, CT.

Saltz, R. 1967. Evaluation of a Foster Grandparent Program. Merrill-Palmer Institute, Detroit.

Saltz, R. 1971. Aging persons as child-care workers in a foster grandparent program. Aging Hum. Dev. 2:314–340.

Schultz, N.W. 1980. A cognitive-developmental study of the grandchild-grandparent bond. Child Study J. 10:7–26.

Scott, B.R. 1974. Grandparent presence as a variable in child development. Unpublished doctoral dissertation, University of Washington, Seattle.

Seña-Rivera, J. 1979. La familia Chicana. In: E. Corfman (ed.), Families Today, pp. 67–128, Vol. I. U.S. Government Printing Office, Washington, DC.

Shanas, E. 1973. Family kin networks and aging in cross-cultural perspective. J. Mar. Fam. 35:505–511.

Shanas, E. 1980. Older people and their families: The new pioneers. J. Mar. Fam. 42:9–15.

Shanas, E., and Streib, G.F. (eds.). 1965. Social Structure and the Family Generational Relations. Prentice-Hall, Englewood Cliffs, NJ.

Silberbauer, G.B. 1972. The G/wi Bushmen. In: M.G. Bicchieri (ed.), Hunters and Gatherers Today. Holt, Rinehart & Winston, New York.

Simmons, L. 1945. The Role of the Aged in Primitive Society. Yale University Press, New Haven, CT.

Staples, R., and Smith, J. 1954. Attitudes of grandmothers and mothers toward child-rearing practices. Child Dev. 25:91–97.

Stehouwer, J. 1965. Relations between generations and the three generation household in Denmark. In: E. Shanas and G.F. Streib (eds.), Social Structure and the Family Generational Relations. Prentice-Hall, Englewood Cliffs, NJ.

Townsend, P. 1957. The Family Life of Old People. Routledge and Kegan Paul, London.

Troll, L.E., Miller, S.J., and Atchley, R.C. 1979. Families in Later Life. Wadsworth, Belmont, CA.

Turnbull, C. 1965. The Mbuti pygmies of the Congo. In: J. L. Gibbs (ed.), Peoples of Africa. Holt, Rinehart & Winston, New York.

Uhlenberg, P. 1974. Cohort variations in family life cycle experiences of U.S. females. J. Mar. Fam. 36:284–292.

U. S. Bureau of the Census. 1979. Characteristics of the population below the poverty level: 1977. Current Population Reports, March 1979, Series P-60, No. 119.

U. S. Department of Commerce. 1977. Social Indicators, 1976. U.S. Government Printing Office, Department of Documents, Washington, DC.

Van der Straeten, S. 1971. De bete kenis van de grootouders voor de Kleinkinderen. Unpublished masters thesis, Catholic University of Louvain, Belgium.

Weatherford, J.M. 1977. Family culture, behavior and emotion in a working class German town. Unpublished doctoral dissertation, University of California, San Diego.

Werner, E.E. 1979. Cross-Cultural Child Development: A View from the Planet Earth. Brooks/Cole, Monterey, CA.

Werner, E.E., and Smith, R.S. 1977. Kauai's Children Come of Age. University of Hawaii Press, Honolulu.

Werner, E.E., and Smith, R.S. 1982. Vulnerable, but Invincible: A Longitudinal Study of Resilient Children and Youth. McGraw-Hill, New York.

West. 1982. Annotated California Civil Code, Section 197.5. West Publishing Co., St. Paul.

Williams, T.R. 1972. Introduction to Socialization. Mosby, St. Louis, MO.

Wood, V., and Robertson, J. 1976. The significance of grandparenthood. In: J. Gubrium (ed.), Time, Roles and Self in Old Age, pp. 278–357. Human Sciences Press, New York.

CHAPTER **6**

Family Day Care

"Those are not his brother and sister?" said Mrs. Boffin. "Oh dear, no, ma'am. Those are Minders." "Minders?" the secretary repeated. "Left to be Minded, sir. I keep a Minding school. I can take only three, on account of the mangle. But I love children, and fourpence a week is fourpence."

Charles Dickens, *Our Mutual Friend*

The daytime care of young children in family day care homes is a very important means of child care in most industrialized countries. It is the predominant form of arranged formal care in the Anglo-Saxon countries (Canada, Great Britain, and the U.S.) and plays a large role in other industrialized nations where housing is not a problem. In return for financial reimbursement, day care is rendered to a child in another family home, usually in the company of a few other young children and often including at least one child who is a relative of the person providing the care (Robinson et al., 1979).

There are few research data concerning family day care, primarily because the bulk of such arrangements in most countries are the private affairs of parents and caregivers, without contracts and institutional supports and often without public regulation or supervision. Although most countries have laws regulating private paid day care—regulations having to do with numbers of children, health, space, and safety—it takes a great deal of effort to discover where such day care is going on.

Family day care constitutes the largest natural system of out-of-home care in the U.S. Of the 7.5 million American families who regularly use some form of child care for 10 or more hours a week, fully 45% place their children in family day care homes. An estimated 1.8 million family day care homes serve almost 50% of all children in full-time care; the greatest proportion of these children are under 3. Family day care also represents the most prevalent mode of after-school care for the more than 5 million school children between 6 and 13 in the U.S. whose parents work (Divine-Hawkins, 1981).

Family day care encompasses a myriad of arrangements between families and caregivers, but from a policy point of view it is useful to distinguish between three types: unregulated, regulated, and sponsored.

An estimated 94% of family day care in the U.S. is provided by some 1.7 million *unregulated* caregivers who operate informally, independent of any regulatory system or administrative structures. *Regulated* providers, although they have been certified by the appropriate governmental agency as meeting state and/or federal standards for day care, are similar to unregulated caregivers in that they are not tied to any administering agency. In 1979, there were approximately 115,000 regulated family day care homes serving an average of three children per home. The third major group of family day care homes are operated by *sponsored* caregivers—licensed or registered providers who operate as part of a day care system or network of homes under the sponsorship of an administrative agency. Sponsored homes are most likely to serve subsidized children (of low-income single mothers) and may also have access to a range of social services, such as provider training and client referral (Singer et al., 1980; Thornell et al., 1981). They account for only 2% of all family day care providers in the U.S.

CHARACTERISTICS OF FAMILY DAY CARE PROVIDERS

Although there is an occasional male among family day care providers (Jackson and Jackson, 1979), the overwhelming majority are women. The National Day Care Home Study (NDCHS), conducted under the auspices of the U.S. Department of Health and Human Services (1981), interviewed some 793 caregivers from three different ethnic backgrounds (black, Hispanic, and white) in three urban areas of the U.S. (Los Angeles, San Antonio, and Philadelphia) and found a median age of 42 years across the three sites, with a range from 16 to 76 years. Although a large proportion of the family day care mothers is composed of young women, often with small children at home, an even larger fraction consists of middle-aged and older women who have already raised their own families, but may have grandchildren and/or other relatives in their care.

Emlen (1977) studied day care providers in Portland, Oregon, and found them to be generally in a later stage of family development than their clients, and saw a complementary fit between the needs of the young working mother with small children and those of the caregiver whose nest was partially or entirely empty of young children. The British studies of "childminders" (Jackson and Jackson, 1979) in Birmingham, Bradford, Huddersfield, Leeds, London, and Manchester report a similar trend.

There seem to be two distinct types of caregivers: *older,* poorer women, often without husbands, taking care of their relatives, along with enrolled children, and *younger,* middle-income married women, taking care of their own young children along with enrolled children. The former tend to be less educated, but more experienced, and rely on family day care as the major source of income; the latter have more formal education, but less experience, and regard family day care as a supplementary source of income (Singer et al., 1980).

Emlen (1977) found that the older caregivers (with less education and marketability) tend to prefer to stay at home and to do that for which they are best prepared by experience and inclination—raising young children. Jackson and Jackson (1979) in their portrait gallery of British childminders distinguished between those who positively sought the work, and those who would find it difficult to earn a living in the larger public theatre.

Both in the American and British studies, more of the older, less educated, and poorer family day mothers were found among non-whites: Hispanic and black caregivers in the American sample (Singer et al., 1980), and Asian and West Indian childminders in the British sample (Jackson and Jackson, 1979).

CAREGIVER JOB PERCEPTIONS

The majority of the family day caregivers, both in the U.S. (Emlen et al., 1971; Singer et al., 1980) and in Great Britain (Jackson and Jackson, 1979) began providing day care services for one of two reasons: either they had young children of their own or among their relatives needing care, or they were approached by someone else (friends, neighbors) and asked to take care of children.

Thus, the typical family day caregiver did not start out from a business perspective, from a sense that there is a market for family day care in the community. She was persuaded to care for children by a friend or relative. About 60% to 68% among the British and American family day care providers interviewed indicated that they considered their work permanent, the most frequently cited reason was that they liked providing care for children and had no plans for other work.

The majority of the caregivers in the NDCHS (Singer et al., 1980) agreed on the importance of affection and discipline in the lives of a child. Greater variability was found in areas concerning the amount of adult supervision or the content of adult teaching. In general, white caregivers were more likely to feel that adults should play an authoritarian role, that young children should be taught useful skills and concepts, and that children should be encouraged to express themselves than their non-white counterparts. Unregulated caregivers tended to stress the importance of an informal, home-like social environment, regulated and sponsored family day care providers stressed the educational aspects of family day care.

CAREGIVERS AS COMMUNITY MEMBERS

More American family day care providers than British "childminders," perceived the city they lived in as a positive environment to raise children, and saw themselves involved in their neighborhoods through schools or churches. The vast majority of the caregivers (some 80%) were satisfied with the adult contact they had; two-thirds reported that parents turned to them for information and advice, and almost half indicated that neighbors sometimes asked them for advice about bringing up children or about child care.

Two recruitment sources are typically used by family day care providers: An informal network of relatives, friends, neighbors, and words of mouth (for the unregistered providers) and also advertisements on local bulletin boards, at supermarkets and laundromats, and in newspapers (for the registered providers). Only sponsored caregivers rely primarily on an affiliated social service agency to fill their homes with children.

With the exception of the sponsored family day care homes, most family day care providers in the U.S. and in England, are not integrated in the "professional" child care community. As a result they are often unaware of child care training opportunities and referral and support services available in their cities (Jackson and Jackson, 1979; Singer et al., 1980).

Despite the fact that by law, every U.S. resident must file a federal income tax return, a large proportion of the family day care providers in the NCDHS reported that they did not. Many of those who filed and declared their income were unaware of the deductions they could take. Some of their counterparts among the British childminders interviewed by Jackson and Jackson (1979) were actually found to operate at a net loss, if one considered their expenditures for heating, supplies, food, etc.

Family day care arrangements are part of a publicly subsidized system of child care in all Scandinavian countries (Bang, 1979; Dodge, 1979), and in France and Belgium (Robinson et al., 1979). There laws have been introduced to regulate the employment of "day mothers," their wages and obligations. Yet in these countries, as in the U.S., the number of publicly subsidized family care homes is far exceeded by the greater number of private arrangements which escape scrutiny and are not subject to official control (Berfenstam and William-Olsson, 1973). This also holds for informal family day care arrangements in socialist countries, such as Poland and the U.S.S.R.

From a provider's perspective, family day care is not a lucrative profession. Data available from the U.S. and Great Britain (Emlen, 1977; Jackson and Jackson, 1979; Singer et al., 1980) show that many caregiver's earnings are below minimum wage standards, or just barely sufficient to make a difference between poverty and a low income budget. Although wages may be low, family day care providers constitute a self-supporting segment of the population. Day care providers work long hours, frequently have no provisions for sick time or vacations and often do not even recognize the benefits for which they are eligible.

In summary, family day care in most industrialized nations consists for the most part of an invisible array of small and varied businesses that operate, by and large, outside of the market mainstream, and yet are often strongly and adversely affected by it. While family day care providers range from professionals and middle class families to single day care mothers with little income they are "for good or ill a service on the whole forged for the poor by the poorer" (Jackson and Jackson, 1979, p. 193).

CHARACTERISTICS OF THE CHILDREN IN FAMILY DAY CARE

Contrary to the frequently held misconception that family day care homes have inordinately large enrollments, the average number of children in a typical American family day care home is three, just as in Mrs. Higden's home in Dickens' time in Victorian England (Emlen, 1972: Singer et al., 1980).

Only 10% or less of the family day care homes surveyed in the NDCHS (1981) had enrollments of more than six children, and Emlen (1972) suggests that this "deviant" subgroup of family day care deserves special study since it appears to run more like a small business than a family household.

In homes in which family caregivers cared for related children (either their own or relatives') there was a decrease in the number of additional children enrolled. Four children were, on the average, enrolled in homes that did not care for related children, compared to 2.3 children in the family day care homes in which related children were present.

Overall half of the caregivers interviewed in the NDCHS cared for infants (53.4%) or preschoolers (50.2%). Toddlers, the most common group in family day care, were found in 62.8% of the homes; only one-third of the caregivers (37.8%) provided after school care for children above age 5.

Almost one-third of the family day care homes had only a single age group in care. Another third had two age groups in care, either an infant/toddler combination (the most common) or toddler/preschooler combinations. The remaining one-third were homes with three or four age groups, but fewer than 5% had children of all age groups from infants to school-age children.

The vast majority of children in the NDCHS (U.S. Department of Health and Human Services, 1980) were of the same ethnicity as their caregivers. This was more common in non-white than white homes, both in American and British studies (Jackson and Jackson, 1979; Singer et al., 1980). One-third of all the children in care came from single-parent families. The highest percentage of children from such homes, almost 50%, were found in sponsored care.

The majority of family day care arrangements are made on a full-time basis 5 days a week, with an average of 9 to 10 hours of care per day. Overall almost 70% of all children in family day homes are in care for 30 or more hours per week. Part-time arrangements tend to be for school-age children only.

Emlen (1975; 1977) who studied family day care arrangements for children under the age of 3, and Vaughn et al. (1980), who looked at such

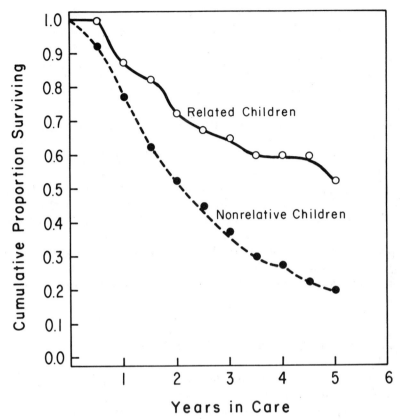

Figure 8. Survival distributions: length of time in care by relative status of child. (From U. S. Department of Health and Human Services, 1980, p. 363.)

provisions for infants (up to age 18 months), found family day care arrangements to be relatively unstable, lasting on the average only 6 months, with half surviving longer than a year.

In contrast, the NDCHS, which included a large sample of children (N = 2812), reports that the average time in family day care is relatively long. The length of time a child stays with a particular caregiver is a function both of the age of the child and of whether or not the child is a relative of the caregiver (see Figure 8).

RELATIVE CARE

The majority of the family day care providers in the NDCHS provided care for related children, either their own (predominant among white family day caregivers) or their grandchildren or (grand) nieces and nephews (predominant among Hispanic and black caregivers).

Providers who cared for young relatives tended to be older than those who did not, as most relative care was provided by grandmothers (mean age, 47). Relative care is concentrated in unregulated homes, and homes that care for related children have fewer children enrolled.

Relative care is related to the age of the child at the start of family day care and to the length of time he or she spends in such care. Children cared for by an aunt, grandmother, or other relative were found to enter such care at younger ages than non-related children.

Among the 1466 children available for a "survival" analysis of length of time in family day care (Singer et al., 1980), 54% were less than 1 year old when they entered a relative's care; only 32% of the children entering a non-relative home were this young. Related children also tended to stay in family day care significantly longer than children not related to the caregiver. One-half of all related children were still in care after more than 5 years. The median survival time was 2 years and 2 months for non-related children. For relatives, on the other hand, the average length of stay in family day care was almost 4 years. Related children started in family day care earlier than non-related children, remained in it longer, and shared it with significantly fewer unrelated children.

PARENTS OF CHILDREN IN FAMILY DAY CARE

Parents are the critical link between the family day care provider and the child. It is therefore important to examine the impact of family day care arrangements on their lives, and a few studies have begun to do just that (Emlen, 1974, 1977; Emlen et al., 1971; Golden et al., 1978; Singer et al., 1980; Steinberg and Green, unpublished manuscript).

The NDCHS (1981) interviewed 348 parents who used family day care in three metropolitan areas—Los Angeles ($N = 105$), Philadelphia ($N = 121$), and San Antonio ($N = 122$)—and found an unusually high level of involvement between parents and day care providers and a high level of agreement between the caregivers' and the parents' responses concerning the children in their care.

In general, the income of the parents in the NDCHS sample was lower than the national average; but among the three ethnic groups represented, whites had a higher income level than Hispanics and blacks. Most parents came from either unskilled or skilled working-class backgrounds and had small families (one or two children). Some 40% were single parents, that is, divorced, separated, widowed, or never married.

Most parents in the NDCHS sample sought day care for their children so they could work, although most of the mothers would have preferred to work part-time or to stay at home while their children were young (see also Emlen,

1974a). They selected *family day care* because it was available, affordable, and offered special attention to their child. Parents preferred care in the child's own home for children under 1 year, family day care for 1 to 3 year olds, and a more structured environment, that is, center care, nursery school, or kindergarten, for older preschoolers. A higher proportion of black parents (61%) than white (36%) or Hispanic (48%) parents had preferences for center care with an educational component.

In general, working mothers using family day care were constrained by the options open to them. The majority reported not having a relative at home or in the vicinity who could take care of their young children. Most parents in the NDCHS sample and in Emlen's (1971, 1974a) studies in Portland, Oregon, located their family day care mother through some personal source—relatives, friends, or neighbors—and would follow the same route again if seeking child care in the future. Among the most important requirements parents looked for in a caregiver were experience with children (rather than formal education), reliability, and the ability to provide for the child's emotional, cognitive, and nutritional needs in a safe and clean environment that was conveniently located. Emlen (1977) found a compensating fit in experience: Women with 2 or more years of experience as working mothers used sitters with little experience as caregivers, whereas mothers who were new and inexperienced as working mothers tended to use experienced caregivers.

Nearly half of all the parents in the NDCHS sample felt that their child had a special need to be with other children. Parents were concerned that those others be children from whom their own child could learn. Among the benefits from the family day care experience the majority of the parents cited their child's social growth, one-third felt that the child's linguistic and conceptual skills had benefitted in family day care, and one-fifth mentioned the home-like atmosphere as a special benefit for their child. Only a few parents (about 13%) would have preferred a greater emphasis on the acquisition of cognitive and linguistic skills. The vast majority (87%) would recommend their caregiver to a friend.

Over three-quarters in the NDCHS sample paid the full cost of child care. In general, whites paid higher fees than blacks, who in turn paid more than Hispanics. Fees for children cared for by a relative or friend did not differ from those of other children in the sample. Nearly all parents had discussed fees with their providers before finalizing the care arrangement. Most parents thought the fees charged were appropriate for the services rendered.

PARENT-CAREGIVER COMMUNICATIONS

The demands of family and friendship sometimes conflict with the parents' needs as consumers and the caregivers' needs as providers. Emlen (1971, 1974a,

1977), in several studies with Portland working mothers, found that arrangements started between friends tended to be used only temporarily, and were less serviceable for permanent child care. The task of renegotiating a prior relationship from one of friendship to one involving a contractual exchange of money for services proved to be hazardous either to the friendship or to the child care arrangement.

By contrast, the most stable family day care arrangements in Emlen's (1977) studies in Portland and in the NDCHS samples in Los Angeles, San Antonio, and Philadelphia were between persons without prior close acquaintance. Although the majority of family day care providers were found within 1 mile of the child's home in Portland (Emlen, 1977), within 2 miles from home in California (Sale, 1972), and within three city blocks or in the same apartment building in Eastern cities, such as New York City (Golden et al., 1978), most parents had *not* been acquainted with their child's caregiver before making arrangements for family day care.

Despite or maybe because of this social distance between parents and family day care providers, relationships which began as a well-negotiated contract between strangers often developed into friendships, and when they did, the child care arrangement tended to endure (Emlen, 1971, 1974a). In such stable arrangements most parents in the NDCHS sample felt that they were in agreement with the caregivers on important aspects of child-rearing. Most frequently shared items between parents and caregivers *before* setting up an arrangement concerned the child's health and food preferences; fewer than one-quarter of the NDCHS sample providers mentioned such information as behavior problems, discipline preferences, or the child's favorite toy or activities.

Once family day care had begun, providers generally reported taking time at the end of the day to talk to parents about their children's behavior and state of health, the activities of the day, and new skills the children had learned. Relatively few child care arrangements were terminated by family day care mothers. In a telephone follow-up 1 year after the initial survey at the Los Angeles site of the NDCHS (Singer et al., 1980) about one-quarter of the caregivers contacted were no longer providing child care. Caregivers' reasons for termination of family day care were most often related to the needs of their own children and family members or changes in their personal life, and very infrequently to problems with day care parents.

To the extent that arrangements were terminated due to caregiver dissatisfaction, major predictors in Emlen et al.'s (1972) longitudinal study of 116 family day care arrangements in Portland were a growing dissatisfaction with the mother's concern for the child, an increasing sense of inconvenience, and an initial and increasing feeling that caring for this mother's child was an emotional drain. Dissatisfaction with the child was not a contributor; rather, the caregiver's concern focused primarily on the attitudes and behaviors of the mothers. Dissatisfied mothers also reported a worsening relationship with the day care provider. Central for both was the other woman's concern for the child, not the child himself or herself.

Most arrangements were terminated by the parents, however, and usually for extrinsic reasons rather than dissatisfaction with the care arrangement, such as changes in residence, jobs, or marital status, which are highly contingent on the circumstances of family life and employment opportunities.

THE EFFECTS OF FAMILY DAY CARE

Critical reviews of the effects of day care have focused mostly on studies conducted in high-quality, university-based day care centers (Belsky and Steinberg, 1978, 1979; Brown, 1978; Etaugh, 1980; Rutter, 1981). There has been a conspicuous lack of assessment of home-based types of substitute care for young children.

Since the late 1970s, a number of studies have appeared in American, British, Canadian, and Swedish publications that begin to give us a glimpse of the impact of family day care on the behavior of children and their caregivers. Some of these studies describe child and caregiver behavior in the context of family day care, others contrast the cognitive, emotional, and social development of children in family type care with youngsters who were exclusively reared by their mothers and/or with children who had supplementary care in centers. Most of these studies lack assessments prior to day care entry, however, and very few are longitudinal in design.

Because the samples in these studies were not randomly assigned to type of care, we cannot determine with certainty whether the effects observed are attributable to type of care (family day care, own home, or center care) or to naturally occurring selection processes. The generalizability of findings from the observation studies described next are limited to the extent that participation of caregivers was voluntary, and the effects of the presence of observers in family day care homes on the behavior of caregivers is unknown. It will be important to see to what extent these findings are replicated in other studies here and abroad.

Caregiver and Child Behaviors in the Context of Family Day Care

The most extensive set of observations of caregiver and child behaviors in family day care comes from the NDCHS (Stallings and Porter, 1980). The behavior of caregivers and children were monitored in 303 family day care homes in three metropolitan areas of the U.S.: Los Angeles ($N = 99$), San Antonio ($N = 115$), and Philadelphia ($N = 89$). Included were black, white, and Hispanic children and family day care "mothers" in regulated, unregulated, and sponsored homes. Caregivers and children were observed as they went about their usual activities for approximately 2 hours during each of two mornings. Behaviors were sampled every 20 seconds for periods of 5 minutes at a time.

Caregiver Behavior in Family Day Care

In general, the observations of the NDCHS showed family day care homes to be positive environments for children. They were generally safe, home-like environments that were less structured and homogenous with respect to children's ages than day care centers. Caregivers spent nearly half of the observed time interacting with the 1- to 5-year-old children in their care, and the time spent seemed appropriate to the needs of children of a given age (see Table 6).

The most frequent type of *direct* involvement with the children was some form of teaching. Of the remainder of the caregiver-child interactions, participation in play and helping were about equal in frequency. Directing, controlling, and conversing with children were less frequent behaviors. Caregivers rarely expressed any negative affect toward the children during the observation periods.

Indirect involvement with the children, such as supervising their play and preparation of meals and play material, also occupied a substantial amount of the caregiver's time, leaving only about one-third of her time for activities such as housekeeping, entertaining herself, and talking to other adults. The caregiver was out of the range of the children only 1% of the observed time period.

The NDCHS found caregiver behavior in family day care to be remarkably stable. This was confirmed in comparison data collected hour to hour, day to day, and week to week, and in comparisons between natural and structured observations.

Differences in Caregiver Behavior in Different Types of Family Care

Some interesting differences in caregiver behavior appeared in comparisons among different types of family care, that is, with relatives and in unregulated, regulated, and sponsored homes.

The presence of the caregiver's own children or a relative in the family day care home appeared to affect the caregiver's behavior toward the other children. Homes in which the caregiver's own child was present tended to be more informal, with more activities that were not centered on the children and activities that were less structured. This also tended to be true for caregivers who cared for a non-resident relative.

On the whole, the types of caregiver activities in unregulated and regulated homes were similar to each other, but teaching occurred more often in sponsored homes. More emphasis was placed on cognitive and expressive activities in these homes, and they were more suggestive of a preschool environment.

In general, caregivers in the NDCHS spent a considerable amount of their time in positive interactions with the children in their care. Other studies in the U.S. and in Sweden suggest that there may well be a greater amount of adult

Table 6. Distribution of the caregiver's time by regulatory status[a]

	Sponsored	Regulated	Unregulated
Direct involvement with children			
Interactions with 1 to 5 year olds			
Teach	17.0	12.8	12.1
Play/participate	8.6	7.3	7.3
Help	9.3	9.5	8.2
Direct	3.9	3.8	3.8
Converse	3.4	3.3	3.0
Control	3.6	3.8	3.5
Subtotal	45.8	40.5	32.9
Interactions with baby	3.4	5.3	2.5
Interactions with school-aged children	0.8	0.7	0.9
Negative emotional affect	0.2	0.2	0.4
Total direct involvement	50.2	46.7	41.7
Indirect involvement with children			
Supervise/prepare	18.4	17.2	14.2
Noninvolvement with children			
Converse	5.5	5.8	6.8
Recreation alone	4.8	5.7	13.0
Housekeeping	17.9	17.8	22.0
Out of range	1.7	1.4	1.2
Subtotal	29.9	30.7	43.0
Total	98.5	94.6	98.9
Activities Facilitated			
Language information	10.6	8.4	7.8
Structured fine motor	6.1	3.1	3.5
Work	1.4	1.3	1.3
Physical Needs	8.2	8.9	8.1
Dramatic play	1.1	0.8	1.2
Music/Dance	2.1	0.7	0.4
Television	1.8	2.6	2.0
Exploratory fine motor	1.2	1.0	0.9
Gross motor	2.2	1.8	1.5
Total facilitation	34.7	28.6	26.7
Positive affect	6.0	5.6	4.6

[a] From U.S. Department of Health and Human Services (1981, p. 29).

input and one-to-one caregiver-child interaction in family day care than in day care centers.

Comparative Studies of Caregiver Behavior in Family Day Care, Center Care, and Own Home Care

A comparison of some 20 family day care programs with 11 center programs in the New York City Infant Day Care Study (Golden et al., 1978) noted that family day care environments were superior to day care centers on a variety of important social dimensions, that is, caregiver-to-child ratio, social interaction, and individual attention.

Cochran (1977) observed Swedish toddlers (ages 12, 15, and 18 months) who were either in day care centers or in home-based care provided by the mother or by a substitute caregiver in her own home with one or two other children. Interactions between adults and children occurred with considerably greater frequency and duration in the homes and day homes than in the centers, thus providing greater opportunity for socialization by adults. The interactions that distinguished homes from the centers were verbal and exploratory in nature. Both family home caregivers and mothers set more limits ("do's and don'ts") than center caregivers on the toddlers' activities, a finding also reported by Howes and Rubenstein (1978) in the U.S.

Prescott (1973) observed that preschool-age children in family day care homes were rated more favorably than children in open and structured day care centers on receiving help and opportunities for tactile-sensory exploring and physical activity. They were lowest of all groups in experiencing frustration, pain, or rejection.

In summary, family day care tends to resemble home-rearing more than center care in amount and quality of adult-child interaction.

CHILD BEHAVIOR IN FAMILY DAY CARE

In the NDCHS, observations of the behavior of the children in family day care homes were divided among the younger children (12 to 35 month olds, $N = 210$) and the older children (36 to 59 month olds, $N = 137$). Where possible, one child in each age range was observed in each home; however, both of these age groups were not represented in every home (see Table 7).

Contrary to the popular stereotype of a caregiver busy with other things while the television set "babysits" the children, the youngsters in the NDCHS spent little time watching television, at least on the morning that they were observed.

Both toddlers and preschool children played with water, sand, paint, dough, and other exploratory materials more often than they engaged in any other activities. This finding is similar to that of Prescott (1973), who observed that children in family day care did more tactile-sensory exploring than children in day care centers or in their own homes. Cochran (1977) also reports that Swedish toddlers in family day care explored more with materials than did center children.

Preschoolers in family day care manifested more involvement with peers than did the toddlers. They talked more with other children, played alone less often, and were less involved with the caregivers. Howes and Rubenstein (1978) observed more positive social skills among preschool children in family day care than among center children, suggesting that perhaps the family day

Table 7. Means and standard deviations for child behavior[a]

Child variable	Younger child ($N = 210$)		Older child ($N = 137$)	
	X	S.D.	X	S.D.
Prosocial activity	0.003	0.006	0.008	0.024
Affectionate behavior	0.007	0.010	0.001	0.003
Distress	0.006	0.009	0.001	0.004
Attention-seeking with caregiver	0.008	0.012	0.006	0.008
Antisocial to other younger children	0.002	0.005	0.001	0.004
Controlled by caregiver	0.021	0.022	0.015	0.019
Controls other young child	0.001	0.003	0.003	0.005
Language/information with caregiver	0.030	0.054	0.040	0.063
Dramatic play	0.007	0.021	0.024	0.038
Looking at book	0.006	0.017	0.009	0.021
Fine motor structured activity	0.066	0.074	0.103	0.095
Fine motor exploration with caregiver	0.009	0.015	0.008	0.016
Fine motor exploration with other young children	0.006	0.010	0.011	0.019
Fine motor exploration alone	0.216	0.122	0.150	0.120
Conversation with other young children	0.001	0.002	0.003	0.006
Conversation with caregiver	0.003	0.010	0.009	0.020
Television alone	0.028	0.055	0.044	0.084
Educational television with someone	0.014	0.040	0.018	0.048
Noneducational television with someone	0.015	0.043	0.015	0.038
Music/dance	0.004	0.009	0.004	0.010
Household work	0.004	0.014	0.007	0.020
Gross motor	0.098	0.084	0.085	0.072
Physical needs with caregiver	0.054	0.052	0.025	0.036
Physical needs alone	0.112	0.096	0.087	0.067
Monitor environment	0.119	0.084	0.088	0.082
Alone	0.626	0.135	0.519	0.140
With other children	0.017	0.023	0.051	0.053
With caregiver	0.147	0.099	0.118	0.101

[a] From U.S. Department of Health and Human Services (1980, p. 390).

care arrangement offers an optimal number and type of peer relationships for the development of these skills.

Overall, children in family day care spent a considerable portion of the observation period playing by themselves. The toddlers were observed playing alone 63% of the time, and the preschoolers played alone 52% of the time. The adult caregiver at that time was usually present (doing other chores), but not directly involved with the child. Very little distress was observed in this arrangement.

Reciprocal Child-Caregiver Effects in Family Day Care

Both child and caregiver behavior were most consistently affected by the group composition, that is, the number and age mix of children in the family day care home. As the number of children in the home increased, interactions of virtually all types between the caregiver and individual children decreased (with the exception of control activities). At the same time, caregiver interactions with two or more children increased. In turn, in homes with more children present, children spent less time interacting with the caregiver, but more time interacting with other children.

When *infants* (below age 12 months) were present, caregivers tended to display more affection, provide more comfort, help more, and attend to physical needs; but they taught and played less with the older children and watched less television with them.

The toddlers, in turn, sought attention less, were alone more often, and interacted less often with the caregiver, but they also did more monitoring of the caregiver-infant interaction. The amount of time children spent with their peers increased as the caregiver became more involved with infants, and the children made more attempts at controlling each other.

As the number of *toddlers* (ages 12 to 35 months) increased, caregivers were more directive and less likely to provide messy materials, like paint, water, or dough. Children in these situations tended to play with their peers more often, but made more attempts to control them, were more antisocial, and showed less affection. In turn, the caregiver spent more time controlling their unruly behavior and less time engaged in developmental activities.

When several *preschoolers* (ages 36 to 59 months) were present, the caregiver facilitated more language learning activities, and all children tended to engage more often in large muscle play, such as, climbing, jumping, and riding tricycles. The younger (1 to 2 year old) children spent more time alone and received less caregiver attention.

When a *school-age* child was present, the 3 and 4 year olds watched less television, and the 1 and 2 year olds engaged in more language facilitating activities. When the age mix was greater, children had more interactions with each other.

COGNITIVE DEVELOPMENT
OF CHILDREN IN FAMILY DAY CARE

The effects of family day care on the intellectual development of children have only been investigated in a handful of studies which included samples of infants, toddlers, and preschoolers, both from middle-class and lower-class homes. Hence the results must be considered tentative.

Rubenstein et al. (1977) compared the effects of mother and substitute care in two groups of healthy, black, 5- to 6-month-old infants who grew up in a low-income urban area. Thirty-eight infants were reared by their mothers and 27 infants had substitute caregivers during the day. Fifteen of the caregivers were relatives, and 12 were non-related babysitters. The substitutes cared for the infants in their own or the infant's home. The groups of mother-reared and substitute-reared infants were comparable in sex of infant, birth order, parental age and education, socioeconomic status, numbers who had fathers living in the home, and number of other children present.

The duration of the regular contact with the infant by the substitute caregiver ranged from 2 weeks to 5½ months, with a mean of 3 months. Observers of the caregivers' behavior noted that with increased contact, substitute caregivers provided more stimulation, were more responsive to the infant's signals, and were more similar to mothers in the expression of positive affect.

The two groups of infants were comparable on 16 out of 17 measures of infant functioning that included the Bayley Mental and Psychomotor Scales, and clusters of behavior ratings from the Bayley Scales of Infant Development, such as social responsiveness and goal-directedness, preference for novel stimuli, and vocal expressiveness. The mother-reared group engaged in significantly more focused exploration at home.

Cochran (1977) compared 60 home-based and 60 day care center-based Swedish toddlers in a naturalistic field study of child-rearing patterns and gathered both observational and developmental data on the children. Sixty of the children were spending 8 to 10 hours a day, 5 days a week, in a comprehensive urban child care center. The other 60 were reared in family settings which took two forms: In 34 cases the child was in its own home with its natural mother, whereas in the other 26 cases the child was in the home of a "day mother" with one or two other children.

The children in family care and group day care were carefully matched with each other at three different age levels: 12, 15, and 18 months (by sex, number of siblings, socioeconomic status, and geographical location of the home). Most came from middle-class homes. A comparison of full-scale mean scores on the Griffith Mental Development Scale showed no significant differences at any of the three age levels across the three settings. Only the hearing and speech subscales differed significantly at 12 months (but not at 15 or 18 months), with the home-based children scoring higher. It was noted that children in both home settings—the day care home as well as their own home—engaged more in cognitive verbal, exploring, and play interactions with their caregivers than center-based children.

In a Canadian study Doyle (1975) compared three groups of 11 children—groups attending day care, reared at home, or being cared for outside the home by a mother surrogate such as a grandmother or babysitter. The children ranged in age from about 6 to 25 months at the beginning of the study, with an average age of about 18 months. There were no significant differences among the three groups in Cattell IQ scores and language development.

The New York City Infant Day Care Study (Golden et al., 1978) focused on the development of 400 high-risk children from predominantly lower-class homes reared either at home or enrolled in one of 31 service-oriented, licensed public and private, community-controlled, group and family infant day care programs. They entered family day care or center programs between 2 and 21 months and were followed longitudinally until 36 months.

At 18 months, children who had been enrolled in child care outside the home between the ages of 2 and 14 months outperformed their home-reared counterparts on the Bayley Mental Development Index (MDI; mean, 100.4, 98.0, and 92.9 for center day care, family day care, and home care, respectively). While only the difference between the center- and home-reared groups were statistically significant at this age, by 36 months the performance of center-reared children on the Stanford-Binet (mean, 99.1) differed significantly from both family day care-reared (mean, 92.0) and home-reared children (mean, 92.6). However, since the maximum difference between the groups is only 7 points, and therefore of questionable functional significance, caution is required in interpreting these findings.

These findings suggest however that poor children in family day care tend to resemble, over time, children reared at home in their scores on standard IQ tests. Experience in group day care may prevent the lower scores (on such tests) generally reported for low-income children after 18 months of age.

In line with the findings by Golden et al. (1978) in New York City, Vroegh (1976) and Saunders and Keister (1972) report that 1 year after entry into day care centers, toddlers from low-income families outperformed their family day care counterparts on measures of cognitive and motor development, such as the Bayley Scales of Infant Development.

Winett et al. (1977) compared preschool-age children and families involved in four child care environments in a Kentucky County: all-day center care ($N = 35$), all-day sitter (family) care ($N = 15$), center/sitter-home (mixed) care ($N = 31$), and exclusive at-home care ($N = 31$). Black families were underrepresented in the home or mixed groups, and tended to send their children either to a sitter or a day care center at least 8 hours a day, 5 days a week. White middle-class children were overrepresented in the "mixed" group where children either stayed with a sitter in family day care or went to a center program between 9 and 15 hours a week. Among measures of cognitive development administered to the children when they were between 3 and 5½ years old (mean age, 4 years, 8 months) were the Peabody Picture Vocabulary Test (PPVT), the Illinois Test of Psycholinguistic Abilities (ITPA), and a Preschool Screening Test.

The results on the child measures yielded significantly higher mean scores on the PPVT for the mixed group (mean, 110.2) than for the day care (mean, 101.5), at-home (mean, 100.9), and babysitter (mean, 98.7) groups. Similar significant differences, favoring the mixed group, were reported for the Pre-school Screening Test and the auditory reception and visual association sub-scales of the ITPA.

It was unclear, however, whether these differences reflected the impact of the higher socioeconomic status of the mixed group or the effects of different child care situation. The authors argue that their results mirror the reality of naturally occurring child care arrangements and that we should rephrase the question "What are the effects of center or family day care on children and their families" to "What kinds of children, from what kinds of families, in which kind of child care settings behave and develop in what sorts of ways?"

Findings regarding outcome on intellectual abilities other than those mea-sured on standard intelligence tests are few in number, but tend to show fairly consistently that for most children family day care appears to foster verbal skills as well as home care, and does so more than center care.

Rubenstein et al. (1977) noted no differences in verbal expressiveness between 5- to 6-month-old infants who were reared either by their mothers or substitute caregivers; Cochran (1977) reports higher scores on the Griffith's Speech and Hearing Scale for home-reared (both mother and family day care based) Swedish toddlers at 12 months than for those in center care. Howes and Rubenstein (1978) noted that American toddlers in family day care had higher frequencies of spontaneous and responsive talk and a higher proportion of contingent talk with their caregivers than children in day care centers. And Feine (cited by Belsky and Steinberg, 1978) suggests that sophisticated vocal-ization is more characteristic of preschool children raised in family day care centers than center care. He, like Cochran (1977), attributes this difference to the greater amount of adult-child interaction in the family day care setting (which should profit the middle-class child more than the lower-class child). Similar findings on tests of language competency were reported in a British study of matched groups of "minded" and "home-reared" 3- and 4-year-old children (Raven, 1979).

In summary, the findings of the effects of family day care on the cognitive development of children tend to suggest that in comparison with home care, family day care arrangements tend to have no adverse effects on the intellectual development of most children. In comparison with center-based care, results are more equivocal and tentative: After 18 months, toddlers and preschoolers from disadvantaged homes who are in center care tend to score higher on standardized tests, such as the Bayley Scales of Infant Development and the Stanford-Binet Intelligence Test than low socioeconomic status children in fam-ily care (or in own home care). Middle-class children, however, were observed to get more verbal stimulation and exposure to adult talk in family day care settings or in a mixed family-center care arrangement. They also vocalized more and achieved higher scores on measures of speech development, auditory reception, and psycholinguistic abilities than children in center care.

EMOTIONAL DEVELOPMENT
OF CHILDREN IN FAMILY DAY CARE

Judging by the few studies conducted so far, family day care does not seem to be disruptive of the child's emotional bond with his or her mother (unless there is serious disadvantage and lack of a stable alternative caregiver arrangement in female-headed, single-parent households). There is some suggestive evidence that family day care, as other forms of substitute care, may have more of a differential effect on the emotional development and well-being of boys than of girls.

Sex-Care Interactions

Some studies on the attachment behavior of children in family care have obtained interactions between type of care and sex of child. No consistent patterns of sex differences have emerged from these studies yet (Brookhart and Hock, 1976; Hock and Clinger, 1980; Portnoy and Simmons, 1978), but other studies comparing children of the same sex in different care settings (Moore, 1975; Moskowitz et al., 1977) indicate that males may be more affected than females by variations in caregiving arrangements, as they are in response to other forms of stress (Rutter, 1970; Werner and Smith, 1982).

Attachment to the Mother as a Function of Type of Care

A number of studies (Cochran, 1977; Doyle and Somers, 1978; Hock, 1980; Hock and Clinger, 1980; Portnoy and Simmons, 1978; Vaughn et al., 1980) in the U.S., Canada, and Sweden, have contrasted the behavior of children in family day care with home-reared and/or center-reared children on adaptations of the Ainsworth et al. (1978) "strange situation" experiment. A stressful situation is created (either in the laboratory or in the home) by repeatedly separating the child from the mother and/or introducing him or her to a strange adult. The assumption is that the child's approach-avoidance responses to the mother and the stranger, as well as his or her exploration of the environment, will reflect the quality of the mother-child relationship. Belsky and Steinberg (1978) have raised some serious questions about the ecological validity of this procedure by pointing to the artificial behavior required by the mother and the stranger.

Not surprisingly, most strange situation type experiments have found no reliable differences in attachment behavior between children reared in family care or other forms of care.

Hock (1980) performed a longitudinal study comparing 72 infants whose mothers were not working and were home most of the day with 83 infants whose mothers worked during part or all of the first year of life. At 12 months the two groups of infants behaved similarly toward their mothers in the Ainsworth experiment and showed no differences in apprehension toward maternal departure. Among the children of working mothers, those who were cared for in another location while the mother was working were not different from those who were cared for at home.

In Sweden, Cochran (1977) observed the behavior of 12- to 18-month-old toddlers in a semistructured separation situation, which took place in the living room of each child's home. The mother and child were playing together on the living room floor, with the mother facing the door. On a silent signal from the observer, the mother got up, and making no verbal comments to the child, left the room through the door, closing it behind her and remained outside for about 3 minutes. The time of onset of searching (visual), seeking (movement), distress (calling), and cry behavior were recorded. No differences were found on the separation/attachment measure between the behavior of toddlers who were cared for by a day mother and toddlers in center care or exclusive home care in their reaction to the separation experience. A comparison of the groups by age (12, 15, and 18 months) also showed no significant differences.

In Nova Scotia, Canada, Doyle and Somers (1978) examined the attachment behavior of 39 toddlers whose ages ranged from 10 to 42 months, with a mean age of 22 months. They came from three different child care environments: family day care by relatives or regular babysitter outside the home or in the home ($N = 11$), care in a child care center ($N = 14$), and home-reared children ($N = 14$). The family day care and center children had begun substitute care for the most part between 6 and 7 months of age.

Frequency of attachment behavior and security of attachment were assessed in laboratory separation episodes that were adaptations of the Ainsworth and Bell (1970) strange situation. The two substitute care groups behaved similarly; both played significantly more and cried less than did the home-reared group when left alone. Children in family day care and center care did not differ in this study from home-reared children in strength and security of attachment, but found brief maternal separations less novel and anxiety provoking than did home-reared children.

Portnoy and Simmons (1978) studied the attachment behavior of 35 white middle-class 3½ to 4 year olds who had experienced different rearing histories in a series of standardized episodes involving separations and reunions with the mother and a stranger. Group 1 children had been continuously cared for by their mothers. Group 2 children were cared for at home by their mothers until age 3, when they were enrolled in group day care. Group 3 children had been enrolled in family day care at 1 year of age and entered a group day care setting approximately 2 years later. No significant differences in attachment pattern were found for children with different rearing histories.

However, a report on children of low-income mothers, most of whom were single parents, points to some stresses in the quality of infant-mother attachment associated with inconsistent out-of-home care. Vaughn et al. (1980) examined the effects of routine daily separations on the formation and maintenance of infant-mother attachment in a population of economically disadvantaged mothers, most of whom lacked the support of an adult male in the home. Three groups were contrasted on the basis of the time in the infant's life when out-of-home care began: 1) before 12 months; 2) between 12 and 18 months; and 3) home care controls. Infant care for both groups of working mothers (1 and 2) was most frequently provided by a relative or friend of the mother in the alternate caregiver's home. Changes in the family care arrangements were common, with at least 80% of the infants experiencing a change in the substitute care that involved either changes in the caregiver, the location of the care, and/or the group composition at the babysitter's home.

All of the infants were seen at both 12 and 18 months in the strange situation procedure (Ainsworth et al., 1978). At 12 months, 47% of the infants whose mothers had returned to work/school before 12 months were classified in the anxious avoidant group (that is, infants avoided contact with the mother after separation or ignored her attempts to initiate interaction), while the other two groups did not differ significantly in security of attachment behavior. Again, at 18 months differences among the three work status groups showed a significant proportion (41%) of anxious avoidant infants in this early working group. By 18 months, both anxious avoidant and anxious resistant attachments were also associated with growing up in non-intact families. A British study of West Indian preschoolers (Stewart Prince, 1967) also reports high rates of withdrawn behavior among the offspring of West Indian mothers who were single parents and left their infants with childminders so that they could go out and work.

These findings suggest that we need to pay special attention to the quality of out-of-home care for the growing number of children from female-headed households in the industrialized and in the developing world. In the U.S., for example, between one-third to one-half of family day care is used by single-parent families (Singer et al., 1980), and trends are similar in Great Britain (Jackson and Jackson, 1979). The proportion of female-headed households is largest among blacks, Puerto Ricans, and Native Americans, but it is on the increase among whites as well. The majority of such families live below the poverty line. In such a setting the cumulative stresses of poverty, work, and absence of an adult male may make the mother both physically and psychologically less available to her infant, and out-of-home care may be less consistent as well. Children in these families are most in need of high-quality care, but least likely to find such care.

Ego Resiliency and Ego Control

In a follow-up study of 3- to 5-year-old children from middle-class, intact families, Schiller (1980) found that substitute child care in the first and second years of life with non-relative caregivers, such as a family day care mother or a sitter, had a positive effect on children's ego resiliency. Children who had received substitute care by a non-relative in a home environment appeared more ego resilient when they were tested at ages 3 to 5 than children who had not received substitute care until 2 years of age or older. These children were better able to adapt resourcefully to circumstances and changes in the environment in their preschool years.

While earlier entry into non-relative care in a home-based setting was significantly associated with less ego resiliency, earlier entry into group care was significantly associated with greater ego control, that is, restlessness, impulsivity, non-compliance, and aggression. Home-based type of care, such as sitter in the child's home or family day care, seemed to be a better care environment for these children in the first and second year of life than center or group care; and the early, gradual exposure to peers and substitute caregivers in home-based care seems to have prepared them better for adaptive functioning when they entered group care between the ages of 3 and 5.

SOCIAL DEVELOPMENT OF CHILDREN IN FAMILY DAY CARE

The scanty evidence available suggests that children in family care do not differ significantly from home-reared children in their social development, but tend to be more "socialized" in the adult sense of the word than children in group center care.

One of the first studies comparing the effects of substitute care in the home with exclusive mothering was conducted by Perry (1963) in Spokane, Washington. The design involved a cross-sectional survey in which a sample of 104 full-time working mothers, with children ages 3 to 5, was obtained by area probability sampling. An ecologically matched control group was obtained by taking 104 of the nearest non-working neighbor mothers of children ages 3 to 5. In addition, "mother substitutes" ($N = 82$) were interviewed. Most of these day care arrangements were made through informal contacts, involving either home care or care out of the home. For all three measures of effects on the child (antisocial behavior, withdrawing tendencies, and psychosomatic symptoms), no significant differences were found between the exclusively mothered children of non-working mothers and the children of working mothers in family day care. The investigators also controlled for two possibly intervening variables: acceptance of and satisfaction with the child, and compensating behavior by the working mothers; still no significant differences were revealed.

Other studies have compared the social behavior of children in family day care with children in center group care. Howes and Rubenstein (1978) observed toddlers' behavior in centers and family day care homes and found that the children in family day care displayed more positive social skills.

Vroegh (1976) came to the same conclusion after monitoring the behavior of low socioeconomic status children, 12 to 36 months of age, who were cared for in a home other than their own for most of the day with that of children who attended a day care center. The behavior of the 114 children was rated every 6 months for 18 months. Home day care children were rated consistently higher in being compliable and likable than children in center care.

Lippman and Grote (1974) compared 66 triplets of 4-year-old children ($N = 198$), matched on sex, race, intactness of family, and amount of mother's education. Members of one group were cared for in homes other than their own for an average of 2 years prior to assessment; another group attended a day care center for about the same length of time; and the third group was reared at home by the natural parents. There were minimal differences among the three groups on variables such as relation to parents, control of impulses, and sex typing. Home-reared children, however, were more likely to cooperate in games in which taking turns was the winning strategy.

Several British studies alert us to the fact that family day care, like home care, cannot be regarded as a homogenous set of experiences. Both vary greatly in style and quality of child-rearing (Bryant et al., 1980; Mayal and Petrie, 1977; Raven, 1981). Many inner-city children looked after by childminders in the action research by Brian and Sonya Jackson (1979) spent long, under-stimulated days in cramped surroundings; some did not get the love and attention they needed, and others experienced repeated changes of caregivers. This was especially true for the poorest—the offspring of single working mothers from the West Indies. Observations of black preschool children referred to London pediatricians and psychiatrists for apparent signs of deafness or speech impairment revealed a number of mental health problems involving impaired social behavior (apathy, withdrawal, unwillingness to explore the environment) among the majority of the children who had been left with unregistered childminders while their mothers (who were often single) went out to work.

Moore (1975) has published the only investigation of the long-term effects of "diffused mothering" versus "exclusive mothering" on a group of middle-class London children from intact families. "Exclusive mothering" was defined as full-time care of the child by the mother to the age of 5, apart from occasional babysitting. "Diffused mothering" was defined as a minimum of 25 hours per week away from the mother over a period of at least 12 months before the age of 5. The substitute care could be in a nursery school, in a day nursery, or with a private individual either in the child's own home or elsewhere. The average duration of such substitute care was 25 months, with a range from 1 to 4½ years. Interviews and questionnaire measures were taken when the children were 6 to 8 and 15 years old, and analyzed separately by sex. For the boys, the findings from the mother's inventory indicated that exclusive mothering tended to result in conformity to adult rather than peer standards, self-control, timidity, and academic interests. In contrast, diffused mothering tended to result in greater non-conformity with parental requirements, and with outgoing, active, social interests that showed a greater peer group orientation. These tendencies were relatively consistent through childhood and adolescence. The group differences for the girls, however, were fewer, smaller, and less consistent.

TRAINING AND COMMUNITY-BASED SUPPORT PROGRAMS FOR FAMILY DAY CARE PROVIDERS

Since the 1970s a number of pilot programs have emerged in the U.S., England, and the Scandinavian countries that have introduced educational and/or social service programs into the provision of family day care.

They are based in local communities, rely mainly on voluntary efforts and contributions by residents of a given neighborhood, and respect the inevitable primacy of the consumer or user who initiates and terminates the arrangement. Some have been partially funded as demonstration projects by government agencies, but very few have been maintained long enough to allow for an evaluation of their effect on the participants in the family day care system, that is, the caregivers and the children.

The interested reader is referred to a number of publications that describe in depth some of the neighborhood-based interventions. Among them are the *Day Care Neighborhood Service* in Portland, Oregon (Emlen, 1972; Collins and Watson, 1976), the *Community Family Day Care Project* of the Pacific Oaks College in Pasadena, California (Sale, 1972, 1973a, 1973b, 1975), and the *Rhode Island Connection: A Family Day Care Training Program* (Goldsmith, 1979). All offer a wealth of ideas to anyone interested in organizing community-based support for family day care mothers. Among the ideas tried successfully in these projects are neighborhood referral services and resource centers for day care providers and users; book, toy, and equipment loans and libraries; community resource manuals and monthly bulletins for family day care providers; link-ups with day care centers and local colleges that provide extension classes in child care and development; and self-help organizations of family day care mothers who provide back-up for each other in person or via the telephone.

A similar wide range of services has been successfully tried in a number of English cities as part of the action research described by Brian and Sonia Jackson in *Childminders* (1979). These British authors also demonstrate the successful use of the mass media in reaching family day care providers, including a thrice weekly television series for day care providers, called *Other People's Children*. They also designed a basic toy set and a model starter kit for family day care mothers which contains information on contracts, registration, and insurance, and key telephone numbers.

Sweden (Berfenstam and William-Olsson, 1973), which provides publicly subsidized family day care and training, has experimented with a special form of family day care called the "three family system." It was started in Stockholm among university students and has been introduced in the other university cities as well, but is not restricted to student families. State subsidies are granted, just as for family day care. The municipality employs a "children's nurse" to take care of the children of three families. Each family holds its dwelling unit at the disposal of the children every third week. The child thus moves to a new private home each week—a small group is preserved and the child is kept in a familiar environment. No comparative data are yet available to judge the effectiveness of this system vis-à-vis the conventional form of family day care or center care.

Since the mid-1970s, a number of family day care training programs have been tried out in the U.S., for example in Rhode Island (Goldsmith, 1979), New York (Goodman and Andrews, 1981), Minnesota (Wattenberg, 1977), and California (Sale, 1975). They range from workshops, seminars, and extension courses at local colleges, vocational schools, and technical schools to television programs and home-centered training based in the neighborhoods in which the family day care mothers live. Many have adopted models of parent training programs that were used earlier in home-based intervention research with high-risk children, for example, by Gordon et al. There have been a few excellent reviews of home-based intervention programs (Goodson and Hess, 1978; Gray and Wandersman, 1980) that show that some of these programs sustain meaningful impressions on the behavior of mothers and children. But research on the effects of such training on the behavior of family day care providers and the children in their care is still scarce.

Only a few studies have begun to look at the effect of training on the behavior of caregivers and children in family day care. The NDCHS (Singer et al., 1980) observed consistent differences across their sub-samples (sponsored, regulated, unregulated) between the behavior of untrained family day care providers and those who had received some training. Training in both the sponsored and regulated homes was associated with more teaching, helping, and dramatic play and with less activity that did not involve interaction with children. In the unregulated homes there was more expression of positive affect and comforting and more interaction with children as well if family day mothers were trained. Toddlers in homes with trained caregivers had to be controlled less often by the caregiver and engaged more often in structured and fine motor activity. For preschoolers, caregiver training was associated with more music and dramatic activities.

Goodman and Andrews (1981) examined the effects of three different educational programs (high, medium, and low structure) and two types of delivery systems (paraprofessional only and paraprofessional plus day care mother) on the cognitive performance of 52 preschool children in family day care. The children all came from working-class backgrounds and were exposed to one of three programs: a high structure program (following the Bereiter-Engelmann approach), a moderate structure program (devised by Levenstein), and a low structure program of friendly visitation. A paraprofessional teacher (a parent with no more than high school education) worked with the target child for 2 hours per week (for approximately 10 months), either alone or with observation by the day care mother, who also worked with the child for an additional 2 hours. The six experimental family day care samples were compared with a family day care control sample and children in three professionally run group centers on the Peabody Picture Vocabulary Test, the Caldwell Preschool Inventory, and Engelmann's Basic Concept Inventory Test in a pre/post-test design. Family day care children exposed to any one of the modest educational programs for 2 to 4 hours a week showed a more significant and consistent enhancement of cognitive skills than did the children exposed to the professionally run group day care centers and the control group of family day care children without any educational intervention.

Thus, even a modest educational program of from 2 to 4 hours a week can turn a family day care arrangement from babysitting or childminding into a valuable educational experience at a substantially lower cost than the professionally run center.

SUMMARY

The effects of family day care on the behavior of children depends both on the quality and stability of the home, as well as that of the substitute care provided. Given an intact home, stable substitute family day care in an environment not too dissimilar from the child's own background seems: 1) to have no deleterious effects on the intellectual development of the child; 2) not to be disruptive of the emotional bond between child and mother; and 3) to have no significant negative consequences on social development, but may actually enhance ego resiliency and positive social skills. There is some evidence that needs to be corroborated by additional studies that stable family type care may be a more appropriate substitute care environment than center care for children in the first 2 years of life.

In the absence of any long-term follow-up studies we can only speculate about the relative disadvantage of unstable and understimulating types of family day care for high-risk children from poor homes, many of whom live in single-parent households.

Modifying factors in children's responses to family day care that need to be more systematically explored are: the socioeconomic and educational background of parents and family day care providers; the number and age mix of the children in the family day home; the age at which the child enters family day care; the effects of sex, ordinal position, and temperament; and whether the family day care provided is by a relative or a non-relative.

An assessment of the long-term effects of family day care on the children and the impact on their families and other social systems (the neighborhood, schools, and the world of women's work) is urgently needed, as is an increase in availability of training and community-based support for family day care providers.

REFERENCES

Ainsworth, M.D.S., and Bell, S.M. 1970. Attachment, exploration and separation: Illustrated by the behavior of one-year-olds in a strange situation. Child Dev. 41:49–68.
Ainsworth, M.D.S., Blehar, M., Waters, E., and Wall, S. 1978. Patterns of Attachment. Erlbaum, Hillsdale, NJ.
Bang, B. 1979. Public day care in private homes. Int. J. Early Child. 11:124–130.
Belsky, J., and Steinberg, L. 1978. The effects of day care: A critical review. Child Dev. 49:929–949.
Belsky, J., and Steinberg, L. 1979. What does research teach us about day care? A follow-up report. Child. Today July-August:21–26.
Berfenstam, R., and William-Olsson, I. 1973. Early Child Care in Sweden. Gordon and Beach, London.
Brookhart, J., and Hock, E. 1976. The effects of experimental context and experiental background on infants' behavior toward their mothers and a stranger. Child Dev. 47:333–340.
Brown, B. (ed.). 1978. Found: Long-term Gains from Early Interventions. Westview Press, Boulder, CO.
Bryant, B., Harris, M., and Newton, D. 1980. Children and Minders. Grant McIntyre, London.
Cochran, M.M. 1977. A comparison of group day and family child rearing patterns in Sweden. Child Dev. 48:702–707.
Collins, A.H., and Watson, E.L. 1976. Family Day Care: A Practical Guide for Parents, Caregivers and Professionals. Beacon Press, Boston.
Divine-Hawkins, P. 1981. Family day care in the United States. National Day Care Home Study Final Report: Executive Summary, U.S. Department of Health and Human Services, Washington, DC.
Dodge, M.K. 1979. Swedish programs for children: A comprehensive approach to family needs. Child Care Q. 8:254–265.
Doyle, A.B. 1975. The effects of group and individual day care on infant development. Paper presented at the Canadian Psychological Association Meeting, Quebec.

Doyle, A., and Somers, K. 1978. The effect of group and family day care on infant attachment behaviours. Can. J. Behav. Sci. 10:38–45.

Emlen, A.C. 1972. Family Day Care Research: A Summary and Critical Review. Pacific Oaks College, Pasadena, CA.

Emlen, A.C. 1974a. Boundaries of the surrogate relationship in family day care: An analysis of the caregiver role. Paper presented at the 51st Annual Meeting of the American Orthopsychiatric Association, April 12, San Francisco.

Emlen, A.C. 1974b. Day care for whom? In: A.L. Scharr (ed.), Children and Decent People, Chapter 4. Basic Books, New York.

Emlen, A.C., and Perry, J.B. 1975. Child care arrangements. In: L. Hoffman and F.I. Nye (eds.), Working Mothers, pp. 101–125. Jossey-Bass, San Francisco.

Emlen, A.C. 1977. Family day care for children under three. Paper presented at the International Symposium on the Ecology of Care and Education of Children under Three, February 23-26, Max Planck Institute for Educational Research, Berlin.

Emlen, A.C., Donoghue, B.A., and Clarkson, Q.D. 1972. The Stability of the Family Day Care Arrangement: A Longitudinal Study. DCE Books, Corvallis, OR.

Emlen, A.C., Donoghue, B.A., and LaForge, D. 1971. Child care by kith: A study of the family day care relationships of working mothers and neighborhood caregivers. Report to the Research and Evaluation Unit, Children's Bureau, U.S. Department of Health and Human Services, Washington, DC.

Etaugh, C. 1980. Effects of nonmaternal care on children: Research evidence and popular views. Am. Psychol. 35:309–319.

Feine, R.J. The differential structural characteristics of sentences formed by preschool children in family and group day care. Unpublished manuscript.

Golden, M., Rosenbluth, L., Grossi, M., et al. 1978. The New York City Infant Day Care Study. Medical and Health Research Association of New York City, New York.

Goldsmith, M.J. 1979. The Rhode Island connection: A family day care program. Child. Today July-August:2–5.

Goodman, N., and Andrews, J. 1981. Cognitive development of children in family and group care. Am. J. Orthopsychiatry 51:271–284.

Goodson, B.D., and Hess, R.D. 1978. Effectiveness of parent-training programs. In: B. Brown (ed.), Found: Long-term Gains from Early Intervention. Westview Press, Boulder, CO.

Gray, S., and Wandersman, L.P. 1980. The methodology of home-based intervention studies: Problems and promising strategies. Child Dev. 51:993–1009.

Hock, E. 1980. Working and non-working mothers and their infants: A comparative study of maternal caregiving characteristics and infant social behavior. Merrill-Palmer Q. 26:79–101.

Hock, E., and Clinger, J.B. 1980. Behavior toward mother and stranger of infants who have experienced group day care, individual care, or exclusive maternal care. J. Gen. Psychol. 137:49–61.

Howes, C., and Rubenstein, J. 1978. Toddler social development in two day care settings. Paper presented at the Annual Meeting of the Western Psychological Association, Spring, San Francisco.

Jackson, B., and Jackson, S. 1979. Childminder: A Study in Action Research. Routledge and Kegan Paul, London.

Lippman, M.A., and Grote, B.H. 1974. Social emotional effects of day care. Project report, Western Washington State College, Bellingham, WA.

Mayall, B., and Petrie, P. 1977. Minder, Mother and Child. Institute of Education, University of London, London.

Moore, T.W. 1975. Exclusive early mothering and its alternatives. Scand. J. Psychol. 16:256–272.

Moskowitz, D.S., Schwarz, J.C., and Corsini, D.A. 1977. Initiating day care at three years of age: Effects of attachment. Child Dev. 48:1271–1276.

Perry, J.B. 1963. Mother substitutes. In: F.I. Nye and L.W. Hoffman (eds.), The Employed Mother in America. Rand McNally, Chicago.

Prescott, E. 1973. A comparison of three types of day care and nursery school home care. Paper presented to Society for Research in Child Development, March, Philadelphia.

Portnoy, F., and Simmons, C. 1978. Day care and attachment. Child Dev. 49:239–242.

Raven, M. 1979. A comparison of the language competency and social behavior of childminded and non-childminded three and four year old children. Unpublished masters dissertation, Institute of Education, University of London.

Raven, M. 1981. Review: The effects of child-minding. How much do we know? Child Care Health Dev. 7:103–111.

Robinson, N.N., Robinson, H.B., Darling, M.A., and Holm, G. 1979. A World of Children: Day Care and Preschool Institutions. Brooks/Cole, Monterey, CA.

Rubenstein, J.L., Pedersen, T.A., and Yarrow, L.J. 1977. What happens when mother is away? A comparison of mothers and substitute caregivers. Dev. Psychol. 13:529–530.

Rutter, M. 1970. Sex differences in children's response to family stress. In: E.J. Anthony and C. Koupernik (eds.), The Child in His Family: Children at Psychiatric Risk, Vol. I, pp. 165–196. Wiley, New York.

Rutter, M. 1981. Social-emotional consequences of day care for preschool children. Am. J. Orthopsychiatry 51:4–28.

Sale, J.S. 1972. Family day care: Potential child development service. Am. J. Public Health 62:668–670.

Sale, J.S. 1973a. Family day care: A valuable alternative. Young Child. 28(4):209–215.

Sale, J.S. 1973b. Family day care: One alternative in the delivery of developmental services in early childhood. Am. J. Orthopsychiatry 43:37–45.

Sale, J.S. 1975. Watch family day care mothers work together to improve services. Child Today 36:22–24.

Saunders, M.M., and Keister, M.E. 1972. Family day care: Some observations. Day Care and Child Development Council of America, Washington, DC.

Schiller, J.D. 1980. Child Care Alternatives and Emotional Well Being. Praeger, New York.

Singer, J.D., Fosburg, S., Goodson, D.B., and Smith, J.M. 1980. National Day Care Home Study. Research Report, Vol. II. Abt Associates, Cambridge, MA.

Stallings, J., and Porter, A. 1980. National day care home study: Observation component. Final Report, Vol. III to the Department of Health and Human Services, Washington, DC. Stanford Research Institute, Stanford, CA.

Stewart Prince, G. 1967. Mental health problems in preschool West Indian children. Maternal Child Care 3(26).

Thornell, C.A., Vernon, E.A., and Glassman, M. 1981. Findings and recommendations. Final report: Day Care Systems Study, Vol. I. Boone, Young and Associates, New York.

U.S. Department of Health and Human Services. 1980. Family Day Care in the United States. National Day Care Home Study, Final Report. Volume II, Research Report, U.S. Department of Health and Human Services, Washington, DC.

U.S. Department of Health and Human Services. 1981. National Day Care Home Study, Final Report: Executive Summary. U.S. Department of Health and Human Services, Washington, DC.

Vaughn, G.E., Gore, F.L., and Egeland, B. 1980. The relationship between out-of-home care and the quality of infant-mother attachment in an economically disadvantaged population. Child Dev. 51:1203–1214.

Vroegh, K. 1976. Infant Day Care: Some Research Findings. Institute for Juvenile Research, Chicago.

Wattenberg, E. 1977. Characteristics of family day care providers: Implications for training. Child Welf. 56:211–229.

Werner, E.E., and Smith, R.S. 1982. Vulnerable, but Invincible: A Longitudinal Study of Resilient Children and Youth. McGraw-Hill, New York.

Winett, R.A., Fuchs, W.L., Moffatt, S.A., and Nerviano, V.Z. 1977. A cross-cultural study of children and their families in different child care environments: Some data and conclusions. J. Commun. Psychol. 5:149–159.

CHAPTER 7

Nurses, Nannies, and Their Kindred

"Do you know who runs the East Side of New York? The Nanny Mafia . . ."

Tom Wolfe, *The Kandy-Kolored Tangerine-Flake Streamline Baby*

There are distinct class differences in the choice of surrogate mothers. Anthropologists and family historians report that motherhood is not everywhere and at all times construed in the same manner. Unequal access to the resources of a complex society (rank, social status, money, and education) allows some women to acquire or buy full- or part-time mother surrogates for their children (Yanagisako, 1979).

Most of the evidence on child care among the affluent comes from scholars working in a relatively new discipline, the "history of childhood" (Cable, 1975; De Mause, 1974; Greenleaf, 1978; Sommerville, 1982). These historians have traced changes in parent-child relationships and class differences in child-rearing from the Middle Ages, through the Renaissance and Industrial Revolution, to the contemporary scene, working with documents that chronicle the family life of the "well-to-do" in Europe and the U.S.

Mother surrogates who are not kin or neighbors, such as nurses, nurse-maids, or nannies, arise in societies that are stratified by class, caste, or ethnicity (Boon, 1974). Most of the evidence we have comes from European family history. On her transatlantic journey to America, the lower-class nurse or nanny underwent a transformation into the black slave "mammy" who served as nursemaid to the children of plantation owners in the antebellum South and the West Indies (Drummond, 1978).

In contemporary life, nannies survive among wealthy families in Europe, in Latin America, and among upper upper-class families in the United States, and they are beginning to make a comeback among the professional elite (Wolfe, 1969). But today we have other contractual arrangements for mother surrogates as well, be they babysitters or foreign "au pair girls" who provide child care for the offspring of upper middle-class families in exchange for language lessons. What distinguishes these nanny-type surrogates from a surrogate or supplementary parent who is kin is a theme of separation rather than inclusion of herself and her small charges in the life of the adults in the family. Let us first take a brief look at the historical development of such an exchange system that divides the care of children of the affluent between "nanny givers" and "nanny takers" (Drummond, 1978).

FROM MEDIEVAL WET NURSE TO VICTORIAN NANNY

Barbara Kaye Greenleaf in her book *Children through the Ages: A History of Childhood* (1978) reminds us that it was in the High Middle Ages (the 11th century) that men for the first time chose to write about domestic life and children as well as about political intrigue and warfare. These medieval writers referred to the childhood of aristocracy who were their principal readers, and up to the 19th century most of what we know about the history of child care is about the offspring of privileged families.

The bulk of historical evidence suggests that ladies of the nobility gave over their infants to wet nurses. There they were nursed for a much longer period than is common today, anywhere from 1 to 3 years, with boys being weaned a full year later than girls. Historians have no ready-made explanation for this disparity, but Greenleaf (1978) suggests that it might stem from a greater concern with the survival of the male child who was more important to medieval society than the female. (This attitude today is still quite prevalent in developing countries where infant and preschool mortality rates are high and one out of every two children dies before they reach age 5.)

By the time the Renaissance began in the 13th century in Italy, the custom of wet nursing had also spread to the newly rich who benefited from the economy. These affluent families made their money in trade, lived in big city houses, and imitated the customs of the medieval nobility. Even the wives of skilled laborers, many of whom worked, preferred to hire wet nurses; it was one of the first luxuries women demanded (Sommerville, 1982).

Most common was the practice of sending an infant out to a peasant woman (*balia* in Italian) who lived at a distance away in the country. The infant was suckled (for pay) by this woman for a period of 2 years. During that period of time, parents rarely visited their children before it was time to take them home. Illegitimate children were sometimes left longer with the wet nurse, for periods up to 5 or 10 years. If a wet nurse became pregnant again, babies had to adjust to another source of milk and care before being weaned and returned to their parents.

In the big city houses of the 17th and 18th century, some wet nurses began to live in the homes of their patrons, and in that case the roles of the wet nurse and the children's nurse were combined. During this period in Western Europe, approximately one-fifth of all children were, in their earliest years, members of domestic groups that contained servants. Of the other four-fifths, about one-half (some 40%) themselves became servants at some time between age 12 and 22. These young strangers were more numerous than domestic kin in European households and always came from a social class below that of their masters. Their young and vigorous personalities must have had an effect on the children in the family (Laslett, 1977).

By the time the American colonies gained their independence, there had arisen a chorus of disapproval against the wet nurse on the European continent, and the wealthy hired instead a nurse/nanny to look after the young children. During the 18th century a separate nursery became increasingly common. Its existence crystallized in England in the first 30 or 40 years of the 19th century—a period of unprecedented growth of wealth and population (King-Hall, 1958). From the middle of the 19th century until World War II, some 2½ million lower-class nannies and nurses reared the young children of the British upper- and middle-classes, and their impact on other English speaking countries and colonies was at its zenith.

A very large number of poor seeking employment and a relatively smaller number of rich families with many children who were to be looked after by servants created a situation in which nursemaids, nurses, and nannies multiplied with great speed. By the end of the 19th century, a British family was barely considered middle-class if the parents did not have at least one nursemaid for their children (Gathorne-Hardy, 1972).

During that same period the nanny made her transatlantic journey to the Americas well, and could be found in the big plantation houses of the American South and the West Indies, and in the city houses of the industrial North and Northeast of the U.S.

THE AMERICAN SOUTH

The children of plantation owners in the American South and in the Caribbean had their own special companions that were play children and nursemaids. We have two sources of information on what it was like to grow up in the "big houses" of the antebellum South—the memoirs of white Southerners that were published after the Civil War, and the recollections of former black slaves who were interviewed in the 1930s—during the Great Depression—as part of the Federal Writer's Project (1941). Together, they project mirror images of a vanished society that reflect the nature of the relationship between white masters and black slaves.

A "play child" was a widespread institution in the antebellum South. Mary Cable (1975) cites an old gentleman raised on a Carolina plantation, who, on his fifth birthday, had been given a pony and a black play child whose duty it was both to serve him and play with him. One of the old ex-slaves interviewed in the 1930s, in turn, remembered being chosen as a play child by the mistress of the house after a contest of running, jumping, and walking on hands among the children in the slave quarters.

At the age of 10 or 12, a black slave girl might be brought into the house to be trained as a nursemaid. Letitia M. Burwell in *A Girl's Life in Virginia* (1895) writes about her childhood before the Civil War:

> My sister and myself, when very small children, were often carried to visit the cabins, on which occasion no young princesses could have received from admiring subjects more adulation . . . Around the cabin doors the young negroes would quarrel as to who should be his or her mistress, some claiming me, and others my sister (p. 2).

Among the duties of these little "indispensables" were the care and entertainment of their masters and mistresses. One ex-slave interviewed in the 1930s recalled that her master's children had been "mostly carried roun on pillows till dey big 'nough to walk. . . ." Letitia Burwell describes the errands required of her servants as she grew older:

> At such establishments one easily acquired a habit of being waited upon, there being so many servants with so little to do. It was natural to ask for a drink of water when the water was right at hand, and to have things brought which you might easily have gotten yourself. But these domestics were so pleased at such errands, one felt no hesitation in requiring them. A young lady would ask black Nancy or Dolly to fan her, whereupon Nancy or Dolly would laugh good-naturedly, produce a large palm-leaf, and fall to fanning her young mistress vigorously, after which she would be rewarded with a bow of ribbon, some candy or sweet cakes (p. 6).

The recollections of the ex-slaves were less paradisiacal. Remembers Katie Darling, an ex-slave from Texas:

> Massa had six children when the war came on, and I nursed all of them. I stayed in the house with them and slept on a pallet on the floor, and as soon as I was big enough to tote the milk pail, they put me to milking, too. Massa had more than 100 cows . . . We'd better be in the cowpen by five o'clock (Tyler et al., 1974, p. 61).

and Abram Sells:

> We children hung around close to the big house, and we had an old man that went around with us and looked after us, white children and black children, and that old man was my great grand-daddy. We sure had to mind him, cause if we didn't we sure had bad luck. . . (Tyler et al., 1974, p. 87).

As the rich white children got older, some planters employed a northern or English governess or tutor to teach them. Parents who could not afford such an expense would send their children to boarding schools in Charleston, New Orleans, or New York (Cable, 1975).

THE NORTHERN CITIES

During the 19th century in the industrial cities of the North and Northeast, the offspring of the rich had many privileges. Here, as in England, families that could afford servants entrusted their children to them most of the time. Among the successful newcomers to American "high society" were many who had

made enormous fortunes during the Civil War—the Rockefellers, the Car-
negies, the Vanderbilts, and many others (Cable, 1975). Their children were
brought up in the style of the European aristocracy, with French or German
governesses and English nannies rather than the Irish nursemaids of previous
generations. Many of these upper-class children were segregated from adult
company on third-floor nurseries and were only summoned to be with their
parents for an hour a day. They generally lived highly regulated lives (Greenleaf, 1978).

In her book *The Little Darlings: A History of Child-Rearing in America*
(1975), Mary Cable describes the daily routine for such wealthy families laid
down in an etiquette book by "Anon," published in 1887: The children were
expected to have breakfast with their governess who was completely in charge of
them, and who would seize every opportunity to correct their manners. She
walked the elder children to school, while the father said "good morning" and
"good bye" to the younger ones. The mother might then spend about an hour
with the children in the nursery and saw them again at lunch. She would eat
with them in the dining room only if there were no guests. The children's
afternoon was spent in walking and other recreational activities. Small children
were taken for walks by nannies or nursemaids to parks where they met only
their "social equals." The choice of such parks in New York changed through
the 19th century with the changing landmarks of the city, from St. John's Park
to Gramercy Park to Central Park where nannies can still be found today
(Wolfe, 1969). At 6 o'clock all children under the age of 13 ate in the nursery,
the older ones ate with their parents.

The regime in the nursery—on both sides of the Atlantic—was quite
strict. There were ice-cold baths, long sessions on the potty, and simple, monotonous meals. Yet despite its austerity and separation from the parents'
world, many adults who were brought up in such a regime fondly recall their
nursery days and developed a strong attachment to their nannies that lasted to
old age.

THE "NANNY MAFIA"

Even today, American upper-class families have adopted the nanny system as
their own. They tend to hire middle-aged, "sensible" English nannies, or if not
English nannies, then French or Irish nannies who are rumored to act more
"British" than the original. German nannies can gain acceptance as well if they
are old and confident enough (Wolfe, 1969).

Like their British counterparts in other capital cities of the world, nannies
who work for upper upper-class American families have a reputation for being
snobbish, and tend to impress on their employers their tastes on what is proper
in children's manners, clothing, carriage, and associations. Their grip on their

small charges and their taste seem to be loosening with the onslaught of television advertisement, however, a pastime that occupies a third of the day of their young charges.

According to Tom Wolfe (1969), the "nanny mafia," which consists of New York's leading nannies, still gathers in Central Park in the playground next to Fifth Avenue at the foot of East 77th Street. Any behavioral scientist brave enough to approach and interview them could make a landmark contribution to our knowledge of class differences in contemporary child care in the U.S. In Europe, "bastions" of nannies can still be found in Paris, St. Moritz, Madrid, Seville, and Vienna. Their employers are mostly foreign upper-class families or members of the diplomatic corps from France, Italy, Spain, Switzerland, and South America (Gathorne-Hardy, 1972).

THE WORLD OF THE NANNY

Nannydom as a widespread institution among the British upper- and middle-classes disappeared in the wake of extensive social reforms after the end of World War II. But it needs to be remembered that the nannies' effects on the children they cared for can still be felt among middle-aged and older members of the British elite, be they men of letters, politicians, civil servants, or scientists.

The same is true for the American upper class who were nannied, for example, former First Lady, Jacqueline Kennedy (Onassis) and her young children when they lived in the White House. It was Caroline Kennedy's nanny who told her that her father had been elected President of the United States and, less than 3 years later, that he had been assassinated (Sadler, 1967). Since the nanny may well make a comeback not only among the wealthy but also among the two-career families of the professional elite, it is worth taking a look at what we know about her world: her role, her partnership with the mother, and her effects on her charges.

A classic and highly readable account of the world of the nanny is the book by Gathorne-Hardy, *The Rise and Fall of the British Nanny* (1972), which appeared in the U.S. in 1973 under the title *The Unnatural History of the Nanny*. It is based on letters and interviews with some 259 English men and women who were nannied as young children and contains information on the lives of 296 British nannies. It also draws skillfully on novels, biographies, and autobiographies of poets, artists, politicians, and statesmen, including Winston Churchill, who pays a moving tribute to his Nanny Everest in his auto-biography.

Mrs. Everest was engaged as nanny by his parents very soon after Winston Churchill was born in 1874. From then, wrote his son, "until her death in 1895, when Winston was twenty, she was destined to be the principal confi-dante of his joys, his troubles, and his hopes." (Churchill, 1966, pp. 33–34).

Churchill was neglected by both his parents: His father, Lord Randolph, was busy with politics, an interest that consumed him, and his mother, a beautiful young American, was caught up in the world of fashionable society. But for the first 8 years of his life, Winston was virtually never separated from his nanny, and shared her exclusive love for 5 years, until his younger brother Jack was born.

Nanny Everest, like most British nannies and nursemaids, came from a working-class background. But invariably British nannies identified with the values and manners of the upper class they served, and through their admonitions and actions they managed to preserve long-standing class distinctions (Gathorne-Hardy, 1972). Only some 5 thousand among the estimated 2½ million nannies and nurses that served in British households during the period from 1850 until World War II were college trained. The majority worked their way up "through the ranks": The classical nanny started as nursery-maid at 12, worked her way up to Under Nurse or Second Under-Nurse, and finally achieved the rank of nanny with a separate nursery far removed from the rest of the house and nursemaids and children under her "command." Here is Gathorne-Hardy's (1972) description of the Nanny's domain:

> Her kingdom . . . consists of a day nursery, a night nursery . . . and possibly the room of her servants. These consist of an Under-Nurse, nursery-maids . . . and possibly a French bonne. Her other subjects are inanimate toys . . . medicine, clothes, hair brushes, chamber pots. The parents are hardly seen at all. Mother may look in for ten minutes . . . Then all the children go down to the drawing room for an hour around tea-time, very clean and very well behaved. That is all.
>
> Above all the feeling of the nursery is that it is separate. Nanny is separate, suspended half-way between the mother and the rest of the staff, half-parent, half-servant. The children may see other adults, but there is always the sense of venturing out. The other servants look at the nursery as a separate and almost alien world . . . Nursery-maids leave it in the role of ambassadors. And this psychic separation is expressed physically. It may have its own staircase, its own door out into the grounds, it may be in a separate wing, a separate corridor, a separate floor, cut off and even silenced from the rest of the house . . . (p. 77).

In contrast to the other servants, the strength of the nanny's position was that she was in charge of the children. This gave her not only considerable influence on the mistress of the house, but the authority of a real mother when the children grew up and she was kept. More often than not, the power was shared between nanny and mother, either in an uneasy truce or a real partnership. But the children knew that the nanny's power, although absolute, was derived from the mother. Her mistress, their mother, by the right of her class position, was the final arbiter.

There were some incompetent and even cruel nannies, who abused their young charges, but on the whole, nannies seemed to have had an intuitive skill with young children. They were remembered as being patient and unruffled, and practiced a firm, regular, disciplined daily routine. This must, at times, have seemed monotonous to the children, but also gave them a great deal of security. And nannies were great storytellers. They also acted as buffers between parent and children during times of family upheavals (as well as wars). On the whole, nannies tended to stay with their families for a great number of years, often becoming nannies to their "children's" children.

Gathorne-Hardy (1972) estimates that only about one-fifth of the nannies sought employment elsewhere each year; most stayed at least 5 years in the employ of the same household, until the youngest child was of school age. Even during the period of relative decline of household help from 1901 to 1939, the nanny was one of the last servants to be relinquished in a British household.

Most nannies, like other old servants, retired back into a branch of their families; few married and had children of their own. Some, after retirement, ran nursery schools, fostered children, worked in orphanages, or ran old people's homes. Sometimes nannies in retirement supported their employers, if the latter had fallen on hard times.

THE EFFECTS OF THE NANNY SYSTEM OF UPBRINGING

In the absence of any longitudinal studies, the effects of the nannies on their charges cannot be directly documented, but only inferred from the interviews and autobiographical statements analyzed by Gathorne-Hardy (1972) and others (Drummond, 1974; Swan, 1974). They have to do with matters of trust and discipline, with conscience and moral values, and with the development of interpersonal skills and attitudes toward sexuality.

These effects, however, cannot be separated from the context in which nannydom flowered: a class-conscious society that separated children from their parents and that inhibited the spontaneous expression of feelings.

There is no doubt that nannied children became attached to their substitute mothers. Although we do not have any observational data or experiments that document the degree and quality of that attachment, we know from retrospective interview data and (auto) biographies that this attachment, at its best, was quite secure and lasted for a lifetime. Infants and toddlers reacted to temporary separations from their nannies with the same type of behavior that is observed when the mother is the principal caregiver, that is, grief and depression, and upon her return, with proximity seeking behavior.

Since there were often several mother figures in their household—the real mother, the nursemaid, and the nanny—the intensity of their emotions was lessened. Nannied children were often better able to cope with stressful situations, such as marital spats and frequent and sometimes prolonged absences of the parents, than children who could only rely on the emotional support of their immediate family. Thus, the nanny system bears some similarity to the system of "multiple mothering" that is practiced in the Israeli kibbutzim. There, children are separated from their parents shortly after birth, and live with their peers in a succession of children's houses, being taken care of by a "metapolet," a caregiver, who meets their bodily needs, plays with them, and disciplines them. Like the nannied children, the children of the kibbutz see their parents for brief periods during the day, during work breaks, and in the evenings (Clarke-Stewart, 1982).

Some of the byproducts observed in such a system of multiple mothering is the tendency for kibbutzniks as well as nannied children to conform to peer pressure, to exhibit some diffidence, and to display less intense emotions in close interpersonal relationships. But the pressures that operated on upper-class British children were not only the strict upbringing by their nannies, but the additional strictures enforced by the "prep" and "public" schools they attended (Gathorne-Hardy, 1972).

Nannies probably played a decisive influence on the attitudes of most upper- and many middle-class British children toward sexuality. Gathorne-Hardy (1972) suggests that the rise and fall of the idea that upper-class women had no sexual feelings, while lower-class women did, coincided fairly well with the zenith and decline of the influence of the British nanny. Nannies brought to the upbringing of upper-class children attitudes toward the body that were typical of the lower-class at that time: They included strict and early toilet training, a passion for cleanliness, and prudery about undressing. But the same lower-class nannies looked after the children's physical needs:

> Nannies wiped bottoms and washed penises. Nannies fed. Nannies wiped up sick. Nannies gave baths and tucked up in bed. It was Nanny's arms that went around little boys, Nanny's breasts and lips they felt, Nanny they smelt. But Nannies were lower class : . . (1972, p. 98).

Thus, nannies may have become the first objects of sexual desire for upper-class English boys and made it possible for them as adults to separate sexuality in a woman ("lower class") from respectability ("upper class"). All of this is speculation, of course. But the American psychoanalyst Jim Swan (1974) reminds us that the "discoverer" of infantile sexuality, Sigmund Freud, also shared the first 2½ years of his life with *two* mothers: his (remote) middle-class Jewish mother and his lower-class Catholic nanny who in his words "provided me at an early age with the means of living and going on living." Freud once remarked to his biographer Ernest Jones, "It seems to have been my fate to discover only the obvious: That children have sexual feelings which every nursemaid knows" (1953–57, p. 350). Swan (1974) suggests that in a way not yet fully appreciated mother and nursemaid share a crucial set of roles in Freud's discovery of the Oedipus complex. The nurse, a working-class Czech Catholic, employed by a bourgeois German Jewish family, had a subordinate status that implied a certain cultural, social, economic, and ethnic separation similar to that of the black mammy who nursed the white children of plantation owners in the slave-holding South (see Figure 9).

Nanny, Babysitter, etc.

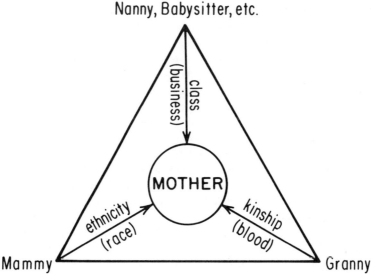

Figure 9.   The maternal complex in the culture of American kinship. (Reprinted by permission of the American Ethnological Society, American Ethnologist 5(1):30–43, 1978.)

For better or worse, the nanny seems to have left an imprint on the intellectual history of the behavioral sciences, not only in psychiatry, but in anthropology as well. For Boon (1974) reports that most of the kinship theories in anthropology have been constructed by (American upper upper-class) anthropologists who were "nannied" and had few close and intimate contacts with their parents while they were young. Notes anthropologist Drummond (1978), "The universal nuclear family has been championed by those who mourn its absence in their own lives" (p. 33).

On the positive side, nannied children were taught order and discipline in their lives and politeness that made social life more pleasant. Among the good manners impressed on them were conscientiousness, fair play, neatness, and punctuality (Gathorne-Hardy, 1972). Nannies also instilled a strict moral code: Authority must be respected, laws must be obeyed, the self shall not be indulged, and the best actions are for the common good. These may seem like rather old-fashioned virtues today, but Gathorne-Hardy suggests that they made not only for certainty in private life, but incorruptibility in public service. In short, the nanny "system" was an experiment in child upbringing that, at its best, produced honorable men and women.

THE BABYSITTER

The American babysitter is a phenomenon that grew out of the dramatic changes in life-style after World War II (Kourany et al., 1980a). In the postwar period, people married at younger ages, moved into suburbs if they could afford it, and had children in unprecedented numbers. Few families could afford full-time servants, however. The babysitter, in a manner, became a nanny surrogate. Her function was most appropriate to the urban and suburban pace of middle-class life. The American middle-class home, notes the Canadian anthropologist Drummond, "is more way station, equipped with individualized living and entertainment centers, where adults host adults, children host children, and everyone is perpetually about to be on his way" (1978, p. 41).

At the height of the "baby boom," the number of sitters in the U.S. steadily increased from an estimated 2 million in 1948 to 6 million in 1960, commanding a total income of some 1 billion dollars. During the lifetime of the post-war generation, a person might expect to play all three roles in the babysitting relationship, first as "sittee," then as sitter, and, finally, as parent (Kourany et al., 1980a).

Today, more often than not the babysitter who provides temporary child care while parents are away is a teenager. A survey by the U.S. Census Bureau (1973) reports that nearly half of all babysitters are under 16 years old, while another third are between 16 and 19 years old. The U.S. Children's Bureau (1974) estimates that over 1 million American teenagers are caring for young children as babysitters.

Among younger children paid babysitting outside of the home is relatively rare. Only 3% of the 764 11 and 12 year olds whose outside-of-school life was studied by Medrich et al. (1982) in Oakland, California, babysat regularly outside of the home, while the majority, including those with paid babysitting jobs, sat with younger siblings. In contrast, Kourany et al. (1980b) and LaBarbera et al. (1980) found that among both high school students in the age range from 14 to 18 and among college students in the age range from 18 to 20, more than 90% had paid babysitting experience. In both, the high school–age and the college–age sample, three times as many females than males reported having worked as babysitters.

College students, however, seem to have less of a personal interest in babysitting than teenagers, and also experience less of a sense of personal accomplishment than adolescents (LaBarbera et al., 1980). For the adolescent babysitters—more than any other age group—babysitting seems to provide a sense of accomplishment in several areas: 1) it provides them with responsibilities that among middle-class Americans are usually restricted to adults; 2) it allows them to gain a degree of financial independence; and 3) it helps them to develop parenting skills (Kourany et al., 1980a, 1980b).

Despite the prevalence of teenage babysitting and its possible impact on the development of adolescents as well as the young children they care for, this generation-old phenomenon has received very little attention in the child development and psychological literature. Only recently, Kourany, a child psychiatrist at Vanderbilt University, and his associates, have begun to explore in a systematic way the "babysitting experience."

In their normative studies with Tennessee high school students, Kourany et al. (1980b) found that the majority of teenage babysitters were either related to the child or family, or knew the child and his or her parents because they were neighbors. Only a minority sat with unfamiliar children.

Adolescent babysitters seem to be more comfortable when the age difference between them and their charges is relatively large. The greatest proportion of the (predominantly female) respondents in the study by Kourany et al. (1980b) preferred to take care of very young children, under 2 years of age (30.4%), or toddlers from 2 to 4 years (28.5%). Replies for the 5- to 10-year-old age group were mixed, showing ambivalent attitudes, and most teenage babysitters preferred not to babysit for youngsters in their teens. Apparently the greater the age difference, the more the adolescent babysitters can be seen as "legitimate" parent figures.

Among the activities adolescent babysitters expected to perform were feeding the children, playing games and reading to them, watching television with them, putting them to bed, and cleaning up toys; they did not expect to clean the house or to do the dishes. While adolescent babysitters seem to have a fairly clear view of their expected duties, they were less confident about dealing effectively with discipline problems that might arise. Nearly half of the babysitters studied by Kourany et al. (1980b) admitted to having gotten angry at the children they sat for, and sizeable proportions of the high school students—a third or more—acknowledged that they had to punish or even spank the children. Thus, while most adolescents were clear about their roles, a surprisingly large number were confronted by "management problems" for which they did not feel adequately prepared. The majority of respondents preferred to sit for girls rather than boys, who were viewed as more aggressive and less easily controlled.

Like unregulated family day care, the responsibility for establishing standards for babysitters rests primarily with the parents, who tend to look for someone they know (in the majority a relative or neighbor) in the hope of finding a temporary substitute who shares their general attitudes toward child-rearing (Spock, 1963). With a babysitter, parents expect to maintain their control over their child's experiences and that the sitter, in turn, will respect the parents' views and give the child the discipline they favor (Steinberg and Green, cited in Clarke-Stewart, 1982).

However, in the absence of regulations governing the relationship between babysitters and the families they serve, occasional abuses of that informal relationship are bound to occur; they may be on the increase, at least in the headlines of the popular press.[5] Among them are instances of child abuse and sexual experimentation by adolescent sitters (usually males) which occasionally come to the attention of child psychiatrists (Kourany et al., 1979).

---

[5] Missouri is the only state in the U.S. with a monitoring placement service with regulations for babysitters.

So far, the sparse community and professional interest in the babysitter and his or her activities have focused mostly on providing information on the "how to" of physical care for young children, including facts on nutrition, health, and safety (Drew, 1973; Hunnisett, 1970; Watson et al., 1971). But it seems to be just as important to examine the impact of the babysitter on a young child's emotional and intellectual development, especially if that child is exposed to a number of sitters. As of now, we have very few data to go by.

Among studies comparing the effects of family day care with exclusive mothering and/or care in a center are a handful of American and Canadian reports that included babysitters in their samples. During the first 2 years of life, children in the care of an unrelated babysitter do not differ significantly from mother-reared children or from infants attending day care on measures of sensorimotor ability and language development, and on behavior ratings, such as social responsiveness, goal directedness, and preference for novel stimuli (Doyle, 1975; Rubenstein et al., 1977). Observers of the caregivers' behavior noted that with increased contact, babysitters provide more stimulation for the infants, are more responsive to the infants' signals, and are more similar to the mother in their expression of positive affect (Rubenstein et al., 1977).

Infants cared for outside of the home, whether by a babysitter or in a child care center, also do not differ from home-reared children in the strength and security of their attachment to their mothers, but they find brief separations from her less novel and anxiety provoking than do exclusively mothered children (Doyle and Somers, 1978). The difference in independence is most marked for the infants who attend day care center full-time, but greater independence from the mother has also been observed when they are in the care of a babysitter (Clarke-Stewart, 1982).

Two studies, one in Chicago (Clarke-Stewart, 1982), one in Kentucky County (Winett et al., 1977), have looked at a variety of care arrangements for preschool children from a mixture of home backgrounds. Among the care arrangements were at-home care by the mother or by a babysitter, care in a day care center or nursery school, or a combination of group care and babysitter arrangements. All these child care arrangements occurred naturally in each community.

In both studies, on measures of intellectual competence, a difference was found between children in home care (with parents, babysitters or day care home providers) and children in center care (day care, nursery school, or combination of center care and babysitter) favoring those in center care (Clarke-Stewart, 1982) or in the mixed center-babysitter care arrangement (Winett et al., 1977). The children who were most likely to benefit from a center arrangement were from poor families; children from affluent families did not gain as much from center care, and did as well in the care of a babysitter.

In summary, the few studies that have monitored the effects of care arrangements for young children that include babysitters who come on a regular basis, have found no negative effects on the children's affective or cognitive development during the first 2 years of life. In comparison with exclusively reared children, such children tend to show a greater degree of independence from the mother, although they are securely attached to her. By the time children reach preschool age, social class differences become apparent. Children from poorer homes tend to do better on academic type tests if they are in center care. For middle-class children it does not seem to make much difference if they are cared for in a center or by a reliable babysitter at home.

STABILITY OF CARE: THE CASE OF THE "AU PAIR GIRL"

Most babysitters care for children who are related to them or whom they know as neighbors, but there is a sizeable minority who sit for unfamiliar families. Changes in care arrangements are particularly likely to happen if the children are over 1 year of age and if care is being provided by an unrelated, unlicensed sitter who is young and inexperienced (Clarke-Stewart, 1982). Such a pattern of unstable child care is now fairly common among professional families in Great Britain and on the European continent (and is being introduced in the U.S. as well). There, child care is often delegated to a series of foreign "au pair girls," among them, college students who visit the country for 6 or 12 months to learn the language. This can subject a child to a series of stressful situations, similar to a rapid turnover of babysitters.

Terrence Moore (1972), from the Center of the Study of Human Development in London, is one of the few investigators who has published longitudinal data on the consequences of relatively stable versus relatively unstable substitute care. He compared children who had three or more successive regimes of substitute care before age 5 with a group who had only one or two substitute caregivers during early childhood. By age 6, the children in the "unstable" care group were markedly more insecure, fearful, dependent, and clinging than children who had been in stable substitute care. However, in some cases the changes in caregivers themselves reflected the unstable circumstances and lifestyles of the families. It is therefore important to replicate this type of study with a larger sample that would allow for the control of a number of variables—such as moves, changes in employment, and marital status—that may affect the caregivers as well as the children.

THE FUTURE OF NANNY SURROGATES

It is not unreasonable to assume that babysitting and its various derivatives (such as the "au pair girl" arrangement) will continue to thrive as an underground activity for either regular or occasional temporary child care. This seems to be true for both middle- and lower-class families (Hill, 1977).

A survey conducted by the Michigan Department of Social Services showed that mothers eligible to receive public assistance funds to care for their children while at work preferred to have babysitters who came into their homes. Many of these were relatives or neighbors, and many of them were teenage girls (Frost and Schneider, 1971). At the same time, middle-class parents continue to hire teenagers when they go out, as they have done for more than a generation. In keeping with changing sex roles, more babysitters are now teenage boys than a generation ago, but the majority of regular babysitting is still being done by adolescent females.

Instruction for the care of young children is occasionally given in high school "parenting" or in home economics classes, or by civic minded groups, such as local hospitals and health departments. But it seems that both the babysitter and the children he or she cares for could profit from greater attention by the medical and child care professions. Education for babysitting needs to go beyond courses on feeding and diapering to address the psychological needs of sitters and young children, including topics that for long have been "taboo," such as child and sexual abuse (Kourany et al., 1980a). Child development research, in turn, has much to learn about the effects of such a relationship on both the adolescent and the young child he or she cares for. Since babysitting is one of the few opportunities that allows American adolescents a preview of adult responsibility and an opportunity to practice parenting skills, it deserves more attention than it has received so far from those who care for the nation's children.

SUMMARY

Mother surrogates who are strangers can be found in societies that are stratified by class, caste, or ethnicity. Here unequal access to the resources of a complex society allows some women to acquire or buy a full-time or part-time mother substitute for her children. Mother surrogates who are not kin, together with their young charges, tend to be separated rather than included in the life of the adults of the household.

From the Middle Ages through the Renaissance to the Industrial Age, affluent families in Europe have entrusted their children to the care of women who came from a lower social status than the mother herself, be they wet nurses, nursemaids, nannies, or modern nanny surrogates. In the Americas, this custom was imported, both in the Northern industrial cities and on the plantations in the American South and the West Indies. There is at least circumstantial evidence from autobiographies and childhood recollections of those who were nannied, that these mother surrogates made a lasting impact on their social values, on their sexual attitudes, and on their ability to form close interpersonal relationships.

The contractual arrangements that succeeded the nanny in the post-World War II area (the babysitter and au pair girls) have not been adequately studied, although they involve nearly every adolescent in the U.S. today. The few studies available have shown that care by a regular babysitter seems to be as adequate as exclusive mothering, and does not negatively affect the intellectual or affective development of young children. However, a rapid turnover of sitters in early childhood may lead to greater emotionality, fears, and dependence when a child reaches school age. The effect of such unstable care is often confounded with other stressful life experiences in the family. There have been occasional reports of child abuse and sexual experimentation by adolescent babysitters, but the extent of this phenomenon and its impact on the young child is not well known.

Babysitting is one of the few avenues by which American adolescents, especially those who grow up in small, middle-class families, can acquire parenting skills and be exposed to adult responsibilities. It deserves more attention by medical, psychological, and child development professionals than it has received so far.

REFERENCES

Boon, J.A. 1974. Anthropology and nannies. Man 9:137–140.

Brant, S., and Callman, E. 1980. Small Folk. Dutton, New York.

Burwell, L.M. 1895. A Girl's Life in Virginia Before the War. F.A. Stokes, New York.

Cable, M. 1975. The Little Darlings: A History of Child-Rearing in America. Charles Scribner's Sons, New York.

Churchill, R.S. 1966. Winston Churchill: Vol. 1, Youth: 1874–1900. Houghton Mifflin, Boston.

Clarke-Stewart, A. 1982. Day Care. Harvard University Press, Cambridge, MA.

Clarke-Stewart, A. The Chicago Study of Child Care and Development. In press.

De Mause, L. (ed.). 1974. The History of Childhood. The Psychohistory Press, New York.

Doyle, A.B. 1975. The effects of group and individual day care on infant development. Paper presented at the Canadian Psychological Association Meeting, Quebec.

Doyle, A.B., and Somers, V. 1978. The effect of group and family day care on infant attachment behavior. Can. J. Behav. Sci. 10:38–45.

Drew, J.B. 1973. Training child care aids. Child. Today September-October:15–36.

Drummond, L. 1978. The transatlantic nanny. Am. Ethnol. 5:30–43.

Federal Writers Project. 1941. Slave Narratives: A Folk History of Slavery in the United States from Interviews with Former Slaves. Typewritten records prepared by the Federal Writer's Project. Rare Book Collection. Library of Congress, Washington, DC.

Frost, J., and Schneider, H. 1971. Types of day care and parents' preference. Final Report: Part VII (ERIC ED 068 195). ORI, Inc., Information Systems Division, Bethesda, MD.

Gathorne-Hardy, J. 1972. The Rise and Fall of the British Nanny. Hodder and Stoughton, London. (Published in the U.S. in 1973 under the title, The Unnatural History of the Nanny. Dial Press, New York.)

Greenleaf, B.K. 1978. Children Through the Ages: A History of Childhood. McGraw-Hill, New York.

Hill, C.R. 1977. The child care market: A review of the evidence and implications for federal policy. (ERIC ED 156 352) ORI, Inc., Information Systems Division, Bethesda, MD.

Hunnisett, F.N. 1970. Babysitters on your toes. Can. Hosp. 47:28–29.

Jones, E. 1953–57. The Life and Work of Sigmund Freud, Vol. 1. Basic Books, New York.

King-Hall, M. 1958. The Story of the Nursery. Routledge and Kegan Paul, London.

Kourany, R.F., Gwinn, M., and Martin, J.E. 1980a. Adolescent babysitting: A 30-year-old phenomenon. Adolescence 15:939–945.

Kourany, R.F., Martin, J.E., and Armstrong, S.H. 1979. Sexual experimentation by adolescents while babysitting. Adolescence 14:284–288.

Kourany, R.F., Martin, J.E., and LaBarbera, J.D. 1980b. Adolescents as babysitters. Adolescence 15:155–158.

La Barbera, J.D., Kourany, R.F., and Martin, J.E. 1980. College students as babysitters. Coll. Stud. J. 14:24–26.

Laslett, P. 1977. Characteristics of the Western family considered over time. J. Fam. Hist. 2:89–115.

Medrich, E.A., Roizen, J., Rubin, V., and Buckley, S. 1982. The Serious Business of Growing Up: A Study of Children's Lives Outside School. University of California Press, Berkeley.

Moore, T. 1972. The later outcome of early care by the mother and substitute daily regime. In: F.J. Monks, W.W. Hartup, and J. De Witt (eds.), Determinants of Behavioral Development. Academic Press, New York.

Moore, T.W. 1975. Exclusive early mothering and its alternatives. Scand. J. Psychol. 16:255–272.

Rubenstein, J.L., Pedersen, F.A., and Yarrow, L.J. 1977. What happens when mother is away? A comparison of mothers and substitute caregivers. Dev. Psychol. 13:529–530.

Sadler, C. 1967. Children in the White House. Putnam's Sons, New York.

Schiller, J.D. 1980. Child Care Alternatives and Emotional Well-Being. Praeger, New York.

Schorsch, A. 1979. Images of Childhood: An Illustrated Social History. Mayflower Books, New York.

Sommerville, C.J. 1982. The Rise and Fall of Childhood. Sage Library of Social Research #140. Sage Publications, Beverly Hills, CA.

Spock, B. 1963. Ladies Home Journal. March.

Swan, J. 1974. Mater and nannie: Freud's two mothers and the discovery of the Oedipus complex. Am. Image 31:1–64.

Tyler, R.C., Lawrence, S., and Murphy, R. (eds.). 1974. The Slave Narratives of Texas, 1st Ed. Encino Press, Austin, TX.

U.S. Bureau of the Census. 1973. Washington, DC.

U.S. Department of Health, Education and Welfare, Children's Bureau. 1974. The Pocket Guide to Babysitting. DHEW Publication No. (OHD) 76-30045, Washington, DC.

Watson, J.W., Switzer, R.E., and Hirschberg, J.C. 1971. My Friend, the Babysitter. Golden Press, New York.

Weatherford, J.M. 1975. Anthropology and nannies. Man 10:308–310.

Winett, R.A., Fuchs, W.L., Moffat, S.A., and Nerviano, V.J. 1977. A cross-sectional study of children and their families in different child-care environments: Some data and conclusions. J. Commun. Psychol. 5:149–159.

Wolfe, T. 1969. The Kandy-Kolored Tangerine-Flake Streamline Baby, pp. 262–272. Noonday Press, New York.

Yanagisako, S.J. 1979. Family and household: The analysis of domestic groups. Annual Rev. Anthropol. 6:161–206.

CHAPTER **8**

Foster Parents

Some half a million American children are in foster care, most of them in homes of foster parents who have no blood or legal ties with them. These foster parents are *not* paid for their services, although they receive reimbursement for some expenses (room and board, clothing, and medical care) for their foster children. The taking in one's family of children of strangers in such numbers is a compliment to the extent of voluntarism in the U.S.—an example that is being emulated in other industrialized countries as well (Fanshel and Shinn, 1978)—but the transformation of the role of foster parents from kith or kin to "hired hands" is a phenomenon of relative recent origin in human history.

In traditional societies, for example in Oceania (Carroll, 1971), in West and East Africa (Goody, 1970; Weisner, 1982) and among Native American tribes (Ishisaka, 1978), *fosterage* usually denotes a kinship obligation. Children of both sexes are sent to relatives, either in the case of the dissolution of the conjugal family by divorce, death, or desertion (*crisis* fosterage), or to be taught the technical skills and moral values necessary for survival in their society (*voluntary* fostering). For example, among the Gonja in Northern Ghana, the majority of adults interviewed by Goody (1970) had been exposed to voluntary kin fostering as children. In this society, after the age of 6, both boys and girls are sent to stay with relatives for a few years to be taught domestic and farming skills. The child's sex determines whether he or she goes to the home of the mother's brother, the father's sister, or the maternal or paternal grandparents. The tie between the foster children and foster parents is based on a reciprocal relationship of service and training. The role models, the discipline, and the instruction are provided by the child's kinsmen and kinswomen. The institution of foster parenthood thus helps to reinforce ties between kin.

A similar practice was common in medieval European society among all classes of Anglo Saxon, Celtic, and Scandinavian families (De Mause, 1974). The custom of fosterage allowed parents to send their young children to another family to be reared and to serve, and then to be returned to the parents around age 17. Among children of the noble classes, both boys and girls at age 7 were sent to the households of relatives (for example a maternal uncle) or to the father's overlord for domestic service, a custom that helped consolidate alliances between families and neighbors. In the Celtic societies, notably Ireland and

Wales, this practice began sometimes shortly after the birth of the child. It prevailed from the Middle Ages until well into the 17th century.

In colonial America, town or city authorities took care of children of indigent parents by apprenticing them or binding them out as servants. The system of "vendering" was introduced about the time of the American Revolution. Citizens who needed help in their households bid against each other for a weekly stipend to be paid by the town in return for offering room and board for a child (Cable, 1975). In England, the Poor Law stepped in when neighborliness no longer sufficed to take care of children who had no families, and they were apprenticed to strangers for work. By the middle of the 19th century, an English clergyman began to make an arrangement with the local Poor Law society to finance the maintenance of such children from workhouses in private foster homes which he found and supervised himself (George, 1970).

In that same year, 1854, a New York philanthropist, Charles Loring Brace, founded the Children's Aid Society and initiated the "placing out" system of poor and homeless city children in the U.S. He began to send trainloads of indigent children from Eastern cities to the frontier states and territories of the Midwest and Far West, where they were taken into the homes of farmers. Subsequently, Charles Birtwell, the director of the Boston Children's Aid Society, prodded first the state of Massachusetts and then President Theodore Roosevelt (in 1909) into the establishment of a system of foster family services for dependent, neglected, and unwanted children. This system was to include selection of appropriate foster homes, placement supervision, and periodic review of cases. With the passage of the Social Security Act in 1935 and the establishment of the Aid for Dependent Children (AFDC) Foster Care Program in 1961, federal monies became available for foster home expenditures. In June 1980, the landmark Adoption Assistance and Child Welfare Act (P.L. 96-272) was passed by the U.S. Congress—a law that substantially redirects the federal role in child welfare and foster care.

Designed to encourage the states to move from reliance on foster care to helping children remain with their families, or if that is not possible, to be placed in adoptive homes, the 1980 Child Welfare Act asserts that foster children may no longer be allowed to "drift" in the foster system without resolution of their legal status and ultimate living arrangements (Calhoun, 1980). The new legislation offers the hope for foster children of a shorter time in foster care, fewer changes in living arrangements, earlier return to their biological parents, or placement in adoptive families or long-term living arrangements. It offers financial assistance to foster parents (including relatives) who wish to adopt foster children with special needs, that is, the growing number of older, handicapped, and minority children placed in foster care. The implementation of this law should make a significant impact on all participants in the foster care system: the foster parents, the foster children, the biological parents, and the child welfare agencies that serve as the community's representative to the foster and biological families and as advocate and legal guardian for the foster child. These agencies tend to be staffed with workers who carry an average caseload of 60 to 70 families and whose average length of employment is about 2 years—shorter than the average length of stay of a child in foster care (Child Welfare League of America, 1979).

WHAT IS FOSTER CARE AND
HOW DO CHILDREN ENTER FOSTER CARE?

The Child Welfare League of America (1975) defines foster care as "a child welfare service which provides substitute family care for a planned period for a child when his own family cannot care for him for a temporary or extended period, and when adoption is neither desirable nor possible." Children may enter foster care through voluntary and involuntary placements. In most instances, parents voluntarily place their children in foster care in order to resolve a family crisis, with the expectation that such placement will be temporary. Frequently this expectation is not realized because social service agencies make little or no attempts to provide services that will restore the family life of the voluntarily placed child (Gruber, 1978; Knitzer et al., 1978). Because surveys have indicated that voluntarily placed children have remained in foster care as long as involuntarily placed children, several states have enacted mandatory periodic review of all children in foster care, as has recently enacted federal legislation (P.L. 96-272, 1980).

Involuntary placements are those in which the child is removed from his home pursuant to a court order, issued at a dispositional hearing, following an adjudication of neglect, abuse, dependency, or deprivation. Depending upon state law, the judge will transfer custody of a child to a child welfare agency for placement or directly commit the child to a foster care setting (Gottesman, 1981).

Of the *parent-related* problems that lead to the placement of children into foster care, mental illness of the primary caregiver accounts for the highest proportion, followed closely by abandonment or desertion of the child, and neglect or child abuse. *Child-related* problems account for fewer than one-quarter of foster care placements. These are usually children whose handicaps (physical or mental) or behavior have placed greater demands on their biological families than the families can meet (Gruber, 1978; Fanshel and Shinn, 1978). Most commonly involved in foster care placement are children from poor homes, from minority groups (blacks, Puerto Ricans, and especially Native Americans), and from families with only one parent, usually a single mother. Also disproportionately represented are children whose parents received AFDC payments (Guerney, 1982). More boys than girls are placed in foster care (Fanshel and Shinn, 1978; Gruber, 1978; Guerney, 1982). Boys in foster care tend also to be younger (mean age, 9.9) than girls (mean age, 11.1).

Table 8. Types of foster care facilities[a]

Foster care facility	No. (in thousands)	%
Foster family home	395[b]	79
Public group home	12	2
Private group home	23	5
Residential treatment center	29	6
Other public child caring institution	21	4
Other private child caring institution	22	4
Total	502	100

[a] Source: *National Study of Social Services for Children and Their Families*, DHEW 1978, P110.
[b] Includes situations of mother and child in same foster family placement.

The foster care system has been affected by the same trends in our society that have increased the need for the other alternate caregivers discussed in this book: the increase of single parent households, of divorces, desertion, and teenage pregnancies, and the fact that more mothers are seeking employment outside of the home. Many children coming into foster care are older (including teenagers) and have more medical, emotional, and educational problems than in earlier decades. Thus, foster care has expanded from temporary custodial care for younger children to a treatment alternative for children with special needs—a task that places a special responsibility on foster parents and calls for additional skills and training (Adams, 1975; Bryant, 1981) (see Table 8).

Unfortunately, children who are placed in temporary foster homes frequently become permanent participants in the foster care system. Two and one-half years is the median length of time children spend in foster care in the U.S., and about 25% have been in it over 6 years (Calhoun et al., 1980). Twenty-two percent of children in foster care have been with at least three foster families—an instability of care quite contrary to a child's need for trusting and stable relationships with caring adults who can act as his or her "psychological parents" (Goldstein et al., 1973).

THE FOSTER PARENTS

In the eyes of the law, foster parents are generally viewed as independent contractors who enter into agreement with public or private child welfare agencies to provide temporary care for children in the agency's custody. In return for reimbursement for some of their expenses (but *not* for their services), they agree to provide care, protection, and training for the foster child, but to release the child to the agency upon request (for discharge to the family, adoption, or replacement). Foster parents are thus confronted with a set of conflicting goals: They are to provide the child with a nurturing relationship and a sense of stability, but at the same time they are to remain unattached because the custody is to be temporary (Gottesman, 1981).

The ambiguities in the definition of the role of foster parents may be one of the major reasons for the difficulties in recruiting and retaining foster families. For example, a study by Friedman et al., (1980) in a Florida county reports that only 6.1% of 260 prospective foster parents who called the child welfare agency during 1 year (August 1977 to July 1978) were eventually licensed, with high attrition rates before and after the orientation meetings which defined the agency's expectations for foster parents. In several California counties the annual turnover rate among foster parents is between 25% and 50% (Boyd and Remy, 1978). Nationwide the median length of service for a foster family is approximately 5 years (Guerney, 1982).

Experienced foster parents tend to resemble family day care providers in their demographic characteristics. They come from working-class backgrounds, have high school educations, and more often than not, are approaching the "empty nest" stage in their family lives. They tend to be middle-aged, and have children of their own who are teenagers or older (Guerney, 1982; Gruber, 1978). A sizeable proportion of such foster parents grew up on a farm (Cautley, 1980; Fanshel, 1966).

More recent studies show that the majority of prospective foster parents or foster parents with first placement experiences are younger than previously reported. For an example, an 18-month longitudinal study of 145 new foster families by Cautley (1980) reports the median age of the new foster mothers as 33, that of the new foster fathers as 36. Most of the biological children of these new foster parents were in the age range from 6 to 12 years. However, in this study, as in others, the older the foster mother, the more likely she was successful in coping with the foster child placed in her home (see also Kraus, 1971; Weinstein, 1960). A British study (Trasler, 1960) found a similar relationship between the age of the foster mother and placement success, with more women between 40 and 45 years of age being successful as foster mothers than younger women.

Success in placement seems to be also related to the number, age, and sex of the children in the foster family. Placements in which a sibling of the foster child is placed as well, or another foster child is present in the home, or the foster parents have two children of their own tend to be more successful than when there is no other child present in the household (Kraus, 1971; Trasler, 1960). However, placements in a family in which the foster parents' own children are of the same age and sex as the foster child(ren) tend to lead to difficulties, especially if the biological children are of preschool age. The position of the foster child as the youngest in the family seems to be the most favorable (Cautley, 1980; Trasler, 1960). These family structure variables, no doubt, reflect the demands on the attention and energy of the caregivers. They affect sib care and family day care arrangements as well (see Chapters 4 and 6, this volume).

While demographic factors have been explored more frequently in relation to the duration of the placement of foster children, the attitudes of the foster parents have been considered more often in their relationship to their effects on the behavior of foster children (Guerney and Gavigan, 1981). The motivation of foster mothers who care primarily for infants seems related to private pleasures involving close association with a "cuddly baby"; the foster mothers who care for older children, on the other hand, tend to verbalize a "social service orientation" that manifests itself in a desire to help deprived children (Fanshel, 1966). Several studies in the U.S. and Great Britain have shown that the motivation of helping and sharing resources with those who might need them tends to be associated with more successful foster parents, the desire for companionship for one's self or one's own children tends to be associated with less successful foster parents (Cautley, 1980; Trasler, 1960; Weinstein, 1960; Wolins, 1963).

Although it is usually the wife who is the prime mover in applying to a child welfare agency for foster parent status, most foster fathers identify strongly with the children placed in their homes (Fanshel, 1966). The sensitivity of the prospective foster father and a child-centered (as contrasted with a self-centered) point of view, and the report of the prospective foster father that major decisions were jointly made with his wife were all significant predictors of success among new foster parents (Cautley, 1980). Other factors related to success among such foster parents were having had child care responsibilities for younger siblings or children, growing up with fathers and mothers who provided good parenting models, and being able to treat children as unique individuals.

In a 5-year longitudinal study of 624 children in foster care in New York, Fanshel and Shinn (1978) appraised their foster families after the foster children had been in care for an average of 10.5 months, with a repeat assessment about 30 months later. Foster parents were rated by agency caseworkers on the following dimensions: age suitability, democratic permissiveness, intellectual climate provided in the foster home, and perseverance-altruism.

The "democratic permissiveness" dimension was positively related to significant gains in (non-verbal) IQ's among the foster children over the full 5 years of the study. A permissive foster family environment seemed to "loosen up" the children and was conducive to their cognitive growth. The "intellectual climate" of the foster home (defined by diversity of interests, large number of community contacts, reasoned discipline) was also related to significant positive changes in the children's behavior over time (toward greater agreeableness, likability, responsibility, and lessened defiance, emotionality, and hostility) as judged by their caseworkers. The foster parents in this longitudinal study were, on the whole, viewed positively by the social workers: The overwhelming majority were rated consistently as "excellent to good" in their provision of physical care, and 85% of the parents were considered "warm and affectionate" toward the foster children. There was also evidence of a great deal of sharing between foster parents in such areas as making the decision to accept the foster child into the home, going to foster parents' meetings, and handling visits of the child's natural parents.

A British study of foster parents by Shaw (1975) concludes that to most foster parents "successful fostering means loving children and being good at looking after them, the ultimate objective being the foster child's absorption into the family." Most foster parents, both in the U.S. and in England, do not distinguish between the roles of ordinary parents and foster parents. Treating the foster child as "one of our own" is one way in which they provide loving care (Parker, 1981).

THE EFFECTS OF FOSTER CARE ON CHILDREN

Among the problems facing researchers interested in assessing the effects of foster care on children is the selection of criteria and comparison groups for evaluation. For example, mental health problems, delinquency, or problems in keeping a steady job may reflect the impact of socioeducational problems (poverty, academic difficulties) rather than placement effects. Children in foster care may do "worse" than children in the community at large, "as well as" foster children discharged back to their biological parents, and "better" than children in residential institutions (Duersson, 1967).

On theoretical grounds, one would assume that long-term separations of a child from his or her own family would have negative psychological effects; the more frequent, longer, and permanent the separation, the greater the *potential* for trauma (Hubbell, 1981). However, these separation experiences seem to be moderated by a host of other variables, such as the age at which the separation takes place, the sex of the child, and the strength of the emotional ties to his biological parents and the foster parents. They also are affected by the (temperamental and intellectual) characteristics that the child brings to the experience, just as they affect a child's adaptation to repeated brief separations, such as in day care or being "nannied." To date, we have few empirical data that can give us an unequivocal verdict on the benefits or harm of foster care for the children placed in it. The few longitudinal and follow-up studies that have been conducted so far, however, seem to point to an amazing resiliency of children in the face of such high "risks" as chronic poverty, parental psychopathology, and family instability.

The most comprehensive data come from the 5-year longitudinal study of 624 children who entered foster care in New York City for the first time (Fanshel and Shinn, 1978). Ranging in age from birth to 12 years, all of the children remained in foster care for at least 90 days. Evaluations of caseworkers and teachers and psychological tests were used to assess the children's adjustment. Data were collected at three points in time: 1) from 90 days in placement through 1 year in placement; 2) after 2½ years in placement; and 3) 5 years from the child's entry into care.

The social workers reported that the children coped relatively well with the separation (with surprisingly low degrees of maladaptive behavior and homesickness), but children who entered foster care between the ages of 5 and 12 were more adversely affected than younger children. Generally the children had fewer problems identifying with their foster parents than with other children and adults. This was particularly true of the older children. Fanshel and Shinn (1978) also compared children who had been reunited with their biological families to those who had remained with their foster parents over the full 5-year period. The school performance and the emotional conditions of both groups (determined by psychological assessment) did not differ significantly. The IQ's of the majority of the children increased commensurately with their time in foster care. This was true for most of the black and Puerto Rican children (two-thirds of the sample), but not for the white children (whose IQ's actually declined). Most of the natural parents of the minority children lived in poverty whereas the foster parents were blue-collar workers; thus the IQ differences between the foster children who remained in care and the discharged children may be in part due to the differences in socioeconomic status between the foster families and the biological families.

A Canadian study by Palmer (1976) assessed the progress of some 200 foster children in long-term care. Palmer found that the majority of the children (but not those with a high IQ) improved in their "behavior" and showed a more satisfactory adjustment to school, community, and work over time. Those children who were able to make a positive identification with their foster parents were more likely to make progress in problem areas and to achieve their potential academically. Significantly related to such a positive identification was a higher socioeconomic status of the foster family, fewer moves experienced by the child, and more contacts with their natural family (which was facilitated by trained caseworkers).

An Israeli study of 56 children (mean age, 11 years) of schizophrenic parents removed from their biological families to the care of foster parents before age 3 reports that these children developed more stable personalities and did better in school than children of schizophrenics reared with their biological parents. The social status of their foster homes was, as in the American and Canadian studies, economically better than the majority of biological families (Landau et al., 1975). Flint (1977) evaluated the adjustment (at age 15) of 31 children who had been reared in a severely deprived (institutional) environment during infancy and early childhood and who were then placed with foster parents, following a therapeutic program some time between ages 2 and 5 years. By age 15, the group as a whole had developed a healthy capacity for affiliation with their foster parents, and the children functioned close to their intellectual potential, although they lagged behind age norms in social maturity.

There are some data that suggest that boys and girls may respond differentially to the experience that leads to foster care (as they do to other forms of alternate care). British epidemiological studies in London and on the Isle of Wight have shown that in middle childhood there was a strong association for boys between antisocial behavior, at home and in school, and a history of a short period (< 6 months) in foster care. This association was much less evident for girls (Wolkind and Rutter, 1973). The data from these studies suggested, however, that it was the long-term parental discord with which these children grew up (and to which they had returned) that led to the antisocial disorder rather than the experience of foster care per se, with boys being more susceptible to the family discord than girls.

But in a communitywide longitudinal study on the Hawaiian island of Kauai, Werner and Smith (1982) noted that girls who had been in foster care in early (2 to 5 years) or middle childhood (6 to 10 years) developed serious mental health problems in late adolescence (17 to 18 years), associated either with delinquency or teenage pregnancy. That study suggests that boys and girls may be vulnerable to stressful life events in the family at different points in their lifetimes. This is a topic that needs to be more systematically investigated in longitudinal studies with larger numbers of children in foster care.

There are hardly any data on the adult status of former foster children and the few that have been reported in the literature tend to lack appropriate comparison groups from the same (low) socioeconomic and ethnic (minority) groups from which foster children are generally drawn (McCord et al., 1960; Mnookin, 1973; Sophie, 1924). Meier's (1965) follow-up of 82 adults who had been in foster care 5 years or more shows that they were "successful" as compared with their own natural parents (many of whom had been incarcerated or institutionalized). As adults the former foster children had a higher incidence of illegitimate births and marital breakdowns than the population at large, but none of their legitimate offspring had been placed in foster care, few needed social services, and nearly all were self-supporting and productive and accepted members of their community.

The single most important finding from several studies of the self-concept of foster children (Emlen et al., 1978; Gil and Bogart, 1982; Weinstein, 1960) seems to be that a *sense of permanence* is one of the best predictors of a child's well-being. This sense of permanence is not necessarily related to the legal permanence of the placement. Whether the child is legally placed in the permanent care of foster parents or adopted, or returned home to his or her biological parents seems to make very little difference in level of adjustment or mental health *if* the caregiving setting provides a real sense of belonging.

THE CHILD'S BIOLOGICAL PARENTS

Studies in the U.S. as well as in Great Britain (Cautley, 1980; Parker, 1980) have shown that the relationship of foster parents to members of the child's own family, particularly the child's mother, is the most difficult aspect of care for some foster families. Relations with and feelings toward the child's biological parents are often ambivalent.

The position of the foster family vis-à-vis the child's own family is an aspect of the foster parent's role for which most new foster families are conspicuously unprepared (Cautley, 1980). Although it may not be appropriate for a caseworker to give a foster family full details regarding the child's family, they need to have some information of the child's experiences, attachments, and reasons for removal (which are often not given), and they need to be prepared for the child's possible reactions to parental visits. Some foster parents are able to welcome and work with the child's natural parents, but many seem to be content that they visit only infrequently (Parker, 1981).

In *Social Work Practice with Parents of Children in Foster Care*, Horejsi (1981) offers a list of suggestions as to how foster parents can be of assistance to biological parents. They include rules about visiting that assure maximum contact, but minimum disruption for the foster child, ways of sharing the child's progress with the natural family, modeling appropriate parenting behavior, and finding or advocating community resources for the natural parents.

These positive proposals seem somewhat difficult to implement in light of the results of several surveys that have shown that once placed, most natural parents are cut off from contacts with their children (Gruber, 1978; Knitzer, 1981). One of the most extensively documented of such surveys was conducted by the Children's Defense Fund (CDF) in 1978. It found that only half of the stratified national sample of 140 counties surveyed had specific written policies about parental visiting, some limiting it to the child's birthday or permitting it only in the courtroom. Parental visiting was often discouraged by fiscal policies which do not permit reimbursement to parents for transportation, although many parents have poverty level or marginal incomes. The problem is aggravated when children are placed at long distances from the biological families, out of the county, or even out of state (some 10% in the CDF report).

Yet visiting between biological parents and their children is one of the most important ways to sustain a relationship. In their longitudinal study of children in foster care in New York, Fanshel and Shinn (1978) found that frequently visited children showed greater gains in IQ scores and positive changes in behavior, noted by the child's caseworker and the classroom teachers. Frequency of parental visiting was also the best predictor of the child's return to his biological family. Other follow-up studies by Sherman et al. (1973), Vasaly (1976), and Weinstein (1960) have all pointed to positive relationships between frequent visits by parents and the likelihood of early discharge of the children to their biological families.

Research on foster care seldom focuses on the child's biological parents, their attitudes, perceptions, and needs. The only major study in this area was reported by Jenkins and Norman (1972, 1975), colleagues of Fanshel and Shinn, in their landmark 5-year longitudinal study in New York. Of the mothers interviewed when their children were first placed in foster care the most common feelings were "sadness" and "worry." Feelings of impotence and futility were also common. There was little difference in the pattern of feelings of "filial deprivation" expressed when both parents of the same child were interviewed separately. Five years later, "sadness" and "worry" were still the most common feelings, expressions of "bitterness" had lessened, but "guilt," "anger," and "shame" persisted. However, there were significant differences between mothers whose children had been placed for "socially acceptable" reasons (physical illness, mental illness, emotional disturbance of the child, and inability of an unmarried mother to assume care for her infant) and mothers whose children were placed for "socially unacceptable" reasons (abandonment, abuse, addiction, alcoholism, incarceration, neglect).

A significantly higher proportion of mothers whose children were placed for socially acceptable reasons evaluated the foster care placement positively and were thankful for it. They reported fewer problems in visiting; gave the child care worker higher ratings on communication, helpfulness, and understanding; and used community services more often and found them helpful. In contrast, a significantly higher proportion of mothers whose children were placed for socially unacceptable reasons were angry about the foster care placement and evaluated it negatively. They reported more problems in visiting and less interest, understanding, and communication by the child welfare worker, and few used community services and/or found them helpful. There was also a relationship between the mother's socioeconomic level and their feelings about the foster care placement: The most positive responses came from mothers from the highest socioeconomic level.

Jenkins and Norman (1975) suggest that these differences in the view of foster care by the biological parents may reflect a number of factors that need to be considered in any evaluation or reform of the "system": Mothers whose children are placed for socially unacceptable reasons may indeed be a more pathological group, and harder to reach and resistant to services by "strangers." But such mothers may also be perceived more negatively by both the foster parents and the child welfare workers and actually *get* inferior services. This is not unique to the U.S.: A British study by George (1970) also draws attention to the social stigma placed on parents who fail to fulfill expected child caring roles, and demonstrates the need for supportive services and housing and family counseling as a foundation for meaningful provision of substitute parenting by the foster family.

Studies of foster care have repeatedly shown that few preplacement services were provided that could have prevented the separation of the children from their biological families and that would have been more appropriate to meet their needs, such as assistance with housing, homemaking and family day care services, after-school recreation, and special education (Gruber, 1978; Knitzer, 1981; Sibbison and McGowan, 1978). While controlled studies of the comparative effectiveness of foster care versus at-home services on a routine basis (as opposed to demonstration projects) have not yet been reported (Guerney, 1982), the cost to the taxpayer of an average stay in foster care of approximately 5 years, at a range from $5,000 to $13,000 per year per child, is undoubtedly greater than what would be required to help a family in crisis.

Few services have also been made available that could increase the self-help skills of the biological parents (usually single mothers) during the time their children are placed in foster care or after their discharge back home. For example, Jenkins and Norman (1975) report that while 5 years after children entered foster care, the majority had been discharged back into their homes, the situation of the mothers had actually worsened financially, and there was little movement toward self-support. Money, health, and housing were perceived to be the major problems before and after discharge among the biological families in this New York study, as they were in another follow-up of foster children in neighboring Rhode Island. Data from that study (Sherman et al., 1973) indicated that significantly more children from families with inadequate housing and income had to be returned to foster care, and that follow-up services after discharge were crucial to prevent the reentry of discharged children into the foster care system.

Current efforts that focus on protective and in-home service for the biological families of foster children and on cooperation between natural parents and foster parents (supported by federal fiscal policies) are encouraging signs that the vicious cycle of "entry-exit-reentry" into foster care can be broken for some children. A description of several programs that have worked in different states of the union (California, Illinois, New Jersey, New York, North Carolina, Ohio, South Carolina, Tennessee, Texas, Washington) can be found in *Children without Homes*, published by the Children's Defense Fund (1978). They include in-home services, emergency services for mothers and children, and activities of parents' rights and child advocacy groups (Jones, 1976; Knitzer, 1981; Knitzer et al, 1978; Murphy, 1976).

The use of foster parents as role models for biological parents is on the increase as well, especially in programs designed to meet the needs of special children, that is, the mildly retarded, the physically handicapped, and the emotionally disturbed (Davis and Bland, 1978). In a comprehensive review of such Special Foster Care Programs (SFCP), Bryant (1981) notes that in the successful treatment programs, both biological and foster parents participate in the planning and treatment of the child, joining with the caseworker in negotiating a contract for the child's eventual return to his natural home (a right guaranteed to the parents under the Education for All Handicapped Children Act of 1975). Thus, Special Foster Care may well influence the evolution of traditional foster family care in the years to come, using specifically stated behavioral objectives and treatment procedures aimed at producing adaptive developmental changes in the children and their families.

FOSTER PARENT TRAINING PROGRAMS

Since the mid-1970s funds for developing and delivering pre- and in-service training programs for foster parents have been provided by the federal government (notably the U.S. Children's Bureau) and many states (Guerney, 1982). These training programs have been generally well attended and received by most foster parents, and evidence that the training is having desirable effects has been demonstrated in a number of studies (Boyd and Remy, 1978, 1979; Freeling-Nelson et al., 1976; Guerney and Gavigan, 1981; Guerney and Wolfgang, 1981; Sands, 1982).

For example, the Foster Parent Skills Training Program (FPSTP) developed for delivery by agency personnel, including foster parents, has been evaluated in a number of pre/post-test and follow-up studies at Pennsylvania State University (Guerney and Wolfgang, 1981). Aimed at parents of foster children between ages five and twelve, it has consistently been shown to: 1) increase the foster-parents' acceptance toward their foster-children; and 2) increase their ability to provide positive responses to them. It has also reduced the use of parental responses considered inappropriate or destructive to the children. These gains in foster parent skills were maintained in follow-up studies 9 months after the end of the training program. Program effects seem also to be positive for parents of younger children or children in their late teens and for foster parents of children with special needs. However, (better educated) foster mothers gained significantly more in "parental acceptance" scores after exposure to the training program than did foster fathers, and maintained treatment gains longer (Guerney and Gavigan, 1981).

In California, Boyd and Remy (1978, 1979) followed 267 child placements and compared the outcomes for homes in which foster parents had obtained training with those without previous training. Training had a positive effect on licensing outcomes and tempered the risk that foster children would be moved about from one placement to another in quick succession. Sands (1982) found that foster training programs had also positive effects on the morale of foster parents: They viewed themselves as less isolated from the community of foster parents and learned more about their legal rights and how to assert themselves through organized efforts.

FOSTER PARENTS' ASSOCIATIONS
AND CLASS ACTION LITIGATION

The National Foster Parents Association (NFPA) and state foster parent associations have provided foster parents with an identity, a structure for the exchange of ideas and information, and the means to work for changes in the foster care program that will benefit both the children and their families. Recent trends in case law demonstrate that persistent efforts of foster parent organizations have succeeded in gaining overdue recognition for them (Gottesman, 1981; Katz, 1976).

In a landmark case, the New York based Organization of Foster Families for Equality and Reform (OFFER) brought a class action suit, heard before the U.S. Supreme Court, challenging the practice of moving foster children who had been in the same foster home for long periods of time without providing an opportunity for a hearing to the foster parents. The highest court of the land was asked to decide for the first time what if any constitutional rights could be asserted on behalf of the "psychological family," created by the relationship between a foster parent and foster child. Without specifically acknowledging the existence of such a relationship, the court did note:

> . . . this case turns, not on the disputed validity of any particular psychological theory, but on the legal consequences of the undisputed fact that the emotional ties between foster parent and foster child are in many cases quite close, and undoubtedly in some as close as those existing in biological families . . . (*Smith vs. OFFER*, 1977, 431 US, 844–845).

The court, however, did not state directly what, if any, constitutional protection the foster parent/foster child relationship should be afforded. It ruled that it was adequately protected by the New York statutory scheme (which was being challenged by OFFER) that provides the right for a pretrial hearing (to the *foster child*) in cases where the relocation is to another foster home and when the child has been in the foster home for 18 months (Gottesman, 1981).

In California, recognition of foster parents has been accorded by the California Court of Appeals (*Katzoff vs. Superior Court, City and County of San Francisco*, 1976). It ruled that the person(s) in the home where the child has been living in a wholesome and stable environment would have first consideration in being awarded custody when the custody to the natural parent would be detrimental to the child. Foster parents have also gained recognition in the area of subsidized adoptions. Under the *Model Subsidized Adoption Act*, foster families, who otherwise may not have been able to do so, can adopt "hard to place" foster children (sibling groups, handicapped, or older children) who can qualify for a subsidy (Katz, 1976).

Class action litigation has also successfully challenged the antifamily bias in the foster care system, an interpretation that federal foster care funds could not be used to reimburse a child's relatives for providing foster care, although they could be used to reimburse strangers. In the past, states adopting this view either did not seek out relatives or reimbursed them at a (lower) public assistance rate rather than the (higher) foster care rate, often making it impossible for them to keep the children within the kin group (Knitzer, 1981). As a result of the Supreme Court decision in the case *Youakim vs. Miller,* (1976), it is now possible for significant numbers of children to be placed with or to remain with their relatives. There is ample evidence that the biological parents prefer to have their children placed with kin rather than strangers (Leichter and Mitchell, 1967; Stack, 1974).

PROMISING DEVELOPMENTS

Since 1976 a movement called Permanency Planning has developed that involves not a temporary placement in foster care but systematic case planning with the following objectives: 1) the home in which the child is placed is intended to last indefinitely, with resulting commitment and continuity in the child's family life; and 2) the family is one in which the child has a real sense of belonging with a "respected" social status in contrast to the "second-class" citizenship typical of temporary foster care. By now, the majority of states are engaged in special projects to overcome barriers to permanency, with the technical assistance of the Regional Research Institute for Human Services at Portland State University (Emlen, 1981).

The passing of the Adoption Assistance and Child Welfare Act of 1980 provides strong financial incentives for the states to use foster care *only* when preventive services in a child's home fail or are refused. In cases necessitating foster care, it ensures that the child is returned to permanent living arrangements as soon as possible. The act mandates that the child must be placed in the least restrictive setting as close to home as possible and with a relative whenever possible. Services must be provided to the child and the family to ensure the earliest possible reunion. Provision must be made for a review of the case of each child in foster care no longer than 18 months after the original placement. This review should determine whether the child returns to his or her biological parents, continues in foster care, or is placed in some permanent setting (including subsidized adoption by the foster parents). The foster parents, the parents, and the legal guardians of the child all have a right to a hearing to challenge any governmental action under this act (Gottesman, 1981).

It remains to be seen how successfully the mandates of P.L. 96-272 are translated into action. The implementation of this law is a challenge to human service professionals, lawyers, and child advocates. Only the future can tell whether it changes significantly the lives of the children and the biological and foster parents who care for them, but it is a much needed first step to ensure

"that children at risk of or in placement are treated in a caring way . . ."
(Knitzer, 1981, p. 7).

SUMMARY

In traditional societies foster parents were either relatives or neighbors; in
modern industrial societies, such as the U.S., Canada, and Great Britain, they
tend to be strangers who volunteer their services, but get some reimbursement
for expenses. The children they care for tend to come from "troubled" homes,
are poor and have often been reared by single parents. A disproportionate
number of children in foster care come from minority backgrounds and are
boys. Although foster care was originally conceived as temporary placement,
many children become permanent participants in a system that has too few
foster homes, too many overburdened child welfare workers, and too little
monitoring of progress.

Foster parents are generally middle aged, come from stable, working-
class backgrounds and have two or more children of their own who are older
than the foster child. The "social service orientation," the democratic permissiveness and the intellectual climate of the foster home all seem to contribute
to positive changes in the behavior of their foster children. The frequency of
visiting by his parents is the best predictor of a child's reunion with his biological family and the child's sense of permanence seems to contribute positively to
his or her adaptation and mental health, regardless of his or her legal status.

Efforts have increased to provide services such as homemaker assistance,
family day care, after-school recreation, and special education to prevent the
separation of the child from his or her biological family. In the case of children
with special needs (the emotionally disturbed, the mentally retarded, the physically handicapped) foster parents are now used as role models for biological
parents instead of placing the children in institutions.

Foster parent training programs and foster parent associations are improving the skills of foster parents, and case law is now as concerned with their
rights as with that of the natural parents. Federal policies are encouraging
foster placement in the home of relatives (who received financial aid) and
subsidize the adoption of "hard to place" children by foster parents. The
emphasis now is on preventive services, early case review and "permanency
planning," with the intent of breaking the vicious "entry-exit-reentry" cycle of
foster care and the "drift" of children through the foster care system.

REFERENCES

Adams, N. 1975. Foster family care for the intellectually disadvantaged child: The
current state of practice and some research perspectives. In: M.J. Begab and S.A.

Richardson (Eds.), The Mentally Retarded and Society: A Social Science Perspective, pp. 267–285. University Park Press, Baltimore.

Adoption Assistance and Child Welfare Act (P.L. 96–272). 1980. United States Congress, Washington, D.C.

Boyd, L.H. Jr., and Remy, L.L. 1978. Is foster parent training worthwhile? Social Sci. Rev. 52:275–296.

Boyd, L.H. Jr., and Remy, L.L. 1979. Foster parents who stay licensed and the role of training. J. Social Service Res. 2:372–387.

Bryant, B. 1981. Special foster care: A history and rationale. J. Clin. Child Psychol. 10(1):8–20.

Cable, M. 1975. The Little Darlings: A History of Child-Rearing in America. Charles Scribner, New York.

Calhoun, J.A. 1980. The 1980 Child Welfare Act: A turning point for children and troubled families. Child Today September-October:2–3.

Calhoun, J.A., Grotberg, E.H., and Rackley, W.R. 1980. The status of children, youth and families. United States Department of Health and Human Services. DHHS Publication #(OHDS)80-30-274. Washington, DC.

Carroll, V. 1971. Adoption in Eastern Oceania. University of Hawaii Press, Honolulu.

Cautley, P. 1980. New foster parents: The First Experience. Human Services Press, New York.

Child Welfare League of America. 1975. Standards of Foster Family Services. Revised edition. Child Welfare League of America, New York.

Child Welfare League of America. 1979. Who Knows? Who Cares? Forgotten Children in Foster Care. Child Welfare League of America, New York.

Davis, L.J., and Bland, D.C. 1978. The use of foster parents as role models for parents. Child Welfare 57(6):380–386.

De Mause, L. (ed.). 1974. The History of Childhood. The Psychohistory Press, New York.

Duersson, A. 1967. Heimkinder und Pflegekinder in ihrer Entwicklung. In: R. Dinnage and M.L. Kellmer-Pringle (Eds.), Foster Home Care: Fact and Fallacies. Humanities Press, New York.

Emlen, A. 1981. The Development of the Concept of Permanency Planning. Regional Research Institute for Human Services, Portland, Oregon.

Emlen, A., Cascioto, J., Clarksen, D., et al. 1978. Outcomes of Permanency Planning for Children in Foster Care. Regional Research Institute for Human Services, Portland, OR.

Fanshel, D. 1966. Foster Parenthood: A Role Analysis. University of Minnesota Press, Minneapolis.

Fanshel, D., and Shinn, E.B. 1978. Children in Foster Care: A Longitudinal Study. Columbia University Press, New York.

Flint, B.M. 1977. A longitudinal study of a group of children reared in a severely depriving environment during infancy and early childhood: Sixteen years investigation. Research in Education. September.

Freeling-Nelson, W., Kissel, S., and Surgent, L. 1976. Parenting for foster parents. Child Psychiatry Hum. Dev. 6:244–250.

Friedman, R.M., Lardieri, S., Murphy, R., et al. 1980. The difficult job of recruiting foster parents. Public Welfare. Summer:10–17.

George, V. 1970. Foster Care: Theory and Practice. Routledge and Kegan Paul, London.

Gil, E., and Bogart, K. 1982. Foster children speak out. Child Today January–February:7–9.

Goldstein, J., Freud, A., and Solnit, A.J. 1973. Beyond the Best Interest of the Child. Free Press, New York.

Goody, E. 1970. Kinship fostering in Gonja: Deprivation or advantage? In: P. Mayer (Ed.), Socialization: The Approach from Social Anthropology, pp. 51–74. Tavistock Publications, London.

Gottesman, R. 1981. The Child and the Law. West Publishing Company, St. Paul, Minnesota.

Gruber, A.R. 1978. Children in Foster Care: Destitute, Neglected, Betrayed. Human Sciences Press, New York.

Guerney, L. 1982. The effectiveness of foster care as supplementary parenting. In: M. Kostelnik and H. Fitzgerald (Eds.), Patterns of Supplementary Parenting, Vol. II. Plenum Press, New York.

Guerney, L., and Gavigan, M. 1981. Parental acceptance and foster parents. J. Clin. Child Psychol. 10(1):27–32.

Guerney, L., and Wolfgang, G. 1981. Long-range evaluation of effects on foster parents of a foster parent skills training program. J. Clin. Child Psychol. 10(1):33–37.

Horejsi, C.R. 1981. Social Work Practice with Parents of Children in Foster Care. Charles C Thomas, Springfield, IL.

Hubbell, R. 1981. Foster Care and Families. Temple University Press, Philadelphia.

Ishisaka, H. 1978. American Indians and foster care: Cultural factors and separation. Child Welfare 57(5):299–308.

Jenkins, S., and Norman, E. 1972. Filial Deprivation and Foster Care. Columbia University Press, New York.

Jenkins, S., and Norman, E. 1975. Beyond Placement: Mothers View Foster Care. Columbia University Press, New York.

Jones, M.A. 1976. Reducing foster care through services to the family. Child Today November–December:7–10.

Katz, S.N. 1976. The changing legal status of foster parents. Child Today. November–December:11–13.

Katzoff vs. Superior Court, City and County of San Francisco. 1976. Cal. App. 3rd 1082.

Knitzer, J. 1981. Child welfare: The role of federal policies. J. Clin. Child Psychol. 10(1):3–7.

Knitzer, J., Allen, M.L., and McGowan, B. 1978. Children without Homes: An Examination of Public Responsibility to Children in Out-of-Home Care. Children's Defense Fund, Washington, DC.

Kraus, J. 1971. Predicting success of foster placements for school-age children. Social Work. 16:63–72.

Landau, R. Daphne, Y., Iuchtman, C., and Arden, V. 1975. The development of children of psychotic parents reared away from home. Israeli Ann. Psychiatry Rel. Discipl. 13(1):48–57.

Leichter, H.J., and Mitchell, W.E. 1967. Kinship and Casework. Russell Sage Foundation, New York.

McCord, J., McCord, W., and Thurber, E. 1960. The effect of foster-home placement in the prevention of adult anti-social behavior. Social Serv. Rev. 34:415–420.

Meier, E.G. 1965. Current circumstances of former foster children. Child Welfare 44: 196–206.

Mnookin, R.H. 1973. Foster care: In whose best interest? Harvard Ed. Rev. 43(4): 599–638.

Murphy, D.A. 1976. Programs for parents of children in foster family care. Child Today November–December:37–40.

Palmer, S. 1976. Children in Long-Term Care: Their Experiences and Progress. Family and Children's Services of London and Middlesex, London, Ontario.

Parker, R.A. (Ed.). 1980. Caring for separated children: Plans, procedures and priorities: A report by a working party established by the National Children's Bureau.

McMillan Press, London. (American edition: 1981: Humanities Press, Atlantic Highlands, NJ.)

Sands, L. 1982. Training of foster parents: A survey study. M.S. thesis in Child Development, University of California at Davis.

Shaw, M. 1975. Children between Families. School of Social Work, University of Leicester, England.

Sherman, E.A., Neuman, R., and Shyne, A.W. 1973. Children Adrift in Foster Care: A Study of Alternative Approaches. Child Welfare League of America, New York.

Smith vs. OFFER. 1977. 431 US, 844–845.

Sibbison, V., and McGowan, J. 1978. New York State Children in Foster Care: Executive Summary. Welfare Research Inc., Albany, New York.

Sophie, T. 1924. How Foster Children Turn Out. State Charitable Aid Association, New York.

Stack, C.R. 1974. All Our Kin: Strategies for Survival in a Black Community. Harper and Row, New York.

Trasler, G. 1960. In Place of Parents: A Study of Foster Care. Routledge and Kegan Paul, London.

Vasaly, S.M. 1976. Foster care in five states: A synthesis and analysis of studies from Arizona, California, Iowa, Massachusetts and Vermont. Social Research Group, George Washington University, Washington, DC.

Weinstein, E.A. 1960. The Self-Image of the Foster Child. Russell Sage Foundation, New York.

Weisner, T.S. 1982. Sibling interdependence and child caretaking: A cross-cultural view. In: M. Lamb and B. Sutton-Smith (Eds.), Sibling Relationships: Their Nature and Significance Across the Life Span, pp. 303–325. Lawrence Earlbaum Associates, Hillsdale, NJ.

Werner, E.E., and Smith, R.S. 1982. Vulnerable, but Invincible: A Longitudinal Study of Resilient Children and Youth. McGraw-Hill, New York.

Wolins, M. 1963. Selecting Foster Parents: The Ideal and the Reality. Columbia University Press, New York.

Wolkind, S., and Rutter, M. 1973. Children who have been "in care": An epidemiological study. J. Clin. Child Psychol. Psychiatry 14(2):97–105.

Youakim vs. Miller. 1976.

CHAPTER 9

Television

The Electronic Babysitter

"Sunny day, keeping the clouds away
On my way to where the air is sweet
Can you tell me how to get
How to get to Sesame Street?"

Signature Song, *Sesame Street*
Children's Television Workshop

During the last half of the 20th century a new family member has joined nearly every household in the U.S. and is about to enter most homes in other parts of the world as well. Not a person, but an object—the television set—now occupies more waking hours of a child's life in America than either parents or school. By the age of 18, a child born today in the U.S. will have spent more time watching television than in any other single activity, besides sleep (Liebert et al., 1982).

Children, at least in the early years, spend considerably more hours per week in front of the television than do adults. Most American youngsters are now exposed to television by the time they are 1 year old, and they are steady viewers with favorite shows of their own by age 3. Viewing time during the preschool years peaks at an average of 2½ to 3 hours per day, just before entrance to elementary school. It drops slightly as school cuts into a child's available time, but then increases steadily again, from about age 8 on, to an average of 4 hours per day during early adolescence. It levels off slightly during the high school years (see Figure 10) (Comstock et al., 1978).

The same basic developmental trend has been found in several studies in the U.S. during two decades, but comparisons between the results of early and more recent surveys suggests an overall increase in children's television viewing time at an increment of about 1 hour per day over the past 20 years (Lyle and Hoffman, 1972).

CULTURAL SIMILARITIES AND DIFFERENCES IN TELEVISION VIEWING PATTERNS

This viewing pattern is similar for children who live in other industrialized countries. In a review of international television use, Murray (1980) found that children's viewing time in Asia, Australia, and Europe steadily increased from

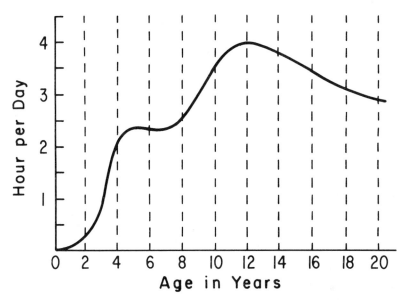

Figure 10.   Constructed curve of average hours of daily television viewing by age. (Reprinted by permission from G. Comstock et al., 1978, Television and Human Behavior, Columbia University Press, New York, and the Rand Corporation.)

early childhood to a peak in early adolescence, followed by a decline. But the number of hours children spent in front of the television varied with the amount and time of programming. In countries with a large amount of television available, such as Australia, Canada, Great Britain, and Japan, children (ages 2 to 11) watch, on the average, about 2 to 3 hours per day. In countries with a more limited television broadcasting time, such as Austria, Germany, Italy, Norway, and Sweden, children watch about 1 to 2 hours daily.

Estimates of "average" television use, however, do not reflect large variations within each age group. For example in the U.S., children from lower social class and minority backgrounds, especially blacks and Mexican-Americans, watch more television than middle- and upper-class whites, and children's viewing habits seem to be more similar to that of their parents' than that of their age peers. If children want to be with their parents or parents with their children, it appears likely that they will meet around the television set. Watching television with their children seems to be one of the few or the *only* shared activity that parents have time and energy for, when the demands of work and child rearing are heavy (Goldsmith, 1978).

Medrich et al. (1982) found a complex relationship between parental and children's viewing habits in their study of out-of-school activities of a multi-ethnic group of preadolescents. Among blacks, (low) family income was the best predictor of children's (high) television viewing time. Among whites, it was the mother's (low) educational level. Only well-educated white and Asian parents systematically limited television viewing for their children (or had children who chose to engage in other activities instead). At every education level, however, single parents were significantly more likely to have children who were heavy television viewers. Single parents were the least likely to have energy to control the television use of their children, given the demands on their time. In their families, television has indeed become "the other parent."

The appearance of television—more than any other technological—innovation has made a significant impact on the rhythm of family life, both in the U.S. and abroad. As early as 1967, Johnson reported that the majority of American families who had acquired a television set changed their sleeping patterns and altered their mealtimes, and that the vast majority (78%) used television as an "electronic babysitter" for their children. Robinson (1972) studied the impact of television in 15 locations in Western and Eastern Europe as well as in Peru and in the U.S. by contrasting the time budgets of set owners with that of non-owners in the same locations. Activities that decreased significantly with television ownership in all countries were time spent in child care, conversation, social gatherings away from home, and sleep. In the U.S., women tend to spend four times as many hours watching television with their children (in proximity, but with little meaningful interaction taking place) as they do on their primary care. For men, the ratio is 10 to 1 (Robinson, 1977).

It comes therefore as no surprise that in a survey of 4- to 6-year-old American children, nearly half preferred watching television to having one of their parents around. When asked "Which do you like better, television or Daddy?" 44% of the preschoolers said they preferred television. Mothers, however, fared better than fathers in that survey: Only one out of five of the children liked television better than Mommy (Chamberlin and Chambers, 1976).

TELEVISION AS SOCIALIZATION AGENT

Television's popularity here and abroad suggests that it is meeting some fundamental needs in its viewers. Noble (1975), a British psychologist, suggests that television viewed at home gives the child or adult the illusion that he or she is meeting people face to face in small social groups. Television, by exposing disparate individuals to the same familiar context (which tends to be repetitive from week to week), may serve to restore a village type of community to modern families who have lost the support of extended kin. It provides a stage with a number of stable characters or role models whom the child can observe and, on occasion, imitate. Thus, television has become a major agent of socialization for the young that contends with the influence of their elders (parents and teachers) and peers (siblings, playmates, and classmates) who, in turn, are also affected by the medium as well as by the child's viewing habits.

During the past decade, there has been a virtual explosion of studies that deal with the viewing patterns and the effects of television on its worldwide audience. A classic book that summarizes research in the early days of television is *Television in the Lives of Our Children* by Schramm et al. (1961). Among more recent "state of the art" reviews are Comstock et al.'s *Television and Human Behavior* (1978), Palmer and Dorr's *Children and the Faces of Television: Teaching, Violence and Selling* (1980), and Liebert et al.'s book *The Early Window: Effects of Television on Children and Youth* (1982), which examines the events leading to the Surgeon General's Report on television and social behavior (1972) and the decade of research afterwards. However, in spite of hundreds of short-term studies on the effects of television on the young, there is a paucity of research with a truly developmental perspective. Only since the mid-1970s have there been some reports from a handful of longitudinal studies which have monitored the impact of television on children's development for periods of from 1 to 10 years.

TELEVISION AS BABYSITTER

Surprisingly few researchers have studied systematically the child care functions of television. That function is especially important for millions of preschoolers and school-age "latchkey" children in the U.S. who spend hours in front of the television set while their parents are away from home at work (Long and Long, cited in Scherer, 1982).

In one of the first systematic studies of television's role as babysitter, Sharon Gadberry (1974) set out to answer the following questions:

1. Are children quieter while viewing television than while playing?
2. What kinds of activities do children engage in during television viewing relative to the kinds of activities that occur during ordinary playtime?
3. Is there less need for parental control and supervision during television than during play?
4. Is there a relationship between a child's viewing rate and his behavior during play and during television viewing?

A team of trained observers visited young boys, ages 4½ to 5½, in their middle-class, suburban homes and compared their behavior while watching television with their conduct while playing with another child. Television viewing proved to be associated with more sitting, less walking, fewer attempts to leave the room, less aggression toward others, and more attention shifts and self-stimulation. Preschool children with high television viewing rates also shifted their attention more during play than children with low television viewing rates. Most important, there was less need for maternal control during television viewing time than during play. Overall, the television behavior of these preschool children was more passive and self-absorbed than playing behavior, and their motor and verbal activity decreased. Both Gadberry (1974) and Essa (1978), who observed mother-child interactions during television watching and play, conclude that television watching significantly affects parental, especially maternal socialization practices, since the presence of television decreased eye contact, verbalization, and child behavior that could be positively rewarded by the parent.

The findings of home observations complement maternal reports in interviews in Denver and New York conducted by Winn (1978) for her research on her book *The Plug-In-Drug*. These mothers confessed that they grew, although sometimes reluctantly, to use television as a babysitter because of its unique ability to pacify young children and because of its ready availability. Parents also aver that babysitters insist on using television, and that their children's overuse of television may be partly due to the sitter's reliance on the television to make her life easier. Thus, even though they may have ambivalent feelings about its use, television enables many American parents to plan for their children's time without too many demands on their own time or presence, and it allows alternate caregivers to occupy the time of the children in their charge without difficulty (Medrich et al., 1982; Singer and Singer, 1981). This seems to hold for other cultures as well: Anecdotal evidence from studies conducted in Great Britain (Himmelweit et al., 1958), in Japan (Goto, 1979), and in Hong Kong (Lam, 1982) all suggest that television is used as surrogate nurse to keep young children at home, distracted, and quiet and that it is considered an ideal "pacifier" by busy parents.

THE DEVELOPMENT OF YOUNG CHILDREN'S LOVE AFFAIR WITH TELEVISION

In an intriguing article called "Piaget Meets Big Bird: Is TV a Passive Teacher?" Fowles and Voyat (1974) remind us that our developmental theories of cognition and socialization pre-date television. As of today, we still know relatively little about what changes television might be bringing about in the nature of cognitive development. They suggest that studies of infants' developing love affair with television might be a good start to making inroads in our ignorance, and a few researchers have begun to do just that.

We now know that infants as young as 6 months not only attend to television but they also respond differentially to the sound and sight that the set provides (Slaby and Hollenbeck, 1977). Infants spend significantly more time looking at television when both sight and sound are on, and remain silent for longer periods of time than when only the picture or the sound effects are provided. If the sound is off, they still tend to look, but they cry more often and longer than when it is on.

Anderson and Levin (1976) conducted a series of studies in which they looked at changes in television viewing across the first 5 years of life. One year olds, accompanied by their parents in a television viewing room (and with toys present) watched an average of only 12% of the children's program shown to them, whereas by age 4 the children watched an average of 58%. The frequency of "looks" at television increased dramatically around age 2½ years. Before that time, toddlers sat usually oriented toward the parent, but at age 2-1/2 and older, they began to sit oriented toward the television set, playing with toys, but glancing up frequently. Their parents likewise reported a sharp increase in television home viewing when their offspring was about 30 months old (Anderson et al., 1979).

McCall et al. (1977) found a parallel age trend in the propensity of 1- to 3-year-old children to imitate a live or a televised adult model's behavior. Before 2 years, infants were more likely to imitate a live than a televised model, but this difference disappeared between ages 2 and 3 years. By that time children imitated televised models as frequently as live models, regardless of their sex, socioeconomic class, temperamental characteristics, television viewing habits, and the presence or absence of siblings.

Anderson and his colleagues (1976, 1979) have also monitored several program features affecting young children's attention to television. Program attributes that were associated with increased attention levels in 1 to 5 year olds were presence of adult women, children, puppets, peculiar voices, auditory changes, animation, movement, lively music, clapping, laughing, rhyming, alliteration, and repetition. Attributes that tended to decrease attention were the presence of adult men, animals, inactivity, and still drawings. Young children tend to "lock in" to what they are watching: The longer a child looks at the screen, the greater is the probability that he or she will continue to look.

In a longitudinal study of three first-born children from middle- and lower middle-class suburban families, Jaglom and Gardner (1981) focused on preschoolers' emerging abilities to "make sense" out of the television medium and to connect its content with the rest of their (real-life) experiences. When they were 2 years old, these children watched and enjoyed cartoons and *Sesame Street* the most, but they were not yet able to identify reliably the characters appearing on the shows. To their eyes the television world was without order and boundaries: Their favorite characters were believed to appear on any channel at any time, and they assumed that their parents could fully control the world inside the box. Events occurring on television were believed to be physically related and influenced by events in the child's own home.

By the time they reached age 3, these children had been exposed to more types of programs and preferred family and situation comedies as much as cartoons and *Sesame Street.* They could now describe characteristic attributes of their favorite characters. In their fourth year, the children began to discuss the interactions between characters and were aware that one character's actions might cause a reaction in the other. They also knew that their favorite shows had a special time, with a beginning and an ending. The television world now was seen as entirely separate from the real world.

By the fifth year, the children had added action-adventure fare to their preferred shows and could distinguish between the news, adults', and children's shows. They could now classify television characters into categories, such as monsters and puppets, and they began to see the reciprocity of their interactions. They could now see some elements that were shared by both the television and the real world, and some that existed only in the television world. They also recognized similarities and differences between television characters and real-life persons. Thus, during the course of their preschool years, children grow into knowledgeable experts of televisionland (Singer and Singer, 1981).

Cross-cultural and longitudinal studies by Salomon (1976, 1977) with American and Israeli children indicate that some of the age-related changes in children's comprehension of television content are most likely attributable to their learning the media "codes" or techniques which represent certain mental skills. For example, the camera's zooming in and out represents the skill of relating parts to a whole, and camera cuts of an object represent the skill of taking a different perspective. Hence, exposure to such codes, especially with "television" naive populations as in Israel (and other developing countries), seems to improve the corresponding cognitive skills of preschoolers and children in the early elementary grades (Hornik, 1981).

EFFECTS OF EDUCATIONAL TELEVISION
PROGRAMS ON YOUNG CHILDREN

Sesame Street

The importance of preschool experience for later educational development has long been recognized. But most 3-, 4-, and 5-year-old children around the world do not attend any formal school. *Sesame Street* was developed by the Children's Television Workshop (CTW) to provide preschool experiences at home that would both entertain and foster intellectual and social development (Lesser, 1974).

Sesame Street, since its first showing in the U.S. in 1969, has become the world's most popular children's television series—the "longest street in the world . . . the only street that winds clear around the globe" (Goldsen, 1976, p. 203). It is now being broadcast in English in over 50 countries, including Canada, the Carribean, Australia, New Zealand, the Far East, Europe, Israel, and Africa. In another 20 countries, the program is broadcast in foreign language adaptations (Palmer et al., 1976). These spin-offs from the original version include *Plaza Sesamo* for Spanish speaking children in the Western hemisphere; *Villa Sesamo*, in Portuguese, for preschool children in Brazil; *Abreto, Sesamo* in Spain; *Bonjour Sesamé* for the millions of French speaking children throughout the world; *Sesamstrasse* for German preschoolers; *Sesamstraat* in the Netherlands; *Sesam* in Sweden; and one of the newest additions, *Iftah Ya Simsim* for children of the Arabic speaking world (Ridha, 1979). Gerald Lesser's book *Children and Television: Lessons from Sesame Street* (1974) gives an excellent "insider's" view of the joint planning and production of the series by experts in child development, educational psychology, preschool education, and television.

To satisfy the requirement of the U.S. Office of Education and various private foundations which funded the planning and production of *Sesame Street*, the Educational Testing Service (ETS) was commissioned to do two series of evaluations of the impact of the first and second year of the show on 3- to 5-year-old children in the U.S. (Ball and Bogatz, 1972). Evaluations of the impact of the program on young children abroad have been undertaken in about a dozen countries, including Canada (Gorn et al., 1976), Mexico (Diaz-Guerrero and Holtzman, 1974; Diaz-Guerrero et al., 1976), Jamaica (Lasker, 1973), the Netherland Antilles (Lasker and Casseras, 1971), Chile (Salas de Bodini, 1975), Great Britain (Blackwell, 1972), West Germany (Kob, 1975), the Netherlands (Van Lil, 1976), Israel (Salomon, 1976, 1977), Japan (Yamamoto, 1976), and Australia (Lemercier and Teasdale, 1973). These were mostly short-term evaluation studies over a period of 6 to 12 months. We have no data yet on how much young children learn anywhere in the world from viewing educational television programs over the typical course of 3 to 4 years before they enter school (Palmer et al., 1976).

The research strategy in the American studies was to design a field experiment by creating randomly designed experimental (viewing) and control (non-viewing) groups. The experimental treatment, called "encouragement to view *Sesame Street*," involved contacting mothers to tell them about the program, sending printed materials, and checking periodically whether or not their children were watching. Control groups were not given specific information about the series, but the unexpected success of *Sesame Street* found many of the control group children watching as well, although without active encouragement. Therefore, in the first year of evaluation comparisons were made between children who had watched frequently and those who did not. In the second year, cities were chosen where *Sesame Street* was available only on cable or UHF channels. Reception capacity was supplied to the experimental group, but not to the control group (Watkins et al., 1980).

Ball and Bogatz (1972) found that children who watched the series either at home or in day care settings achieved significantly higher gains on the assessment tests than those who were not exposed to it. Children who rarely or never watched gained less than those who watched on the average more than five times a week. Younger children gained more than older children. Disadvantaged children who watched frequently gained as much as advantaged frequent viewers and gained more than did disadvantaged infrequent viewers. Boys and girls, English and Spanish speaking children, and rural and urban dwellers showed equivalent gains in skills taught directly in the series (for example, recognition of letters, numbers, counting, and vocabulary). After the second year, frequent viewers had also significantly higher scores on a verbal IQ test and more positive attitudes toward school, and were rated higher in their performance by first grade teachers than infrequent viewers. Similar results have been reported from Australia and West Germany. But Cook et al. (1975), who reanalyzed the ETS data and additional evaluation studies in *Sesame Street Revisited*, issue a word of caution: Because the "experimental" design of the original *Sesame Street* evaluation drew mothers into involvement with the series, the positive results cannot solely be attributed to the effects of educational television. Cook and Conner (1976) found significantly greater gains for children whose mothers were "encouraged" than for control groups whose mothers were not encouraged, even when the frequency of viewing by the children was the same.

A similar finding was reported by Salomon in Israel (1977). Children whose mothers had been encouraged to watch *Sesame Street* with them showed more improved performance on measures that assessed the learning of the specific skills stressed by the series than did children whose mothers had not been encouraged, especially among those from lower-class homes. That the involvement of an alternate caregiver—for example, a day care provider—also contributes to young children's gain from educational television was demonstrated by Diaz-Guerrero and Holtzman (1974) in Mexico City. They evaluated the impact of *Plaza Sesamo* on 3 to 5 year olds from low socioeconomic status homes who attended day care centers. The experimental children who had teacher monitors and observers from the research staff showed superior learning gains over control children without that exposure. In contrast, a larger field experiment in Mexico under less controlled conditions produced no significant gains for rural and urban children from lower-class and blue-collar homes who watched *Plaza Sesamo* for up to 12 months. Diaz-Guerrero et al. (1976) ascribe the negligible educational impact of the series in their second study to the absence of adult encouragement and reinforcement, especially in the homes of disadvantaged children.

The Electric Company

By 1971, CTW began to air *The Electric Company,* an educational television program whose intended purpose was to provide supplementary instruction in basic reading skills (primarily sound-symbol analyses of the printed word) for 7- to 10-year-old children with reading problems (Gibbon et al., 1975). Within 2 months of the series' premiere, it was used in about 25% of American elementary schools, and by the second season, it was shown in about 35% of the nation's elementary schools (Children's Television Workshop, 1971–1980).

The degree of *The Electric Company*'s success was evaluated using the same research design and the same researchers as *Sesame Street* (Ball and Bogatz, 1973). The effect of home viewing turned out to be negligible. But on a reading test battery designed by ETS, it was found that first through fourth graders who viewed the program in school attained significantly higher scores than non-viewers. Again, it is likely that effects of the program were enhanced by the teacher and the reinforcement of the television lessons in the curriculum (Liebert et al., 1982).

In summary, evaluation of the effects of planned television programming for young children, such as *Sesame Street* and *The Electric Company*, here and abroad indicate that children can learn intellectual skills from programs designed to be both entertaining and instructional. Home viewing seems to be effective in teaching preacademic skills to young children and to disadvantaged children, but it is not effective in teaching reading skills to school-age children with reading problems. In all cases learning from watching the televised series was enhanced when an interested parent or alternate caregiver was available (Watkins et al., 1980).

3-2-1 Contact

In January 1980, CTW began broadcasting *3-2-1 Contact*, a series geared toward 8 to 12 year olds to help them: 1) experience the joy of scientific exploration; 2) become familiar with various styles of scientific thinking; and 3) to appeal especially to girls and minorities, so they would recognize that science and technology is open to their participation (Lesser, 1980). This series has since been seen in an estimated 15 million homes in the U.S., but research has yet to determine the degree to which it has achieved its stated objectives (Liebert et al., 1982).

THE EFFECT OF HOME VIEWING OF COMMERCIAL TELEVISION ON CHILDREN'S SCHOOL ACHIEVEMENT

With regard to input/output studies, there is little evidence that watching commercial television programs at home affects achievement in school in areas other than reading skills (Hornik, 1981). Studies conducted in rural Canada by Schramm et al. (1961) and by Williams et al. (1977) suggest that the youngest students (second and third graders) with access to television who live in areas where television is not yet universal have an advantage in vocabulary over children without access to television, but that this apparent advantage is lost within a couple of years (either of schooling or of introduction of television). In a developing country, El Salvador, three separate cohort studies by Hornik (1978), lasting 2 to 3 years, have shown that the introduction of television may actually have a negative effect on the growth of reading skills of older (junior high school) children. Students whose families did not own a television set at the outset of the study, but did own one at the end of the first year, showed less growth in reading ability than either students whose families owned a set all along or students whose families did not own a set at any time during the study. Hornik (1981) cautions us that one reason for the lack of definitive results in this important area of educational research is the failure of most researchers to do follow-up investigations after an initial survey or short-term study. His concern is also relevant to most studies of the effects of television on children's social behavior.

THE PROSOCIAL EFFECTS OF EDUCATIONAL AND COMMERCIAL TELEVISION PROGRAMS

Social learning theory has influenced recent research on the effects of prosocial content of television programs watched by children, that is, programs emphasizing the fostering of goodwill and helping and sharing, and programs aimed at counteracting negative sex and ethnic stereotypes. Most of these studies have been of a short-term nature. We know little about the effects of viewing prosocial programs at home, under natural conditions, for prolonged periods of time (Moore, 1977).

The majority of studies on the prosocial effects of television were conducted over a period of several weeks or months in day care centers, Head Start programs, nursery schools, kindergartens, and early elementary grades, and were monitored by research staff and alternate caregivers, such as day care providers and teachers. Behaviors studied were the children's interactions with their playmates and classmates before and after exposure to short viewing periods of television programs that model altruistic and cooperative behavior, behavior that was also encouraged by the adults present during the studies.

The most frequently viewed television series in these investigations was *Mister Rogers' Neighborhood*, a program that was specifically designed to teach children positive attitudes and behaviors toward their fellow human beings. The characters on this show are friendly, readily understand the feelings of others, resist temptations, obey rules, cope constructively with stress, and recognize the worth of each individual. The pace of the host of the show, Fred Rogers, is slow and reflective. He looks directly into the camera, and addresses each child as "my friend" (Stein and Friedrich, 1975).

About a dozen studies have used this program to test hypotheses about the ways in which children might learn prosocial behavior from television. One of the first studies (Friedrich and Stein, 1973) compared the effects of daily viewing of *Mister Rogers' Neighborhood,* aggressive cartoons, or neutral programs on the play behavior of nursery school children. Children who saw the prosocial television program increased in their task persistence as compared with the other two groups. Children from low socioeconomic level homes also displayed more cooperative and friendly behavior in free play. In other studies using the same television series, similar increases in prosocial behavior have been found in preschool–age and elementary school–age children, but changes toward an increase in positive behaviors were more pronounced for groups of children who received additional help in understanding the objectives of the television program and who rehearsed or modeled this behavior with the encouragement of adults and/or peers (Collins and Getz, 1976; Cosgrove and McIntyre, 1974; Friedrich and Stein, 1975; Friedrich-Cofer et al., 1979; Huston-Stein and Wright, 1979; Singer and Singer, 1976; Tannenbaum, 1977).

Although it would seem that the best source of information on the long-term effects of viewing prosocial behavior would be the study of children who are regular viewers of such a program at home, only three studies report home viewing data (Coates et al., 1976; Friedrich and Stein, 1973; Singer and Singer, 1981). The first two (which were short-term studies) do not suggest consistent or marked effects of home-viewing on school behavior. The Singer and Singer (1981) study, which was based on a year long analysis of television viewing at home and behavior at the nursery school, suggests that watching prosocial television programs correlated highly with cooperativeness with peers, low aggression, and higher imagination among 3- to 4-year-old middle-class nursery school children.

Although teaching prosocial behavior was only a secondary goal of the *Sesame Street* series, some segments emphasize cooperation and taking another person's view. A handful of studies in the U.S. and abroad have evaluated the impact of such prosocial messages on young children (Coates et al., 1976; Goldberg and Gorn, 1979; Leifer, 1975; Paulson, 1974; Palmer et al., 1976; Silverman and Sprafkin, 1980). Evaluations of these materials indicated that children do learn concepts like cooperation and often imitate the televised behavior if they are put in a situation like the one on television, but there is as yet little evidence of generalization. Paulson (1974) is one of the few investigators who exposed day care center children to viewing *Sesame Street* episodes for a whole year. The effect of the viewing on cooperation was assessed in six test situations which replicated problems requiring cooperation that had been shown on the program. A seventh situation was added to assess the generalization (of cooperation to new situations). The viewers in this study scored significantly higher than non-viewers on cooperation in the six test situations that resembled *Sesame Street* episodes, but they did not differ from non-viewers in the test situation that had not been modeled on *Sesame Street* nor in their free play behavior.

Television programs like *Sesame Street* do seem to influence children's attitudes toward minorities, however. In Canada, inserts were produced that portrayed friendly interactions between blacks and whites, Asians and Canadian Indians, and French and English speaking Canadian children. These segments increased the viewing children's willingness to play with children from other races, relative to children who did not view the segments (Goldberg and Gorn, 1979; Gorn et al., 1976). In the 1970s the *Big Blue Marble* series presented colorful vignettes of children around the world. This program, as well as *Vegetable Soup,* which presents a favorable picture of many ethnic groups, was found to make child viewers in elementary school in the U.S. to be more accepting of children of different races (Mays et al., 1975; Roberts et al., 1975).

Reports on the use of television to improve children's sex role attitudes are more mixed. The West German-produced segments of *Sesamstrasse* did not help to alter stereotypical ideas on the roles of males and females (Palmer et al., 1976). The American produced television series *Freestyle,* aimed at showing boys and girls in "non-traditional" roles, was shown to be successful in making grade school children more accepting of girls engaged in "masculine" jobs and boys engaged in traditionally female activities, such as caring for younger children (Johnston et al., 1980).

A few studies in the U.S., Australia, Canada, and Great Britain have also explored the prosocial effects of commercial television programs such as *Lassie* and *The Waltons,* which are watched by more children than the programs of the Public Broadcasting System (PBS) which airs *Sesame Street* and *Mister Rogers' Neighborhood* (Baran et al., 1979; Murray and Ahammer, 1977; Rushton and Owen, 1975; Sprafkin et al., 1975). These studies suggest that prosocial television can have the effect of facilitating sharing and helping behavior in children (in kindergarten and the elementary grades), but that the behavior of television models seems to have a less durable and weaker effect than that of live models (Rushton and Owen, 1975). The influence of prosocial television episodes seems limited to situations similar to those presented in the program, and tends to be ephemeral unless enhanced by examples and explanations of adults in the child's lives (parents, peers, teachers) who "practice what they preach" (Murry and Kippax, 1978).

THE EFFECT OF
TELEVISION VIOLENCE ON CHILDREN'S BEHAVIOR

It has been estimated that the average American child between the ages of 5 and 15 will witness on television the violent destruction of more than 13,400 fellow human beings (Chamberlin and Chambers, 1976). This tentative count does not include the cartoon characters that the child will see battered, smashed, or self-destruct since starting television viewing in infancy. Not surprisingly, one of the most extensively researched and hotly debated topics has been the effect of viewing such television violence on children's behavior.

The interested reader is referred to major review chapters in Comstock et al. (1978), Palmer and Dorr (1980), and Liebert et al. (1982) for an introduction to research on this explosive topic. Also available from the Superintendent of Documents, U.S. Government Printing Office, is a report entitled *Television and Behavior: Ten Years of Scientific Progress and Implications for the 80's* (Signorielli et al., 1982). Within the constraints of this chapter, I will only briefly summarize the current status of the television violence issue (since the mid-1970s) and examine a few longitudinal and cross-national studies that have added another perspective to the many short-term studies done in the U.S.

A pool of the findings of 67 major studies conducted over two decades (1956 to 1976) on the relationship between viewing television violence and aggressive behavior revealed a significant association in 77% of the studies involving more than 30,000 persons (Andison, 1977). This relationship was found across ages, methods of data collection, measures of aggressive behavior, time periods, and countries of investigation. There is no doubt that television violence has "a large effect on a small percentage of youngsters, and a small effect on a large percent . . ." (Liebert et al., 1982, p. 129).

The proposition that certain background factors "predispose" some children to react more strongly to television violence than their peers was first raised in the Surgeon General's Report on television and social behavior (1972) and has been addressed by Dorr and Kovaric (1980) in a chapter entitled "Some of the People Some of the Time—But Which People?" These researchers, after an exhaustive review of the available evidence of the past three decades, came up with four major conclusions:

> *First,* we conclude that television violence seems to be capable of affecting viewers of both sexes and varying ages, social classes, ethnicities, personality characteristics, and levels of aggressiveness. *Second,* we conclude that males and females are equally likely to be influenced by exposure, but that within each sex those who are more aggressive are more likely to be influenced. We will also advance the tentative conclusion that "middle aged" children, those between the ages of about 8 and 12, are somewhat more likely to be affected than are either younger or older youth. *Third,* we conclude that in actual behavior, boys are more likely to be aggressive than girls, and by definition, delinquents and others who are measured as more aggressive in their daily behavior are more aggressive than are obvious comparison groups. *Fourth,* we conclude that in terms of actual viewing of and preference for televised violence boys are likely to exceed girls, and members of the working class are more likely to exceed those of the middle class (pp. 193–194).

Among the most extensive data available on the long-term effects of television violence is a longitudinal study by Lefkowitz et al. (1977). These investigators were able to assess the relationship between watching television violence and aggressive behavior both at the beginning of the study (when the 875 children were 9 years old) and 10 years later when 460 of the original group were followed up at age 19. For the boys the relationship between viewing television violence in the third grade and aggression 10 years later was significant ($r = 31$), while the one between aggression in the third grade and violence viewing when they were 19 was not. The data from the girls did not reveal significant relationships between television violence and aggressive behavior at either ages 9 or 19.

As a follow-up report for the 10-year study, Eron and Huesman (1980) conducted a 3-year longitudinal study with first and third grade children. While the earlier study had shown a significant relationship between television violence viewing only in boys, the more recent data with younger children showed significant relationships between the viewing of television violence and aggressive behavior in girls as well. But the correlations between the two variables decreased with age for the girls and increased for the boys (see also Singer and Singer, 1981). Regardless of sex, there were higher correlations of a child's aggressiveness (based on peer ratings) with the child watching of male actors' violence than with the child's viewing of female actors' violence (Huesman et al., 1978).

Dorothy and Jerome Singer (1981) examined the issue of television violence at even younger ages. They completed a 1-year longitudinal study of the relationship between television viewing and aggressive behavior in 3- and 4-year-old preschool children. Television viewing habits of the children were determined on the basis of parents' diaries for three 2-week periods over a year. The children's aggressive behavior during free play periods in nursery school were observed and recorded three times throughout the year. Partialling out the influence of background factors (socioeconomic status, ethnicity, IQ, and sex) diminished only slightly the significant but small association between "action-adventure" television viewing and aggressive behavior in preschool. As in the Lefkowitz et al. (1977) study, Singers' (cross-lagged) correlations indicated that it was more likely that violence viewing led to aggressive behavior than that aggressive children preferred violent programs. The preschool children identified as the most aggressive in this study came from homes where the parents were not concerned about monitoring their children's television viewing habits and exerted no control over the television set. A unique cross-cultural longitudinal study of the impact of television violence on a previously unexposed community in the remote Canadian North was reported by Granzberg and Steinbring (1980). Three communities, two Manitoba Cree Indian and one Euro-Canadian, were involved. Data on three measures of aggression were obtained prior to and after introduction of television to one Cree community and subsequently compared to similar data from the unexposed Cree community and the Euro-Canadian community with 20 years of television exposure. When children were classified by amount of daily exposure to television violence, in the experimental community (into which television had been newly introduced) high exposed children increased in aggressive attitudes, in comparison with low exposed peers in the Cree and in the Euro-Canadian communities.

In a study of Finnish children in the first and third grades Eron and Huesman (1980) found a significant correlation for boys between television viewing and aggression when the television model was male, but not when she was female. Both Scandinavian and British studies (Brown and Linné, 1976; Greenberg, 1975) report correlations between television violence viewing and aggressive behavior in preschool and school-age children that are remarkably similar to those reported for American children. Heavy viewers of television violence among European children, as in the U.S., came from families where parents, especially mothers, did not restrict their children's television viewing.

In summary, the predictions of social learning theorists have been supported by a number of field studies (as well as naturalistic experiments) in all industrialized nations where there is ample access to television: Television arouses children, shapes their values, and increases the potential for imitation of aggressive and antisocial acts seen on the television screen. These effects, at any age, seem to be strongest for heavy television viewers with the fewest restrictions on their television viewing by their family. Lefkowitz and Huesman (1980) conclude:

> Regulation in some form is necessary, and at least one of three basic actions is ineluctable: (a) a systematic and methodical regulation by *parents* of children's exposure to television; (b) *self-regulation* with respect to the portrayal of violence by the television industry; or (c) *government regulation* of this feature of television programming (p. 177).

CHILDREN, PARENTS, AND TELEVISION COMMERCIALS

American children, ages 2 to 5, are exposed to about 22,000 commercials a year, and their older brothers and sisters, ages 6 to 11, to about 20,000 per year (Adler et al., 1980). The three commercial networks in the U.S., the American Broadcasting Company (ABC), the Columbia Broadcasting System (CBS), and the National Broadcasting Company (NBC), make their profits by selling air time to advertisers who want to sell their products. In the U.S., children's programs are, on a percentage basis, one of the most profitable segments of commercial television because production costs and risks are lower than for prime-time shows. The biggest spenders on commercials for children are the toy manufacturers and the cereal and the candy companies. Melody (1973), in his book *Children's Television: The Economics of Exploitation*, observes that television programs in the U.S. are a bait to lure the viewers into a position where they can be exposed to persuasive messages.

In other countries, there are numerous variations to running the television business (Murray, 1980; Murray and Kippax, 1979). For example, Canada, Japan, and Australia also rely on heavy use of advertising to generate revenues. In the Scandinavian countries (Denmark, Norway, Sweden) and in Israel, there is no television advertising at all, and other Western European countries, such as Austria, France, Italy, and West Germany, have little advertising since broadcasting in these nations (as in Eastern Europe) is government funded and controlled. In the most populous developing country, the People's Republic of China, all television stations are owned by the government, but limited advertising brings in some revenue.

In response to the avalanche of television advertising in the U.S., Action for Children's Television (ACT), a nationwide, non-profit consumer organization founded in Boston in 1968 by a group of mothers, has prodded the National Science Foundation into funding and reviewing research on the effects of television commercials on children (Liebert et al., 1982). Among comprehensive reviews of this topic is a book by Adler et al. (1980), *The Effects of Television Advertising on Children*, and a chapter with the same title by Atkin (1980), who has done much research in this field. Most of the research evidence that has accumulated so far deals with children's understanding of the selling intent of commercials, the effects on children's behavior of food and toy advertising, and the effects of such advertising on family relationships.

Research provides a consistent line of evidence that young children (below age 8) do not comprehend the selling intent of commercials. Children between 6 to 9 years seem to understand it a bit more than 4 or 5 year olds, but even most 7 year olds believe that television commercials tell the truth (Ward et al., 1977). As children get older, their trust in commercials declines, but even by age 10, most children accept technical claims of a medical or nutritional nature (Atkin, 1980). At each age, heavy viewers of commercials are more likely to believe ads than do light viewers.

Correlational studies in which the amount of exposure to television advertising has been related to children's attitudes and behaviors show consistently that frequent viewers more than infrequent viewers ask to go to advertised fast-food restaurants, report liking advertised food, request advertised cereal, and consume advertised cereals, candies, and snacks, believing them to be highly nutritious (Atkin, 1980). Heavy viewers of television advertising are also far more likely to request that parents buy advertised toys for them than light viewers. Among the message components of commercials, premium offers seem to maximize the effects of television advertising on young children.

One of the consequences of the persuasiveness of the "electronic babysitter" is that television commercials can lead to parent-child conflict and unhappiness in young children. Atkin (1980) reviews a number of studies that show that American parents reject approximately one-third to one-half of children's requests for television-advertised products. This leads to occasional mild parent-child conflict in about one out of every two families. Children who are heavy viewers of television advertising have considerably more conflict with their parents about this issue, regardless of their age.

Between one-third and one-half of the children report becoming unhappy, disappointed, or angry after denial of their requests for food and toy products advertised on television. The rate is highest among children who watch the most commercials. Some children become dissatisfied when they compare their own situation with the life-styles portrayed in commercials or when the actual products do not live up to the advertised image (Atkin, 1980).

Advertising may also teach or arouse children's aggression. A content analysis by Schuetz and Sprafkin (1979) shows that aggressive incidents, mostly involving nonhuman characters, occurred 114 times in the 242 commercials they studied, with three times as much aggression per minute of advertising as per minute of programming.

There has been an increasing interest in developing children's "critical viewing" skills to enable them to protect themselves from adverse television influences. Door et al. (1980) pioneered a curriculum to teach the following critical evaluation skills: 1) to decrease children's belief that television programs are real; 2) to increase children's tendencies to compare what they see on television with other sources of information; 3) to decrease television's credibility by teaching children about its economic and production aspects. These skills are taught in six 1-hour sessions to small groups of children in kindergarten and second/third grade. Singer et al. (1980) have also developed and taught an eight-lesson critical viewing curriculum for third to fifth grade children and their teachers. The effectiveness of such critical viewing programs in decreasing the negative and enhancing the positive effects of television for children remain to be determined.

TELEVISION AND THE TRAINING OF CAREGIVERS

During the course of their year-long longitudinal study of the effects of television on aggression and imagination of preschoolers, Jerome and Dorothy Singer (1981) developed one of the first training programs to assist in parent control of television viewing. Suggestions for such parent training have been made by the Parent Teacher Association (PTA). Three parent intervention groups—Television Training, Imaginative Training, and Cognitive Training—were designed to influence subsequent child behavior and television viewing patterns. Training manuals,[6] films, and videotapes were prepared to provide parents with exer-

---

[6] Copies of the three manuals and the supplementary materials are available from the Yale University Family Television Research and Consultation Center at the cost of reproduction and mailing.

cises either: 1) to stimulate preschool children's imagination; 2) to help develop cognitive skills (within a Piagetian framework); and/or 3) to deal with the implications of research concerning the effects of prosocial and violent television programs and commercials on children, with guidelines for television viewing. The three parent training groups met in three group meetings in the spring and in a review session in the fall. They also received periodically supplementary training material for use at home throughout the year.

The results of this intervention study showed some increase in the imaginative play of the children of mothers exposed to imaginative and cognitive training, but the results for the television control training group was disappointing. The middle-class parents who participated in this study were uncomfortable with controlling their child's television viewing. Even by age 3 and 4 the use of television as a companion and babysitter had become so much a part of their family life that direct efforts at change were not only ineffective, but were actively resisted. The Singers' (1981) data support the view that direct efforts at controlling and limiting of children's television viewing may not be as effective as teaching parents or other caregivers more active things to do with their children, such as games and exercises that foster imagination.

Television is now being used around the world to increase the skills of alternate caregivers for children. In the U.S., there are television training programs for Head Start teachers (Friedrich and Stein, 1975), family day care providers (Goldsmith, 1979; Wattenberg, 1977), and foster parents (Sands, 1982, personal communication). In Great Britain, Brian and Sonia Jackson have also demonstrated the successful use of television in reaching "childminders" with a thrice weekly series called *Other People's Children* (1979).

International and private agencies are assisting the developing countries to tap the vast reservoir of educational television to teach caregiving skills as well (Arnover, 1976). The Children's Television Workshop has prepared the *Latin American Health Minutes*, a series of 50 1-minute programs designed to be used as spot messages on television to promote improved health practices. They are being broadcast in Spanish and Portuguese throughout Latin America where about 50% of the people now have access to television. They deal with important issues in maternal and child care, for example, the nutritional value of breastfeeding and the importance of accident prevention (Palmer, 1979).

The United Nations Educational Scientific and Cultural Organization (UNESCO) has helped launch an experiment in television satellite communication in thousands of rural villages in India, the second most populous country on earth. Here educational television is broadcast in many languages (English, Hindi, Gujurati, Marathi, and Urdu) and seeks active participation from adults and children in a variety of programs which present music, drama, and dance, and offer training in literacy and handicrafts (UNESCO, 1979). In Africa, south of the Sahara, the United Nations Children's Fund (UNICEF) is assisting the national television studios in the production of health and educational programs for the benefit of young children and their caregivers (Gaudras, 1982). Television's positive potential is tapped around the world to the benefit of children and their caregivers, but these international efforts have yet to be evaluated systematically.

SUMMARY

Television has become the newest child care arrangement in human history. As it spreads throughout the world, it has become an "electronic babysitter," which is used by parents and alternate caregivers alike. Young children now spend more time watching television than with their parents, and television viewing in the U.S. consumes more of a child's time than any other activity besides sleep. Television, for better or worse, has the capacity to influence children's attitudes, behavior, and consumer habits. It has become a major socialization agent, which contends with the influence of adults (parents and teachers) as well as peers (siblings, playmates, and classmates) in affecting the development of young children. While much concern has been expressed about the negative effects of television violence and advertising, the positive role of television's educational and prosocial content is now being explored on a worldwide scale. This role can be enhanced by the encouragement of adults and peers, whether parents or alternate caregivers, and by (self-) regulation of the television industry. Urgently needed are investigations with a developmental perspective that monitor the process by which the family mediates the effects of television, and evaluation studies of programs which teach parents and alternate caregivers skills to enhance the positive effects of television and counteract its negative effects.

REFERENCES

Adler, R.P., Lesser, G.S., Krasny Meringoff, L., et al., 1980. The Effects of Television Advertising on Children: Review & Recommendations. Lexington Books, Lexington, MA.

Anderson, D.R., and Levin, S.F. 1976. Young children's attention to *Sesame Street.* Child Dev. 47:806–811.

Anderson, D.R., Alwitt, L.F., Lorch, E.P., and Levin, S.R. 1979. Watching children watch television. In: G. Hale and M. Lewis (eds.), Attention and the Development of Cognitive Skills. Plenum, New York.

Andison, F.S. 1977. TV violence and viewer aggression: A cumulation of study results: 1956–1976. Publ. Opin. Q. 41:314–331.

Arnover, R. (ed.). 1976. Educational Television: A Policy Critique and Guide for Developing Countries. Praeger, New York.

Atkin, C.K. 1980. Effects of television advertising on children. In: E. L. Palmer and A. Dorr (eds.), Children and the Faces of Television: Teaching, Violence, Selling, pp. 287–305. Academic Press, New York.

Ball, S., and Bogatz, G.A. 1972. Summative research on *Sesame Street:* Implications for the study of preschool children. In: A. D. Peck (ed.), Minnesota Symposium on Child Development, Vol. 6, pp. 3–17. University of Minnesota Press, Minneapolis.

Ball, S., and Bogatz, G. 1973. Reading and Television: An Evaluation of *The Electric Company.* Educational Testing Service, Princeton, NJ.

Baran, S.J., Chase, L.J., and Courtright, J.A. 1979. Television drama as facilitator of prosocial behavior: *The Waltons.* J. Broadcast. 23:277–287.

Blackwell, F. 1972. Reactions to *Sesame Street* in Great Britain. Independent Television Authority, London.

Brown, R., and Linné, O. 1976. The family as a mediator of television effects. In: R. Brown (ed.), Children and Television. Sage Publications, Beverly Hills, CA.

Chamberlin, L.L., and Chambers, N. 1976. How television is changing our children. Clearing House 50:53–57.

Children's Television Workshop: Research Bibliography: 1968–1979. CTW, Research Division, New York.

Children's Television Workshop: *The Electric Company:* Television and Reading: 1971–1980. A mid-experimental appraisal. CTW, New York.

Children's Television Workshop. 1980. International Research Notes. CTW, New York.

Coates, B., Pusser, H., and Goodman, I. 1976. The influence of *Sesame Street* and *Mister Rogers' Neighborhood* on children's social behavior in the preschool. Child Dev. 47: 138–144.

Collins, W.A., and Getz, S.K. 1976. Children's social responses following modeled reactions to provocation: Prosocial effects of a television drama. J. Personal. 44:488–500.

Comstock, G., Chaffee, S., Katzman, N., McCombs, M., and Roberts, D. 1978. Television and Human Behavior. Columbia University Press, New York.

Cook, T.D., Appleton, H., Conner, R.F., et al. 1975. *Sesame Street* Revisited. Russell Sage Foundation, New York.

Cook, T.D., and Conner, R.F. 1976. The educational impact. J. Commun. 26:155–164.

Cosgrove, M., and McIntyre, C. 1974. The influence of *Mister Rogers' Neighborhood* on nursery school children's prosocial behavior. Paper presented at the Biennial Southeastern Conference of the Society for Research in Child Development, March, Chapel Hill, NC.

Diaz-Guerrero, R., and Holtzman, W.H. 1974. Learning by televised *Plaza Sesamo* in Mexico. J. Educ. Psychol. 64:632–643.

Diaz-Guerrero, R., Reyes-Lagunes, I., Witzke, D.B., and Holtzman, W.H. 1976. *Plaza Sesamo* in Mexico: An evaluation. J. Commun. 26:145–154.

Dorr, A., and Kovaric, P. 1980. Some of the people some of the time—but which people? Televised violence and its effects. In: E.L. Palmer and A. Dorr (eds.), Children and the Faces of Television: Teaching, Violence, Selling, pp. 183–199. Academic Press, New York.

Dorr, A., Graves, S.B., and Phelps, E. 1980. Television literacy for young children. J. Commun. 30:71–83.

Eron, L.D., and Huesman, L.R. 1980. Adolescent aggression and television. Ann. N.Y. Acad. Sci. 347:319–331.

Essa, E.L. 1978. The impact of television on mother-child interaction and play. Diss. Abstr. Int. 393:5–8, 2568.

Fowles, B.R., and Voyat, G. 1974. Piaget meets Big Bird: Is TV a passive teacher? Urban Rev. 7:69–80.

Friedrich, L.K., and Stein, A.H. 1973. Aggressive and prosocial television programs and the natural behavior of preschool children. Monogr. Soc. Res. Child Dev. Serial No. 38.

Friedrich, L., and Stein, A. 1975. Prosocial television and young children: The effects of verbal labeling and role playing on learning and behavior. Child Dev. 46:27–38.

Friedrich-Cofer, L., Huston-Stein, A., McBride-Kipnis, D., Susman, E.J., and Clewett, A.S. 1979. Environmental enhancement of prosocial television content: Effects on interpersonal behavior, imagination, play and self-regulation in a natural setting. Dev. Psychol. 15:637–646.

Gadberry, S. 1974. Television as babysitter: A field comparison of preschoolers' behavior during playtime and during television viewing. Child Dev. 45:1132–1136.

Gaudras, A.M. 1982. The shocking image. Project Support Communication Newsletter, Information Division, UNICEF 6:2.

Gibbon, S.Y., Palmer, E.L., and Fowles, B.R. 1975. *Sesame Street, The Electric Company* and reading. In: J.B. Carroll and J.S. Chall (eds.), Toward a Literate Society: A Report from the National Academy of Education, pp. 215–247. McGraw-Hill, New York.

Goldberg, M.E., and Gorn, G.J. 1979. Television's impact on preferences for non-white playmates: Canadian *Sesame Street* inserts. J. Broadcast. 23:27–32.

Goldsen, R. 1976. Literacy without books: The case of *Sesame Street*. In: R. Arnover (ed.), Educational Television: A Policy Critique and Guide for Developing Countries, pp. 203–221. Praeger, New York.

Goldsmith, A.E. 1978. The relationship between television viewing behavior and social development in early childhood. Diss. Abstr. Int. 38(9A):5300.

Goldsmith, M.J. 1979. The Rhode Island Connection: A family day care program. Child. Today. July-August:2–5.

Gorn, G.J., Goldberg, M.E., and Kanungo, R.N. 1976. The role of educational television in changing intergroup attitudes of children. Child Dev. 47:277–280.

Goto, K. 1979. Children and the world of mass media. Courrier March:10–12.

Granzberg, G., and Steinberg, J. 1980. Television and the Canadian Indian. Technical Report, Department of Anthropology, University of Winnepeg, Manitoba.

Greenberg, B.S. 1975. British children and televised violence. Publ. Opin. Q. 38: 531–547.

Himmelweit, H., Oppenheim, A.N., and Vince, P. 1958. Television and the Child: An Empirical Study of the Effect of Television on Young Children. Oxford University Press, London.

Hornik, R. 1978. Television access and the slowing of cognitive growth. Am. Educ. Res. J. 15:1–15.

Hornik, R. 1981. Out of school television and schooling: Hypotheses and methods. Rev. Educ. Res. 51:193–214.

Huesman, L.R., Fisher, P.E., Eron, L.M., et al. 1978. Children's sex role preferences, sex of television model and imitation of aggressive behaviors. Paper presented at the International Society for Research on Aggression, Washington, DC.

Huston-Stein, A., and Wright, J.C. 1979. Children and television: Effects of the medium, its content and its form. J. Res. Dev. Educ. 13:20–31.

Jackson, B., and Jackson, S. 1979. Childminders: A Study in Action Research. Routledge and Kegan Paul, London.

Jaglom, L.M., and Gardner, H. 1981. The preschool television viewer as anthropologist. In: H. Kelley and H. Gardner (eds.), Viewing Children through Television, pp. 9–30. Jossey-Bass, San Francisco.

Johnson, N. 1967. How To Talk Back to Your TV Set. Little, Brown, Boston.

Johnston, J., Ettema, J., and Davidson, T. 1980. An Evaluation of *Freestyle:* A Television Series Designed to Reduce Sex Role Stereotypes. Institute for Social Research, Ann Arbor, MI.

Kob, J. 1975. Begleituntersuchung zur Fernsehserie *Sesamstrasse*. University of Hamburg, Hans Bredow Institut, Hamburg.

Lam, M.C. 1982. Changing Patterns of Child-rearing: A Study of Low-income Families in Hong Kong. Social Work Department of the Chinese University, Hong Kong.

Lasker, H. 1973. *Sesame Street* among the mountains of Jamaica. Harvard Grad. School Educ. Bull. 17:18–22.

Lasker, H., and Casseras, B. 1971. Report on the impact of *Sesame Street* in Curaco, Netherland Antilles, January, Curaco.

Lefkowitz, M.M., and Huesman, L.R. 1980. Concomitants of television violence viewing in children. In: E.L. Palmer and A. Dorr (eds.), Children and the Faces of Television: Teaching, Violence, Selling, pp. 163–181. Academic Press, New York.

Lefkowitz, M.M., Eron, L.O., Walder, L.O., and Huesman, R. 1977. Growing Up To Be Violent: A Longitudinal Study of the Development of Aggression. Pergamon Press, New York.

Leifer, A.D. 1975. Research on the socialization influence of television in the United States. In: Television and Socialization Processes in the Family. A documentation of the Prix Jeunesse Seminar. Internationale Zeitschrift fur Medienpsychologie und Medienpraxis, 9 (Special English Edition).

Lemercier, K.I., and Teasdale, G.R. 1973. *Sesame Street:* Some effects of television on the cognitive skills of young children from lower SES backgrounds. Aust. Psychol. 8: 47–51.

Lesser, G.S. 1974. Children and Television: Lessons from *Sesame Street.* Random House, New York.

Lesser, G.S. 1980. The Rationale for a TV Series on Science and Technology, pp. 1–2. CTW International Research Notes, CTW, New York.

Liebert, R.M., Sprafkin, J.N., and Davidson, E.S. 1982. The Early Window: Effects of Television on Children and Youth, 2nd Ed. Pergamon Press, New York.

Lyle, J., and Hoffman, H.R. 1972. Explorations in patterns of television viewing by preschool children. In: E.A. Rubinstein, G.A. Comstock, and J.A. Murray (eds.), Television and School Behavior, pp. 257–271, Vol. IV: Television in Day to Day Life: Patterns of Use. U.S. Government Printing Office, Washington, DC.

Mays, L., Henderson, E.H., Seidman, S.K., and Steiner, V.S. 1975. On meeting real people: An evaluation report on *Vegetable Soup.* New York State Education Department, Albany. (ERIC Documentation Reproduction Service N. ED 123 319.) ORI, Inc., Information Systems Division, Bethesda, MD.

McCall, R.B., Parke, R.D., and Kavanaugh, R.D. 1977. Imitation of life and televised models by children one to three years of age. Monogr. Soc. Res. Child Dev. 42(5, Serial No. 173).

Medrich, E.A., Roizen, J., Rubin, V., and Buckley, S. 1982. The Serious Business of Growing Up: A Study of Children's Lives Outside School. University of California Press, Berkeley.

Melody, W. 1973. Children's Television: The Economics of Exploitation. Yale University Press, New Haven, CT.

Moore, S. 1977. The effects of television on the prosocial behavior of young children. Young Child. 32:60–65.

Murray, J.P. 1980. Television and Youth: 25 Years of Research and Controversy. Boys Town Center for the Study of Youth Development, Boys Town, NE.

Murray, J.P., and Ahammer, I.M. 1977. Kindness in kindergarten: A multi-dimensional program for facilitating altruism. Paper presented at the Biennial Meeting of the Society for Research in Child Development, March, New Orleans.

Murray, J.P., and Kippax, S. 1978. Children's social behavior in three towns with differing television experience. J. Commun. 28:19–29.

Murray, J.P., and Kippax, S. 1979. From the early window to the late night show: International trends in the study of television's impact on children and adults. In: L.

Berkowitz (ed.), Advances in Experimental Social Psychology. Academic Press, New York.

Noble, G. 1975. Children in Front of the Small Screen. Sage Publications, Beverly Hills, CA.

Palmer, E.L. 1979. Research for the Latin American Health Minutes, Vol. 2, pp. 7–9. CTW International Research Notes, CTW, New York.

Palmer, E.L., Chen, M., and Lesser, G.S. 1976. *Sesame Street:* Patterns of international adaptation. J. Commun. 26:109–123.

Palmer, E.L., and Dorr, A. (eds.). 1980. Children and the Faces of Television: Teaching, Violence, Selling. Academic Press, New York.

Paulson, F.L. 1974. Teaching cooperation on television: An evaluation of *Sesame Street* social goal programs. AV Commun. Rev. 22:229–246.

Ridha, M.J. 1979. Project Profile: *Iftah Ya Simsim* for the Arab World, Vol. I; pp. 13–17. CTW International Research Notes, CTW, New York.

Roberts, D.F., Harold, C., Hornby, M., et al. 1975. *Earth is a Big Blue Marble:* A report of the impact of a children's television series on children's opinions. Unpublished manuscript, Stanford University, Stanford, CA.

Robinson, J. 1972. Television's impact on everyday life: Some cross-national evidence. In: E.A. Rubinstein, G.A. Comstock, and J.P. Murray (eds.), Television and Social Behavior, pp. 410–431, Vol. IV. Television in Day-to-Day Life: Patterns of Use. U.S. Government Printing Office, Washington, DC.

Robinson, J. 1977. How Americans Use Time. Praeger, New York.

Rushton, P., and Owen, D. 1975. Immediate and delayed effects of TV modeling and preaching on children's generosity. Br. J. Social Clin. Psychol. 14:309–310.

Salas de Bodini, S. 1975. Análisis descriptivo de algunas funciones básicas del pre-escolar a traves de un programa de television. Unpublished thesis, Catholic University of Chile.

Salomon, G. 1976. Cognitive skill learning across cultures. J. Commun. 26:138–144.

Salomon, G. 1977. Effects of encouraging Israeli mothers to co-observe *Sesame Street* with their five year olds. Child Dev. 48:1146–1151.

Scherer, M. 1982. The loneliness of the latchkey child. Instructor 1:39–41.

Schramm, W., Lyle, J., and Parker, E. 1961. Television in the lives of our children. Stanford University Press, Stanford, CA.

Schuetz, S., and Sprafkin, J.N. 1979. Portrayal of prosocial and aggressive behavior in children's commercials. J. Broadcast. 23:33–40.

Signorelli, N., Gross, L., and Morgan, M. 1982. Violence in television programs: Ten years later. In: Television and Behavior: Ten Years of Scientific Progress and Implications for the 80's. U.S. Government Printing Office, Washington, DC.

Silverman, L.T., and Sprafkin, J.N. 1980. The effects of *Sesame Street*'s prosocial spots on cooperative play between young children. J. Broadcast. 24:125–147.

Singer, J.L., and Singer, D.G. 1976. Can TV stimulate imaginative play? J. Commun. 26:74–80.

Singer, J.L., and Singer, D.G. 1981. Television, imagination and aggression: A study of preschoolers. Earlbaum, Hillsdale, NJ.

Singer, D.G., Zuckerman, D.M., and Singer, J.L. 1980. Helping elementary school children learn about TV. J. Commun. 30:84–93.

Slaby, R.G., and Hollenbeck, A.R. 1977. Television influences on visual and vocal behavior of infants. Unpublished paper, National Institute of Mental Health, Bethesda, MD.

Sprafkin, J., Liebert, R., and Poulos, R.W. 1975. Effects of a prosocial televised example on children's helping. J. Exp. Child Psychol. 20:119–126.

Stein, A., and Friedrich, L. 1975. Impact of television on children and youth. In: E.M.

Hetherington (ed.), Review of Child Development Research, pp. 183–256, Vol. V. University of Chicago Press, Chicago.

Surgeon General's Scientific Advisory Committee on Television and Social Behavior. 1972. Television and Growing Up: The Impact of Televised Violence. Report to the Surgeon General, Public Health Service. U.S. Government Printing Office, Washington, DC.

Tannenbaum, B. 1977. The effects of peer pressure and prosocial/antisocial television content on children's social behavior. Diss. Abstr. Int. 37:94, 5243.

UNESCO, 1979. Special issue: Children and the world of mass media. Courrier, March.

Van Lil, J. 1976. Audience Size and Evaluation of *Sesamstraat* and other Children's Programs. Netherlands Broadcasting Foundation, Hilversum.

Ward, S., Wackman, D., and Wartella, E. 1977. How Children Learn To Buy: The Development of Consumer Information Processing Skills. Sage Publications, Beverly Hills, CA.

Watkins, B.A., Huston-Stein, A., and Wright, J.C. 1980. Effects of planned television programming. In: E.L. Palmer and A. Dorr (eds.), Children and the Faces of Television: Teaching, Violence, Selling, pp. 49–69. Academic Press, New York.

Wattenberg, E. 1977. Characteristics of family day care providers: Implications for training. Child Welf. 56:211–229.

Williams, T., et al. 1977. The impact of television: A natural experiment involving three communities. Symposium presented at the meeting of the Canadian Psychological Association, June, Vancouver, BC.

Winn, M. 1978. The Plug-In-Drug. Bantam Books, New York.

Yamamoto, T. 1976. The Japanese experience. J. Commun. 26:136–137.

CHAPTER 10

Alternate Caregivers for Children

A Perspective

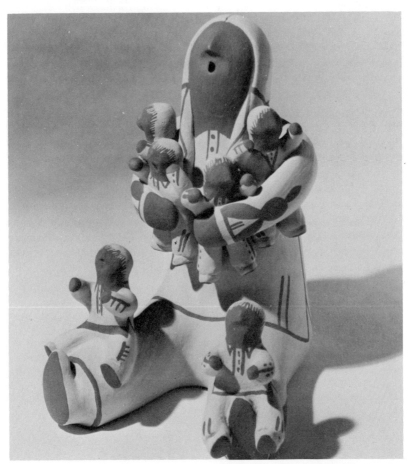

*"Whether any adult will become the
psychological parent of any child
is based on day-to-day interaction,
companionship and shared experience. . ."*

J. Goldstein, A. Freud, and A. J. Solnit
Beyond the Best Interest of the Child

On a typical workday in the U.S. most children spend a sizeable amount of their waking hours being cared for by someone other than their biological parents. This experience they share with most children in the world. The individuals who provide affection, instruction, and nurturance in the home when parents are not available or occupied with work may be older brothers and sisters, grandparents, aunts, neighbors, nannies, or domestic help. In the case of the latchkey children, the television set may become an "electronic babysitter." But these alternate caregivers have remained nearly invisible to people who do research, write about and make social policy for children and their families.

Their attention, instead, has focused mostly on the exceptions rather than the rule: On the decreasing number of children who are reared exclusively by their parents, and on the minority who are in center based care, whether in day care centers, nursery schools, or residential institutions. Thus, when it comes to child care arrangements, "we seem to know most about that which we have the least of, and, conversely, least about what we have the most of" (Belsky, 1980, p. 84).

This book attempts to close some of the gaps in our awareness of the "invisible" caregivers—the kith, kin, and hired hands—and their influence on the lives of children. In this final chapter we discuss some of the implications of what we have learned about such alternate caregivers for the parents, for social policy, and for social action on behalf of children and their families. We also suggest some research priorities that need to be addressed if we want to have a more solid base of knowledge in the future about the long-term effects of shared child care on children, their parents, and the society in which they live.

SHARED CHILD CARE: THE EVIDENCE SO FAR

We have examined, in a comparative fashion, the role of alternate caregivers in our evolutionary past, in history, and on the contemporary scene both in the industrialized and in the developing world. We have noted that both demographic and economic factors put constraints on the availability of alternate caregivers and account for differences in the choice of alternate child care arrangements between parents who live in relative affluence and parents who live in relative poverty.

Worldwide there seems to be a preference for "in-home" care by parents who share the rearing of their offspring with others, and a preference for close (maternal) relatives and neighbors over strangers. Only the relatively affluent can afford to hire paid help, and such help usually comes from social strata below that of the mother, if she is in control of that choice (as is true for our primate "cousins"). The exceptions are foster care where an agency makes the choice for the parents, and subsidized center care for mothers who receive government aid, for example, Aid to Families for Dependent Children (AFDC).

Under demographic conditions of relatively high fertility and mortality, such alternate caregivers are mostly young (pre-adolescent or adolescent) females who have not yet had children of their own and learn parenting skills by caring for other people's children. In societies with low fertility and mortality, there is a larger reservoir of "experienced" alternate caregivers who are middle-aged and older, and in the post-reproductive stage of life. They include grandmothers, aunts, and other kin and neighbors whose own children have grown up, leaving their families in the "empty nest" stage.

A cross-cultural perspective reveals three different types of shared child care being practiced in contemporary societies (Rutter, 1972): 1) care in which the mother is the primary caregiver, but assisted by one or a few subsidiary caregivers; 2) care that is shared fairly equally among a few stable persons; and 3) care by a large number of persons that tends to be discontinuous. The first and second form of shared child care has been predominant in human history (and our evolutionary past) and is prevalent in the world today, both in developing and in industrialized countries.

The empirical data that we have reviewed suggest that in the context of these two types of care infants and young children are able to form a moderate number of secure, affectionate relationships with persons other than their biological parents, be they older siblings, grandparents, relatives, family day care providers, nannies, or nanny surrogates (Smith, 1980). In such a stable and continuous relationship, alternate caregivers can have a positive effect on a growing child's trust, independence, and social and cognitive development, and they can foster resilience in coping with stressful life events. Such stable alternate caregivers have proved to be important sources of support for children with special needs, that is, the emotionally, physically, and mentally handicapped; children of teenage parents and single mothers; and children who suffer from a prolonged and traumatic disruption of their family unit because of divorce, parental illness, or child abuse.

The third form of shared child care, consisting of discontinuous relationships with a large number of caregivers (who have little or no control over the context of care) is more recent in human history and found mostly in industrialized societies, for example, in repeated foster care placements or in rapid turnover of "childminders." The available evidence suggests that this form of care tends to be associated with more negative consequences for children's development, making it difficult for them to develop a secure sense of belonging and trust (Rutter, 1981; Smith, 1980).

CHILD CARE PACKAGES

In many situations, both in the U.S. and abroad, parents use two or more alternate caregivers for their children, and "mix" different child care packages for children at different ages. Among intact families of working parents, such arrangements may involve care by each spouse in turn while the other works, with assistance from relatives and neighbors, informal child care arrangements with friends, hired babysitters, family day care, nursery school, and after-school care (Rapaport and Rapaport, 1978).

Kamerman (1980), in her study of working mothers with young children who came from lower-class, working-class, and professional backgrounds, found that for the majority of these women (especially single mothers) child care involved considerable planning and organization, as well as management and transportation problems. Examples of the variety (and ingenuity) of child care arrangements found in her survey (for 327 children below age 10) were: 1) for *infants* (below age 1)—father's care and neighbor's care, father's care and family day care, in home care by "au pair girl"; 2) for *toddlers* (ages 1 to 3)—in-home care by grandmother and care in aunt's home, care by a relative and family day care provider supplemented by a teenage babysitter; 3) for *preschoolers* (ages 3 to 5)—care by neighbor and nursery school attendance; in-home care by grandparent and care in relative's home and nursery school attendance; in-home care by "au pair girl" and nursery school attendance and back-up care and transportation by a neighbor; 4) for *kindergarten-age child* (age 5)—care by a neighbor and by two friends of the mother, as well as attendance at kindergarten.

More than half of the children in this study experienced at least two different types of alternate care while their mothers worked, and close to one-fifth were cared for by three to four different caregivers. While preschool-age children (3, 4, and 5) were particularly likely to experience multiple forms of child care, the toddlers and infants (below 3) were exposed to the greatest diversity of alternate care. For children under age 3, professional two-parent families were likely to use paid in-home child care by a nanny, "au pair girl," or "domestic." Working-class two-parent families were more likely to share child care between parents who worked different shifts, and used some form of relative care, either in their own homes or in homes of relatives, or family day care. Single parents were most likely to use a day care center because many were eligible for government subsidized care, which was more available in centers.

We have no comparable data on after-school care arrangements for older children (ages 6 to 12), but we can surmise from the reports of the National Day Care Home Study (U.S. Department of Health and Human Services, 1981), from a study of out-of-school activities of preadolescents by Medrich et al. (1982), and from reports on latchkey children (Scherer, 1982) that this involves a combination of "family day care" by relatives or neighbors, programs provided by Boys and Girls Clubs and the YMCA and YWCA, or return home to watch television alone or with siblings until the parent(s) returns from work. Difficult as the arrangements for alternate child care is for working parents of young children, the problem changes but does not diminish as their children reach school age (Children's Defense Fund, 1982a; Medrich et al., 1982).

The few family impact studies that have been conducted so far (for example, Rapaport and Rapaport, 1978) suggest that parents who use in-home care arrangements are saving money and are able to entrust their children to familiar persons rather than strangers. Work satisfaction in women has been found to relate positively to satisfaction with substitute child care, and so has the perceived quality of parent-child relationships (Peters and Belsky, 1982). But if relatives and friends are involved as alternate caregivers, these arrangements can be vulnerable to breakdown due to illness or other emergencies. In families where each spouse takes turn caring for the children while the other works, parents tend to be fatigued and have little time together if no dependable alternate child caregiver is available in or near the home (Giele, 1979). The search for satisfying child care arrangements tends to be the central problem for all working parents, but especially for working mothers who are single heads of household (Kamerman, 1980).

IMPLICATIONS FOR SOCIAL POLICY

"Family policy may be defined as what the state does, by action or inaction, to affect people in their roles as family members, or to influence the future of families as an institution" (Kamerman and Kahn, 1978, p. 495). In contrast to Marxist and socialist countries, such as Cuba, Israel, the People's Republic of China, the U.S.S.R., and many East and West-European countries, the U.S. does not have a comprehensive national policy that focuses on children and their families. In the pluralistic context of the U.S., social policies and social action programs for children and their caregivers emerge out of the advocacy and power play of several conflicting interest groups, that is, federal, state, and local governments, taxpayers, lawmakers, and professional and parent organizations. A pessimist might deplore the lack of efficiency in this process; an optimist would point to the greater room it leaves for variability and flexibility under conditions of rapid social change (Werner, 1979).

The closest "consensus" that has been reached so far on the national level in the U.S. about child care can be found in the recommendations by the 1980 White House Conference on Families, participated in by well over 100,000 Americans from all walks of life and all states of the Union. Three of the 60 recommendations (which were supported by the overwhelming majority of the delegates) are most relevant to our discussion:

> 43. That federal, state and local government and private industry redirect and expand current funding for quality child care to provide family support and preventive services for all families who require these services including, but not limited to, child care services that would prevent the removal of children from their own homes and into institutions and foster care settings.
> 44. In order to assure that child care programs involve families and reflect their diverse values and choices for their children, it should be the policy of government at all levels to promote the development of alternative forms of quality care, both center and home based. Families must be central to any child care program for ideal impact on children's development.
> 45. To ensure the safety, health and developmental potential of children, quality licensing standards for all child care programs should be required on the local, state, and federal levels and these standards should require that child care personnel be adequately trained and receive wages which fit the level of qualifications and competencies required (Dempsey, 1981, p. 150).

These are only general recommendations that have not generated much substantive action so far. But if it so chooses, government can use a number of direct and indirect policy measures to enhance the quality of home-based child care and to support the role of alternate caregivers (Kamerman and Kahn, 1978; Ricciuti, 1976). They include income transfer (supplementation or substitution), tax allowances and tax credit, provisions for direct child care services, regulation and licensing, training programs for caregivers, and—last but not least—the reform of family law. Using a combination of these measures, government can provide the means, the skills, and the rights for quality child care, and eliminate barriers that stand in the way of support of alternate caregivers for children.

At present, the federal government makes the largest impact on child care through income transfer programs and tax credits: The greatest number of children are affected by the AFDC program. Up to $160 dollars per child per month for child care services paid by the parent(s) are disallowed when the "means tested" AFDC benefits are calculated (which vary from state to state). Most of these families use in-home care provided by relatives, friends, or neighbors.

The child care tax credit allows employed parents with children under age 15 a tax credit for a portion of work-related child care. The percentage of credit depends upon income, and ranges from 30% of expenses for incomes under $10,000 to 20% for incomes of $28,000 and up. Since 1978, tax credit is allowed for child care expenses paid to relatives who are not dependents, for example, grandparents.

The 1980 Adoption Assistance and Child Welfare Act provides for reimbursement for foster care expenses to relatives and for subsidized adoption of "hard to place" foster children by foster parents (including relatives) with the support of the government. The federal and state governments fund training programs for foster parents and, through ACTION (a volunteer service agency), training and a small stipend to elderly low-income foster grandparents as well. State and federal government agencies also establish regulatory standards for foster parent homes and licensing standards for family day care providers.[7]

Most important, recent family law reforms in various states have extended the rights of relatives and foster parents who provide care for children. They include grandparents and great-grandparent visitation rights to their (great) grandchildren in case of divorce, and the rights of foster parents to pre-placement hearings and to a preferred status for permanent placement of a foster child in their family, if parents relinquish the child.

However, in contrast to many European countries, the U.S. does not have a deliberately created, uniform child care benefit service "package." Public response and the marketplace have instead created one set of programs supporting child care services for the poor, and a different package for others that includes market-based family day care and tax credits (Kamerman and Kahn, 1981).

Many European countries (for example, France, East Germany, West Germany, Hungary, and Sweden) have additional components in their child care benefit package and extend them to all families, regardless of income. They include child care or family allowances, special allowances for single mothers for supplementary child care, paid maternity or parental leave, specified numbers of days of paid sick leave so that parents can take care of ill children, supplemental after-school care, flextime (flexible work schedules) for both working parents, and a shorter workday. The governments of these countries have provided such services because their citizens were willing to pay higher taxes than people in the U.S., and their social policies have been predicated on the assumption of a steady rate of growth in the gross national product. Whether these assumptions will still prove valid for the remainder of the century is anybody's guess.

In summary, an exception among the industrialized countries of the world, the U.S. does not have an explicit policy for children and families.

---

[7] A complete list of federal programs supporting child care can be found in Appendix C of *The Child Care Handbook*, published by the Children's Defense Fund (1982a).

However, the continuing entry of women with young children into the labor force, as well as the rise in "non-traditional" family forms, especially single-parent households, will necessitate a public as well as a diversity of private responses to the need for alternate forms of child care. Certainly the demand for "quality care" will increase as the members of the "baby boom" generation (born between 1946 and 1964) reach the peak of their childbearing, child-rearing, and employment responsibilities in the 1980s and 1990s—even if economic constraints persist (Kamerman and Kahn, 1981). The questions raised in response to this demand by policy analysts have been succinctly stated by Dempsey (1981): "How much can we afford, irrespective of desires and even needs?" "How will priorities be set?" and "How will family well-being be considered in the priority setting process?"[8]

THE ROLE OF ADVOCACY AND PUBLIC INTEREST GROUPS

The setting of priorities can be influenced by a number of advocacy and public interest groups that "speak out" on behalf of children and their caregivers. One of the most articulate and effective is the Children's Defense Fund (CDF), a private national organization, with headquarters in Washington, DC, which is supported by individual donations, as well as corporate and foundation grants.

The objective of CDF's work is to ensure that the needs of children and their families are placed "higher on the nation's public policy agenda" (CDF, 1982a). It seeks to accomplish its goal through research, education, monitoring of federal and state policies and practices, and through litigation. Its staff of professionals includes economists, policy analysts, and lawyers, as well as child care, child welfare, education, health, and mental health professionals. Since 1979 CDF has published a monthly newsletter on its activities (*CDF Reports*) and a number of publications on special issues in its four program areas (Child Care and Family Support Services, Child Health and Mental Health, Child Welfare, and Education). Two of the 1982 publications, *The Child Care Handbook: Needs, Programs and Possibilities* (1982a) and *Employed Parents and their Children: A Data Book* (1982b), provide a wealth of information for the interested reader on issues of work-family linkage, and on high-quality child care programs that include home-based care for sick children, family day care networks, and after-school care programs in neighborhoods in different regions

---

[8] Since the 1950–1965 period, the increase in public welfare programs has exceeded the rate of growth of the gross national product in the U.S., and this has accelerated markedly in the 1965–1975 period. Not the children's, but the elderly's share of the federal budget will rise through the rest of this century, reaching 32% in the year 2000 from existing programs, 42% in 2015, and soar to 63% by 2025, without any new programs (Harris, cited in Dempsy, 1981, p. 138).

of the country. Through the Children's Network, CDF also provides information and support to local organizations and community leaders across the nation.

There are many other public interest groups in the U.S. concerned with the quality of home-based child care by kith, kin, and family day care providers. They include the Child Welfare League, grandparents' rights organizations, state and national foster parent organizations, and Action for Children's Television, the nationwide, non-profit consumer organization (founded by a group of mothers) which is concerned with improving the quality of the "electronic babysitter." All are attempting to affect policy through advocacy, testimony at congressional committees or in state legislatures, petitions to government regulatory agencies, and litigation. With tight budgetary constraints on programs for children and their families, coalitions between these sometimes competing public interest groups may become more prevalent in the future. Judging from their past and present record, the advocates who seem to be the most effective, such as the CDF and the lobbying activities of organized labor, have joined public interest and self-interest as driving forces (Steiner, 1976).

On the international scene, a number of voluntary organizations, for example, the University of London based Child-to-Child programme and the American Friends Service Committee (AFSC) have begun to focus their attention on the care of children by older siblings, relatives, and neighbors, and have provided educational material and training for them. They are being joined by United Nations agencies, such as the ILO, UNICEF, and UNESCO, whose concerns are the child care problems of working mothers of young children. It remains to be seen whether the support of naturally occurring alternate child care arrangements by relatives and neighbors will increase with the help of such organizations. In the past they have tended to export Western concepts of day care and nursery schools to the countries of the developing world—facilities that are too often affordable only to the affluent and well educated (Werner, 1979).

NEEDED RESEARCH

Most research on the roles and effects of alternate caregivers in the lives of children and their families has been conducted within the isolation of narrow disciplinary boundaries, whether in anthropology, child development, economics, family history, law, psychology, psychiatry, sociology, or social welfare. Consequently, many of the findings are still fragmented and scattered in a variety of publications that are often inaccessible to those to whom they should matter most—parents, policy makers, and concerned citizens.

Conspicuously absent in most research on supplementary and surrogate parenting is a conceptual framework that would bring order into the accumulated empirical data and suggest directions for future research. Yet there are a number of theoretical models that can be applied to the study of alternate caregivers, ranging all the way from the evolutionary perspective of the sociobiologists to social learning theory to Whitings' psychocultural model, which stresses the importance of the (economic, legal, and political) maintenance system in shaping the behavior of children, parents, and alternate caregivers.

Another useful model that uses a "systems" approach is Bronfenbrenner's (1979) conception of the ecology of human development. He views the development of the individual child within the context of a series of concentric circles, each embedded within the next. The *microsystem* encompasses "the complex of relations between the developing person and environment in an immediate setting containing that person." Most research on alternate caregivers so far has focused on such microsystems, whether on day care centers (Belsky, 1980) or, in the case of home-based care, on sibling dyads, grandparent-grandchild relations, and family day care or the foster family home. With few exceptions, research within such microsystems has also been of a short-term nature.

The *mesosystem,* according to Bronfenbrenner (1979), "comprises the interrelations among major settings containing the developing person at a particular point in his or her life." In spite of the fact that today most children are exposed to child care "packages," few studies of supplementary parenting have examined the impact of such a mix of care environments on each other, for example, of sib caregiving on parental caregiving, of the grandparent's surrogate parent role on both mother and child, and of the impact of family day care providers on parents, children, and relatives who may extend in-home care as well.

Even rarer are studies that examine the *exosystem,* that is, the impact of "other social structures—both formal and informal—that do not themselves contain the developing person, but impinge upon or encompass the immediate setting in which that person is found and therefore influence, delimit or even determine what goes on there" (Bronfenbrenner, 1979). The workplace and work schedules of the parents, the transportation system to and from home to work and alternate child care setting, the mass media, and agents of government who deal with alternate child care providers (for example, child welfare workers and providers of training programs for family day care, foster parents, and foster grandparents) would be part of that exosystem. With few exceptions, among the surveys done by the CDF, we have no systematic research on the impact of work, neighborhood, and mass media on the quality of alternate care extended to children in the home.

Finally, the *macrosystem* "refers to the overarching institutional patterns of culture or subculture, such as economic, social, educational, legal and political systems, of which micro- , meso- , and exosystems are the concrete manifestations" (Bronfenbrenner, 1979). Such a macrosystem may take explicit form in written laws and regulations or in a less formal ideology. In spite of its special importance in determining how families are treated in such a system and what priorities are accorded to their needs, we have very few studies so far that examine the impact of the macrosystem on alternate caregivers and on children and their parents. With the exception of the research of a few persons interested in family and child policy (Giele, 1979; Kamerman, 1980; Kamerman and Kahn, 1978, 1981) and publications by the CDF (1982a, 1982b), we know little about the impact of the macrosystem on alternate child care. Yet recent developments in family law and state and federal legislation, including changes in tax law and income transfer programs, are affecting the options for alternate child care to an unprecedented degree.

But there are also some important biological variables that moderate the impact of alternate care provided within the larger social context. They include the age at which the child is placed in alternate care and the temperamental characteristics and sex of the child. A number of studies on the effects of non-maternal care (reviewed by Etaugh, 1980) have shown consistently that the behavior and development of boys seems to be more significantly affected by variations in caregiving environments than that of girls. Most of these studies have been based on short-term investigations. What we need in the future are investigations of the long-term impact of alternate care on both sexes, an issue that becomes especially important in the wake of one of the most important changes in the macrosystem, that is, the rapidly changing sex roles in the contemporary Western world. Greater social equality between the sexes has led to increased male investment in parenting, but it may also lead to greater social inequality among women, that is, between the (more affluent) "nanny takers," who can afford to hire surrogate mothers for pay, and the (poorly paid) "nanny givers," who provide such care for other people's children.

THE SPECIAL CASE OF LATCHKEY CHILDREN

Most research on alternate child care arrangements in the home has focused on the care of young children, below the age of 6 years. However, the growing number of school-age children who need some form of care before and after-school hours is becoming a national and international concern as well. It is estimated that in the U.S., some 15% of all children between the ages of 6 and 13 years are "latchkey" children who return to empty homes after school and have no one to care for them but themselves or another sibling. The label and the situation date back to the beginning of the 19th century and the onset of the industrial revolution, when children left on their own wore their house keys around their neck. What is new at the end of the 20th century is the astonishing number of children involved: a conservative estimate of some 2 million in the U.S. alone today, with some 4 million projected in the next decade.

In spite of the numbers of children involved and the attention given to them in the news media, there has been very little research so far on the way latchkey children cope with their relative isolation. In one of the rare studies comparing such children with parent-watched peers in the Washington, DC, area, educators Lynette and Thomas J. Long found loneliness and concern over safety to be among major characteristics of latchkey children (cited in Scherer, 1982). The latchkey children they studied neither did more chores nor watched more television than their peers for whom after-school care was available; but they took more responsibility for the care of younger brothers and sisters. On occasion, this led to sibling abuse—a response similar to that of isolated adults who are alone with small children all day.

In response to the needs of latchkey children, a number of after-school programs are being developed by community agencies with the help of senior citizens and college student volunteers, as well as by Boys and Girls Clubs, foremost the YMCA and the YWCA. Model YMCA Child Care programs are now being pilot tested in a number of metropolitan areas of the U.S. and Canada. Among them are Boston, Chicago, Houston, Los Angeles, Miami, Minneapolis, New York, Oakland (California), Pittsburgh, and Toronto. The *Child Care Handbook* (1982), published by the CDF in Washington, DC, the Wellsley College Center for Research on Women in Wellsley, Maine, and the "YMCA of the USA" Program Resource Office in Rosemont, Illinois, all provide information on how to start such programs. Clearly this is an area that deserves more research and public attention.

LOOKING AHEAD

In the future, the range of child care alternatives available to families is likely to increase. Although the dichotomy between child care services utilized by the poor and the more affluent will continue, there will be an increasing need for child care that ensures flexible hours and includes after-school care, night care, and weekend care for families at all socioeconomic levels (Peters and Belsky, 1982).

The percentage of children in center care will slowly rise, but the overwhelming majority of parents will continue to prefer care for their children in their own home or in the home of a relative or family day care provider in the neighborhood. With such an arrangement, which is usually more convenient and often less costly than center care, parents will expect to maintain control over the care of their children and a consensus between themselves and the other caregivers on how to raise their offspring (Clarke-Stewart, 1982). Child care professionals can make a contribution to this partnership by providing training, educational material, referral, and support services for home-based as well as center-based child care.

Worldwide the demand for alternate caregivers will continue to grow, both because of an increase in the number of young children and the number of women in the paid labor force. How well this demand will be met by either private or public efforts will depend a great deal on how high the needs of children and working mothers will rank on each nation's policy agenda in the closing decades of this century.

REFERENCES

Belsky, J. 1980. Future directions for day care research: An ecological analysis. Child Care Q. 9:82–99.

Bronfenbrenner, U. 1979. The Ecology of Human Development. Harvard University Press, Cambridge, MA.

Children's Defense Fund. 1982a. The Child Care Handbook: Needs, Programs and Possibilities. Children's Defense Fund, Washington, DC.

Children's Defense Fund. 1982b. Employed Parents and Their Children: A Data Book. Children's Defense Fund, Washington, DC.

Clarke-Stewart, A. 1982. Day Care. Harvard University Press, Cambridge, MA.

Dempsey, J.J. 1981. The Family and Public Policy. Paul H. Brookes, Publisher, Baltimore.

Etaugh, C. 1980. Effects of non-maternal care on children: Research evidence and popular views. Am. Psychol. 35:309–313.

Giele, J.Z. 1979. Social policy and the family. Annu. Rev. Sociol. 5:275–302.

Goldstein, J., Freud, A., and Solnit, A.J. 1973. Beyond the Best Interests of the Child. Free Press, New York.

Kamerman, S.B. 1980. Parenting in an Unresponsive Society: Managing Work and Family Life. Free Press, New York.

Kamerman, S.B., and Kahn, A.J. (eds.). 1978. Family Policy: Government and Families in Fourteen Countries. Columbia University Press, New York.

Kamerman, S.B., and Kahn, A.J. 1981. Child Care, Family Benefits and Working Parents. Columbia University Press, New York.

Medrich, E.A., Roizen, J.A., Rubin, V. and Buckley, S. 1982. The Serious Business of Growing Up: A Study of Children's Lives Outside School. University of California Press, Berkeley.

Peters, D.L., and Belsky, J. 1982. The day care movement, past, present, and future. In: M. Kostelnik and H. Fitzgerald (eds.), Patterns of Supplementary Parenting, Vol. 2. Plenum Press, New York.

Rapaport, R., and Rapaport, R.N. (with Bumstead, J.) (eds.). 1978. Working Couples. Harper & Row, New York.

Ricciuti, R.N. 1976. Effects of Infant Day Care Experience on Behavior and Development: Research and Implications for Social Policy. Department of Human Development and Family Studies, Cornell University, Ithaca, NY.

Rutter, M. 1972. Maternal Deprivation Revisited. Penguin, Harmondsworth, England.

Rutter, M. 1981. Social-emotional consequences of day care for preschool children. Am. J. Orthopsychiatry 51(1):4–25.

Scherer, M. 1982. The loneliness of the latchkey child. Instructor. May:39–41.

Smith, P.K. 1980. Shared care of young children: Alternate models to monotropism. Merrill-Palmer Q. 26:371–389.

Steiner, G.Y. 1976. The Children's Cause. Brookings Institution, Washington, DC.

U.S. Department of Health and Human Services. 1981. National Day Care Home Study, Final Report: Executive Summary. U.S. Department of Health and Human Services, Washington, DC.

Werner, E.E. 1979. Cross-Cultural Child Development: A View from the Planet Earth. Brooks-Cole, Monterey, CA.

Index

Academic achievement
  commercial television and, 197–199
  grandparent contact and, 96–97
  see also Cognitive development
Achievement motivation, in sibling caregivers, 68–69
ACTION, 219
Action for Children's Television (ACT), 204, 221
Adolescents
  babysitters as, 157–161, 162
  effect of grandparents on, 98–99
  prosocial behavior of, 66–67
Adoption Assistance and Child Welfare Act, 169–170, 182, 219
Advertisements, on television, 203–205
Advocacy groups, 220–221
Affiliation motivation, in sibling caregivers, 68–69
Africa, educational television and, 206–207
After-school programs, for latchkey children, 214, 224
Aging, perception of grandparenthood and view of, 102–103
Aggression, television and
  advertising and, 205
  television violence and, 200–203
Agricultural societies
  domestic groups of, 40
  grandparents in, 86
  sibling care in, 59–60
Aid to Families with Dependent Children (AFDC), 215, 218
  Foster Care Program, 169–170
Allofathers, 16
  see also Alloparental care, among primates
Allomothers, 16
  see also Alloparental care, among primates
Alloparental care, among primates
  benefits and costs of, 28–29

child abuse prevented by, 26
great apes, 17
  chimpanzees, 17, 18–20
  gorillas, 17, 20, 26
  social organization, 17–18
high-risk offspring and, 25–27
by males, 27–28
New World monkeys, 16–17, 25
  marmosets, 25
  tamarins, 25
Old World monkeys, 17
  Japanese macaques, 21–22
  langurs, 23–24
  rhesus monkeys, 22–23, 26, 26–27, 27–28
social organization, 17–18
Alloparental care, among social mammals, 16
  see also Alloparental care, among primates
American Friends Service Committee (AFSC), 221
American South, child care in, 150–151
Apes, *see* Alloparental care, among primates
Arunta, patrilocal extended family of, 39
Ashanti, matrilocal extended family of, 39
Asia, television viewing time in, 188–189
Asian-Americans; sibling caregiving among, 61
Attachment, 9–10
  as consequence of sibling caregiving, 64–66
  family day care and, 134–136
  grandchild-grandparent bond and, 101
  to grandparents, 95–96, 101
Aunting, 16
  chimpanzees and, 19–20
  gorillas and, 20
  Japanese macaques and, 21
  rhesus monkeys and, 22–23